D0457768

SERENGETI
HOME

KENYA

TANZANIA

Serengeti National Park

Mara River

Isuria Escarpment

Lamai
Kogatende
Wogakuria
Bologonja R.
To Keekorok

Mugumu
Klein's Camp

To Musoma
Lobo

Lake Victoria
Ikoma Fort
To Musoma
Orangi River

Grumeti River
Kirawira
Musabi
CORRIDOR
Kilimafeza
To Loliondo

Ndabaka
Banagi
Mgungu River

To Mwanza
Seronera

Mbalageti River
Barafu Kopjes

Duma River
Lake Magadi
SERENGETI PLAINS
Gol Mountains
L'engai Crater

Moru Kopjes
Naabi Hill

Simiyu River
Lake Lagaja
Olduvai Gorge
Ngorongoro Crater

Lemugrut Mountain

To Arusha

SERENGETI
NATIONAL PARK

0   10   20   30 miles
0   10   20   30   40   50 k

—— Main roads
—— Present boundary
–– – Old boundary

SERENGETI HOME

by KAY TURNER

WITH A FOREWORD BY
Professor Bernhard Grzimek

THE DIAL PRESS / JAMES WADE

NEW YORK

Published by
The Dial Press/James Wade
1 Dag Hammarskjold Plaza
New York, New York 10017

Copyright © 1977 by Kay Turner
All rights reserved. No part of this book may be
reproduced in any form or by any means without the
prior written permission of the Publisher, excepting
brief quotes used in connection with reviews written
specifically for inclusion in a magazine or newspaper.

Manufactured in the United States of America
First printing

Designed by Paula Wiener

Library of Congress Cataloging in Publication Data

Turner, Kay.
   Serengeti home.

   Includes index.
   1. Turner, Kay. 2. Game wardens—Tanzania—
Serengeti Plain—Biography. 3. Serengeti Plain,
Tanzania. I. Title.
SK255.T3T87   639'.9'0924 [B]   77-3908
ISBN 0-8037-8173-3

For all those who, like Myles,
have devoted their lives to the
protection of wildlife in East Africa

There is a pleasure in the pathless woods,
There is a rapture on the lonely shore,
There is society, where none intrudes,
By the deep sea, and music in its roar:
I love not Man the less, but Nature more,
From these our interviews, in which I steal
From all I may be, or have been before,
To mingle with the Universe, and feel
What I can ne'er express, yet cannot all conceal.

Byron, *Childe Harold* (1812)

Acknowledgments

This book was started for my children, Lynda and Michael, who shared most of the years we spent in the Serengeti but were too young to remember some of them. I am particularly indebted to my husband, Myles, for his loving support and encouragement, and for the photographs which illustrate this story.

I would also like to record my gratitude to Professor Bernhard Grzimek, who did me the honour of writing the Foreword; to Dr. John Owen, who was an inspiration both in his conservation ideals and human values; to Wilfred Thesiger, Sandy Field, and Dr. Hugh Lamprey, who read some of the text and offered invaluable advice; to Harold Hayes for his professional encouragement in the early stages of my endeavour; to many friends whose suggestions have been greatly appreciated; and to my publishers Malcolm Barnes and James O'Shea Wade for their patience and interest.

I wish to thank Professor Grzimek for the use of one of his photographs, 10a, and Anthony Smith and Ralph Thomson for extracts I have quoted from their works.

Foreword

When my son Michael and I first visited the Serengeti twenty years ago, we found Myles Turner and his young wife living there in the only permanent house in the whole of that vast area. Michael and I slept in a metal shed nearby, which was very dusty and, in the daytime, unbelievably hot. Like the Turners, who pushed their baby in her pram for walks along the dusty tracks at Banagi, we had to take care not to disturb the lions which roamed around our two houses. The Turners helped us in our work through many years and we became good friends.

Many books on Africa have been written in recent years, but few women have experienced the kind of life which Kay describes. This book is an account of her impressions and experiences during the years she lived in the Serengeti, amongst the huge herds of wild animals that roamed there. It makes absorbing reading, and is a simple, vivid tale, written by someone who loves nature, in particular the Serengeti.

The lions are still there, the grazing animals have become more numerous, and there are many more people living in the Serengeti today. Seronera—once uninhabited—is now the center of a community housing nearly two thousand workers, including scientists, wardens, building contractors, Parks personnel and their families. Tens of thousands of tourists visit the Serengeti each year to admire its wonders.

Of course, Myles, Kay, and I prefer the old times, when the Park was still wild and untouched. But we have to acknowledge that the animals are safer now, in that they are more effectively protected by the laws of the country. Under an independent government the number of National Parks in Tanzania has increased in a way we had not foreseen in the early days of their creation.

In this achievement of progress and development Myles and Kay Turner played a major part. They encouraged and taught the trainees in their care, worked together with them, and were rewarded by the enthusiasm and eagerness of their successors to carry on the work which they had begun.

When Myles and Kay left the Serengeti, a big part of their hearts remained behind in those great, wide, undulating plains where the sun burns and the country is in turn devastated by fire and turned green again by the rains.

This book may help others to understand why the Turners loved the Serengeti and provide a glimpse of the country in which they spent nearly two decades of their lives. It is a country unique in the world today, a huge sanctuary where thousands upon thousands of wild animals live in freedom. May these vast migratory herds continue to survive and wander across the Serengeti long after we are all gone and forgotten.

BERNHARD GRZIMEK

Contents

Map of Serengeti, ii
Acknowledgments, vi
Foreword by Professor Bernhard Grzimek, vii
1 Banagi, 1
2 Background, 13
3 Early Days, 27
4 Poaching, 41
5 Jason, 63
6 Bushbabies, 72
7 Seronera, 88
8 Wild Pets, 102
9 Lions, 128
10 Making Friends, 141
11 Bush Flying, 154
12 Safaris, 171
13 Visitors, 185
14 Last Days, 201
    Epilogue, 209

Chapter 1

Banagi

Hundreds of gazelles sped away from under the wing of the little plane as it skimmed above the grass runway at Seronera and circled round for a second attempt at landing. I looked out of the window with interest. This was my first visit to the Serengeti, a vast wildlife park in Tanganyika, now Tanzania; my husband Myles had recently been appointed warden in charge of its western section, but had not yet arrived to assume his new post. It was 1956 and we had been married for just six months.

Myles was still working as a professional hunter at the time, and was then escorting Prince Abdorreza Pahlavi, the Shah of Iran's brother, on a hunting safari in southern Tanzania. In his absence a friend and I accepted an invitation to join a safari party flying to the Serengeti. We were met by a hunting car and taken 11 miles to Banagi, the Park headquarters, where one European warden and a score of Africans lived. This isolated station, consisting of a row of small round staff quarters and a mud-brick bungalow built more than twenty years earlier by the Game Department, would soon be my home. At Seronera, where we had landed, there was a self-catering safari lodge that could accommodate twelve visitors in six grass-roofed *rondavels* (round one-roomed houses). Except for Ikoma, an African village 20 miles from Banagi, there was no other habitation nearby. Our closest township was Musoma, a small government administrative center on the shores of Lake Victoria, 110 miles northwest

1

of Banagi; and our nearest European neighbour lived at Ngorongoro Crater, 90 miles south.

In those days few tourists visited the Serengeti; looking round, I could not say I blamed them. The country was parched and colourless, and the car soon filled with tsetse flies that stung us sharply. It was a hot day in October, and dust swirled behind us on the dry air. Those animals we saw were standing deject-edly in the shade of thorn trees; I could not imagine what they found to eat in that sun-baked sea of scrub bush.

My companion, an elegant air hostess, was aghast that anyone could consider living in so lonely and uncivilized a place. At Banagi the whole station looked deserted and forgotten. Grass and bush grew to 3 feet or more up to the house, which had fallen into disrepair. Large sections of plaster were lying where they had come apart from the walls, and quantities of bird droppings from the little swifts' nests lay inches deep along the verandah floor. No furnishings of any kind softened the bleakness of the neglected old building, except for a few hard chairs and tables. The air smelled musty and reeked of bats. Flies buzzed round and settled again, and stifling waves of heat rolled in from the bush. A huge prickly pear stood ugly and stark against the cloudless sky, obstructing the view across to Banagi Hill.

Although a little taken aback by my surroundings, I felt in-wardly excited and undaunted by the thought of living in this wild place. A previous applicant considered for the post of war-den had visited Banagi with his wife, who was a doctor of medi-cine with four children, and they had turned it down as being too isolated. But I was young and had never lived in the wilder-ness before, and, having experienced one brief and memorable safari in the African bush in Kenya, I was eager for more of this adventurous life. I had lived for eight years in Africa when I married Myles, yet I was a newcomer to his world of wild ani-mals and remote places. My early life had been spent in Malaya, until the Japanese invasion of Singapore during World War II, and in India, from where my parents moved in 1946 to East Africa. I was fourteen years old at the time.

At Banagi we were met by an African clerk, who told us the warden was on safari and would not be back that day. After measuring the windows for curtains and taking notes of what was needed to make the old house habitable, we thanked him and returned to the plane.

Two months later, aboard a 5-ton truck and accompanied by a cheerful African cook engaged in Arusha, I set off with a huge amount of household supplies on a journey of over 200 miles to join my husband in the Serengeti. Our party consisted of the driver, his assistant, our cook, and two loquacious African labourers. Myles had gone to Banagi a month earlier to take over from the bachelor warden who had lived there since 1953.

Arusha was our National Parks headquarters, a small friendly town nestling under the jagged 15,000-foot peak of Mount Meru, 170 miles south of Nairobi in Kenya, and the administrative center for Tanzania's northern province. In the years that followed we visited Arusha only on rare occasions, passing through on our annual holidays to the coast or to Myles's home in the Kenya Highlands.

Lumbering along the dusty, potholed track on that first journey by road to the Serengeti, I was overwhelmed by the magnitude and beauty of our surroundings. We climbed the escarpment wall of the Great Rift Valley that extends almost the length of Africa, and looked across Lake Manyara shimmering below us. Steeply forested mountain slopes tumbled down to the lake's gleaming surface and faded smudgily into the distance; elephants and buffaloes fed in the forest glades and birds wheeled in the sky above. Six years later this idyllic place was proclaimed a National Park.

Leaving Manyara, we climbed to the highlands, with the distant peaks of Kilimanjaro and Meru visible behind us amongst the clouds. We wound our way through cool mountain forests, where trees stood veiled in "witches washing," a pale green moss hanging from their boughs. Thin wisps of cloud trailed amongst the trees, sunlight filtered through their leaves, and occasionally we saw buffaloes grazing in open glades, raising their heads to watch us pass. Creeping upward to 8,000 feet, we at last reached the crest and came upon a sudden view of Ngorongoro Crater, 2,000 feet below. Stopping at every viewpoint along the crater rim, I looked in wonder at this walled depression, a caldera 12 miles wide that enclosed a garden of sunlit plains, forest, hills, and shining lake. Thousands of wild animals peacefully roamed the floor of the crater—an area covering more than 100 square miles. As we watched, a shaft of sunlight pierced the cloud and pointed its golden rays into the huge bowl.

Journeying on to the northwestern side of the mountain, we came to a curve in the road and saw the Serengeti sprawling out from our feet towards an indistinct horizon. It was an astonishing sight: breathtaking and immense, like the sea, it had no focal point but rolled for mile after mile in a quivering heat haze, broken only by a low profile of distant hills. The boundless space, unspoilt wildness, and great vaulting sky gave me a feeling of joy and incredulity. To the east lay the Gol Mountains, their colours changing from shades of blue and mauve to pearly grey under the passing clouds. Although we were to travel the same road many times thereafter, the impact of that scene as we rounded the bend and began the long descent to the plains never lessened.

The road down was far worse than the ascent. From the moment we left the crater our truck crawled along the appalling track in a following wind, enveloped in a dense cloud of dust. At the base of the mountain, winding through the acacia trees, the track seemed no better, and finally disappeared altogether. Each safari vehicle had then made its own path as best it could across the lava dust plains, which quickly disintegrated into holes and corrugations. With windows tightly closed, it grew hotter and dustier every minute.

My discomfiture was partially forgotten when we crossed Olduvai Gorge, a repository of ancient relics from the Stone Age of hominids and other extinct creatures. Islands like ruined castles rose from the arid gorge, their layered structure telling its history. Among the many prehistoric species that had been identified from their fossilized remains by Louis and Mary Leakey were the Deinotherium, an elephant with tusks in its lower jaw pointing downwards; the Sivatherium, a huge giraffe with branching antlers; and the Metachizotherium, an ungulate related to the rhinoceros and horse, with five-toed clawed feet. The walls of the gorge revealed that the Serengeti Plains were built up of five successive beds of deposit on a base of black basaltic lava, and that the first two of these beds consisted of depositions that were laid down in an old lake basin. The development of human culture was being traced by the abundance of artifacts found in each bed, ranging from crude choppers and hand axes to small knives and bevelled flint tools. This link with man's beginnings lent the place an atmosphere of antiquity. The heat was intense and hung heavily over the desolate scene.

Leaving Olduvai, the road in those days passed Shifting Sands, a hill of volcanic ash 100 feet high, blown continually westward by the wind. It is believed to move some 25 yards a year, burying scarab beetles and other insects as it creeps imperceptibly onwards. We climbed to the top of the rise and watched the dust trickling over its highest ridge, our footsteps on the sunbaked hill sending little rivers of sand flowing silkily down its westward face.

Continuing our journey, the specks I had thought to be shrubs materialized into thousands upon thousands of gazelles, wildebeest, and zebras, their satiny hides gleaming in the sun. Like windblown leaves they crossed and recrossed before us, spread in a carpet of animal backs, swishing tails, and tossing manes for as far as we could see. This was my first sight of the migration—the seasonal movement of animals from the wooded country to the plains. The spectacle never failed to stir me, for it seemed miraculous that there should still exist a place where one could stand amidst surging masses of unmolested wildlife in its natural state. Watching the animals streaming across the plains, grunting in continuous waves of sound, was a strangely uplifting experience. The sun poured its brilliance over the endless scene, and the tensions of human life slackened and evaporated under the effects of wonder and warmth.

Stretching for 60 miles from Olduvai to Seronera, the Serengeti Plains cover an area of roughly 2,000 square miles and are virtually a sea of grass, devoid of trees or shrubs. The gently undulating country rolls away to a horizon that merges with the arching sky. In the center of the plains a wooded hill, Naabi, rises like an oasis in the desert. On long journeys we often stopped there and imagined how idyllic it would be to live at Naabi, looking out upon the sweeping landscape and the roaming herds of game. But with the beauty and sense of freedom went also the constant wind, the lack of water, and the emptiness of the plains for six months of the year when the animals returned to the woodlands.

Nearing Seronera towards the end of that first journey, our truck driver pointed to a small dark smudge under a distant tree, accurately identifying it as a lion. I was impressed by this seemingly magical ability to name an animal I had not even known was there, let alone its species. Yet in time I too found it possible to identify a distant speck by its shape and size, and with such familiarity grew a greater sense of intimacy and under-standing of the bush.

We crossed the Seronera River and were now amongst the woodlands. Spreading branches of flat-topped acacias provided pale circles of shade, and yellow fever trees were lit by an eve-ning sun that turned the grass to gold. The sun sank rapidly, dazzling the eye with its orange light along the horizon and illu-minating the towering cumulus clouds in a blaze of mauves, purples, scarlets, and delicate pinks. Towards the east an almost full moon hung in a turquoise sky; zebras galloped through bright fields of grass, their hides reflecting the rose-coloured light. It was the most beautiful sunset I had ever seen. Forget-ting the weariness of twelve hours in our cumbersome truck, I watched the radiant colours fade until just one cloud shone from the darkening sky.

Another 10 miles took us through open bush, and it was late evening when we rounded a bend and jolted over loose stones on the slopes of Banagi Hill. With a leap of excitement I saw across the river the sun-bleached green roof and white walls of our low bungalow blending into its surroundings. We crossed the river and climbed to the house where Myles stood waiting on the verandah steps.

"Welcome to Banagi!" he called, laughing at my dust-covered appearance as I clambered from the truck cab.

I was home. Looking across the wilderness that surrounded us, I sensed the loneliness of our isolation and felt a twinge of apprehension. But my misgivings were far outweighed by a feel-ing of eager anticipation for our future in this strange country. There was so much to do, so much to learn, and I wondered how I would adapt to this exciting new life. Although I did not realize it, we were at the beginning of sixteen years in the Serengeti, the most spectacular wildlife sanctuary on earth.

Later that evening, too restless to sleep, I listened to the noises of the African night. A drinking place on the lawn had already been installed, made from part of a corrugated iron tank, and it attracted animals from all around. Impalas snorted, zebras barked, lions roared. It was the first time I had heard them in the bush, and I thrilled at the thought that this magnificent wild country was to be our home.

At Banagi the lions visited us frequently and roared nearly every night. One lion had a habit of first calling from a great distance, gradually moving closer and roaring louder until we could hear his deep grunting breaths beneath our window. The Africans in their tightly shuttered houses were frightened by these nightly prowls, and Myles liked to tease them about the sinister intentions of the "Phantom," as the lion came to be known.

Not long after we arrived, two uranium prospectors visited us and we invited them to dinner. Seated at the candlelit table, our conversation was suddenly interrupted by a roar that shook the old house to its foundations. The faces of our guests turned ashen and an abrupt silence fell as all eyes turned towards the open door leading to the verandah. Myles raced for his flashlight. Shining it from the doorway, we saw two supremely indifferent lions at the foot of the verandah steps, gazing out across the moonlit bush with their great shaggy heads averted. As we watched, one of them lowered his head and uttered a second resounding roar. A small lamp, carried by a ranger walking to our house from the African lines below, suddenly bobbed away in hurried retreat. Leaving the door open, we returned to our meal and listened to the roars, which continued spasmodically for some time, providing an unusual entertainment for our guests.

In those early days the Serengeti was not on any direct route between towns and we lived in almost total isolation. At times we felt shut off from the outside world. Mail reached us once a month on visits to Musoma for supplies; visitors seldom came, and those who did were usually in hunting parties passing through or officials on duty. Except for the sounds of birds and occasional animals, the Serengeti was a quiet and very peaceful world, with a wildness that gave it the charm of mystery.

Our comforts were few. There was no water-borne sanitation and no lighting plant; we used paraffin lamps and cooked on a wood-burning stove. Much of our time was spent in the bush. At

Banagi as on safari we hauled our water, pumped the lamps, and stoked the fires for cooking and bathing. The house was really an extension of camping in the bush, with the advantage of more living space, greater comfort, and such luxuries as books and music from a battery-operated record player.

Until we acquired a trailer, bathwater was rolled in drums from the saline river a quarter mile below the house; for drinking we collected rainwater off the roof in two corrugated iron tanks, each holding 500 gallons. These tanks were locked in the dry weather, and water was rationed carefully to our small community of Africans. The rivers at such times were the colour of dark chocolate and they carried a risk of bilharziasis, a parasitic disease which could be debilitating to those infected. In 1971, when doctors treated Myles for excruciating kidney pains suffered for two days on safari, they found that he had been infected by bilharzia for possibly fifteen years. Mosquitoes, too, were a menace and transmitted malaria, which the station kept under control with regular doses of prophylactics. Myles was frequently afflicted, but I seemed unaffected by this all too common fever, although I only remembered to take the anti-malaria drug when pregnant. Tsetse flies abounded, some of which carried trypanosomiasis, the dreaded sleeping sickness that occurred from time to time in the Serengeti. Yet despite our remoteness and lack of medical facilities we thrived.

During the 1950s roads were either poor or nonexistent; visits to Musoma took a whole day, sometimes two, depending upon the weather. Sections of road would be washed away in the rainy seasons, river gullies became dangerous in flood, and at times we waited several hours before attempting to drive through a raging torrent. Once, some hours after we had managed to cross one of these deep ravines, a Catholic White Father plunged in and was later found downstream drowned in his small Volkswagen. With this in mind I would shut my eyes when the Land Rover churned through the river and water poured under its doors and round our feet. The crossings were narrow, so Myles used always to align the wheels of the Land Rover before entering the water; once in, there was no turning against the strong current. Even so, we would sometimes emerge from the river on the extreme edge of the concrete drift, having been swept sideways by the force of the water.

At Banagi there was little to do outdoors in our recreation hours except walk or go fishing; occasionally Myles hooked a catfish or tilapia, which was permitted to Park officials. In the wet seasons I enjoyed collecting wildflowers and arranging them in vases. I also planted vegetables that were surrounded by a bamboo fence to keep out the animals. These had just begun to look promising when one night a porcupine broke in and turned my garden into a disaster area. Myles wrote in his diary: "Devastation was complete, and in sombre silence we viewed the ravished carrots, uprooted spinach and tomatoes, chewed-through avocado pear and pawpaw trees, and mutilated morning glories."

The exposed and uneaten carrots appeared to have grown in a "U" shape, for Banagi had been built on a limestone ridge, with only a foot or two of surface soil. Stones and rocks filled the earth, vegetables changed direction when they met them, and digging holes for flowering shrubs was a back-breaking task. But eventually we succeeded in clearing a lawn that stretched to the road and in growing a few hibiscus, frangipani, bougainvillea, and oleander shrubs that struggled to survive against the attentions of animals at night. Zinnias, marigolds, and other hardy plants added a touch of colour near the house, and for a while we had a rock garden where nasturtiums grew, around the prickly pear tree. But later we preferred an uncluttered view of Africa and dug out the rocks a previous warden had laid. Soon only grass covered the place where the prickly pear once had stood.

The house itself had considerable atmosphere, and conveyed a feeling of great age and forbearance. There was at times an eeriness, a throbbing stillness broken only by the scuffling of the swifts in their crowded nests along the verandah. At such times the house seemed filled with shadows from the past; but this was by no means disquieting, for it was also a friendly house and endeared itself far more to us than the new bungalow we acquired at Seronera three years later.

Looking to the south from the verandah, we faced a hill rising 1,000 feet across the river that largely obstructed the splendid views so typical of the Serengeti. We wondered why the house had been positioned in this puzzling way and assumed it was because of the two rivers that coursed on either side. One, the

Mgungu, flowed permanently, providing a constant source of water, dark and brackish in the dry weather; the other, the Orangi, ran pure in the rainy seasons only, and we swam in the deeper pools when it was high. The surrounding country typified the scrubland areas of the Park—mainly acacia trees, open bush, and gently rolling hills. Along the rivers there grew wild date palms, wild figs, and other magnificent trees, resembling a miniature tropical jungle, with brilliantly coloured kingfishers and fish eagles adding a final touch of exotic beauty. While Myles angled for the bewhiskered catfish, I found it soothing to sit by the cool rivers at the hottest times of year and watch for the hippos or a crocodile that sometimes broke the surface of the water.

The country around Banagi was a special haunt of old buffalo bulls that lived within the relative safety of our small settlement. We once watched two young lionesses attack an old bull within sight of our house. After a tremendous battle, accompanied by clouds of dust and rousing bellows, two very shaken lionesses fled towards the river chased for a short distance by an outraged buffalo, snorting with indignation. We grew used to seeing these bulls on our evening walks, knowing that if we ventured too close they might charge. But with familiarity came indifference: I seldom gave a thought to walking into dangerous animals.

One day, two years after our arrival, we were pushing our first child in her pram when I saw a pair of lions crouched low in the stubby grass a few feet from the dusty track. They had already seen us and we were too close to stop and turn without disclosing our awareness of them. Instinctively I looked away, the breath catching in my throat with shock as I interrupted our conversation to say in a low voice: "Don't look now, but we're being watched!"

"What by?" asked Myles casually, keeping his eyes from searching round.

"Two lions, and they're very close to the track."

All this was said in normal conversational tones as we continued walking nonchalantly along the road. We were now alongside the lions and my heart beat wildly at the thought of what might happen. From the corner of his eye Myles could see their raised noses and tawny manes lying almost flat with the grass, while four wide eyes watched our progress intently. We strolled past, talking quietly, and the lions remained motionless, thinking we had not seen them.

There was only one track through the bush, and with the large pram we had no alternative but to return along it. After a reasonable time we turned and headed back towards the house. I felt this might prove too much for the disturbed lions, and it was almost too much for me as we drew alongside once more. But again they flattened themselves into the grass and allowed us to pass within a few feet of where they lay.

When we were safely past I asked Myles what he would have done had the lions charged. Having read much on the subject of bullfighting, he answered seriously: "I'd have whipped off my jacket and executed a Veronica to the right!"

In those days the Serengeti was divided into two parts, east and west. It comprised the Crater Highlands, the plains, and a section 10 to 25 miles wide leading from Banagi to Lake Victoria that was known as the Corridor. In 1957 a Committee of Enquiry was sent to investigate clashes between the Park authorities and the Maasai, a nomadic warlike tribe who used the land for grazing their huge herds of cattle. Their investigations were largely based upon a survey conducted in 1956 under the auspices of the Fauna Preservation Society of London by Professor W. H. Pearsall, who had brilliantly assessed the situation and made recommendations for settling the dispute. The Park boundaries had been originally established by the government in 1951, and the Maasai were assured they would not be evicted from the Crater Highlands. Scattered throughout much of the Park lay their *manyattas*—mud and cattle-dung dwellings surrounded by thorn bush, behind which their wandering livestock were enclosed for the night. Although professing to kill no game, they often speared lions that were likely to menace their cattle, and they also had first option on any available water or grazing during dry seasons. It soon became clear that human beings and wild animals were incompatible in a National Park.

The findings of the Committee of Enquiry led to an agreement whereby the western Serengeti should be extended north to include some 2,000 square miles of land up to the Kenya border, and west by the addition of an area measuring approximately 1,000 square miles. Myles was familiar with this country from his hunting days, and although new to his job when Professor Pearsall visited the Park, he urged that these areas be included in the Serengeti. The committee further decided that the eastern Serengeti, enclosing the Crater Highlands, should be excised from the Park and designated a conservation unit area, thus continuing to offer protection for the wild animals living there. The Maasai could still use the area, but would be required to relinquish all of their rights to live and graze their herds of cattle in the western Serengeti.

Although losing Ngorongoro was a bitter blow to all conservationists, the enlargement of the western Serengeti proved providential. With the advent of airplanes, the movement of game was recorded and studied, and the northern and western areas were discovered to be essential to the migratory animals of the Serengeti in their cyclic wanderings, which always took them beyond the borders of the Park. In 1957, when the Committee of Enquiry made its recommendations, little was known of the ecology and distribution of game in the Serengeti; in retrospect, it was remarkable that such an astute decision should have been taken at a time of ignorance about the migratory routes followed by the animals. It was fortuitous that the 1957 agreement should have resulted at least in an area twice as large as the original boundaries of the western Serengeti, for the enlarged Park allowed much greater protection for the migratory animals than had previously been afforded; and there was to be no second chance to renegotiate the Serengeti boundaries. Scientists later revealed that in fact an area almost double the size of the present-day 5,600 square miles was needed to contain all of the country used by the migratory animals.

As a result of these changes we moved in 1959 to Seronera, the new headquarters for the Serengeti. After nearly three decades of use Banagi was virtually abandoned and allowed once more to fall into disrepair. In later years the old house was used from time to time by scientists, and in 1960 the station enjoyed brief distinction with the construction of the first research laboratory in the Park. For me, the feeling of absolute isolation and bush living always remained at Banagi.

Chapter 2

Background

Myles's love of Africa seemed to stem from an ancestor, George Thomson, who explored southern Africa during the early nineteenth century. Born in northern England in 1921, Myles displayed all the instincts of the hunter, and from the start it was apparent he would not settle to the life of an English country gentleman. During the depression years of the 1920s, when his father decided to settle in Kenya, Myles, aged five, was brought to Africa; it was the only place he ever wanted to be.

Much of his childhood was spent riding through country which then teemed with wildlife, shooting whatever game he fancied. He would set out on horseback and not return for days, spending nights with friends on distant farms. As there were no telephones, it must have been an anxious time for his mother, who was aware of the lions and rhinos in the area; but she knew also that this was the life her son loved. Intensely curious, he read extensively, and to his fine library of books he added a growing collection of rare works on Africa by early explorers and hunters. He was educated at the Prince of Wales School in Nairobi, 120 miles from his home in Nanyuki.

During World War II Myles served in Ethiopia and India, and in 1946 he joined the Kenya Game Department, thinking it was too late by then to work for the veterinary degree he had earlier planned.

His three years as a game control officer were spent mostly on farms around Mount Kenya, shooting buffaloes that raided the crops at night. It was an exciting occupation; he was tossed twice and run over many times by these huge animals when tracking them in mountain forests. A pack of dogs was trained to follow the scent of buffaloes; sometimes accidents occurred while the dogs held an animal at bay, leaping round the buffalo and preventing Myles from placing an accurate shot without hitting one of them. As if knowing its real enemy, the buffalo invariably charged the moment it saw man. But the dogs also served a useful purpose in harassing the buffalo before it got a chance to use its formidable horns.

During the years he worked for the Kenya Game Department Myles shot over eight hundred buffaloes, and he learned to respect their courage, strength, and intelligence above all other animals. Their determination, coupled with their acute sight, smell, and hearing, made them intimidating adversaries and, in Myles's opinion, the most dangerous of the "big five"—elephants, rhinos, lions, leopards, and buffaloes.

In 1950 he became a professional hunter after a year's service under two of the doyens of hunting, Sydney Downey and Donald Ker. In those days there were about twenty-five "white hunters" (as they were then called), and to be accepted into their exclusive band required considerable skill and training. Licences were granted by the Game Department on the recommendation of the Professional Hunters' Committee, after a long apprenticeship and by the proposal of two existing professionals, who were stern judges.

For six years Myles conducted safaris into the far corners of the African bush, exploring areas he would not otherwise have seen. One safari took him from west to east, and he also ranged widely over the Congo (now Zaire), Sudan, Chad, French Equatorial Africa (now Central African Republic), Kenya, Tanganyika (now Tanzania), and Uganda. It was an absorbing life and many clients became his friends. In the end, however, shooting animals began to pall and the thrill of hunting changed to a strong compulsion to look after them. Myles was thirty-one when he decided to devote his time to the conservation of wildlife.

After working for Myles's employers, Ker & Downey Safaris Ltd., one of the foremost safari companies in Africa, in 1953 I planned to leave Nairobi and travel the world. In those days my future husband was taciturn and not easy to know; we exchanged

no more than a dozen words during the months I worked for
his company. A week before I left Kenya, a friend invited me to
the Amboseli Game Reserve and he asked Myles to join the
party. It was my first experience of an African wildlife sanctuary,
and those five exciting days were the most exhilarating of my
life. In Myles I found a friend with whom there was that instant
recognition of affinities, as if I had always known him; but his
shy nature and reputation for avoiding women made me think
there was small chance that we would meet again. We said
goodbye, and I knew that I was leaving the only true friendship
with a man that I had ever known. Standing in the corridor of
the train as it drew out of Nairobi, and watching the country I
loved slide past, I could not hold back my tears.

For a while I avoided entering my compartment, which was
to be shared, until I had regained some composure. Later my
sympathetic companion solemnly handed me a small glass of
brandy from a hip flask, and I discovered she was Audrey
Moore. Her husband had been a game warden in Tanganyika
during the 1930s. They had once lived at a place called Banagi in
the Serengeti Game Reserve, now a National Park, and she was
the only European woman ever to have lived there. As we
talked, I told her of Myles, whom I gloomily predicted had left
my life for ever. The following morning my charming companion
was gone, the train having stopped in the dead of night at her
destination, Voi, in the Tsavo National Park.

Four years later, calling at an Army Depot near Myles's childhood home in Kenya, I met Audrey again. After greeting one
another with delight, she suddenly asked: "Did you marry him?"

"Yes," I said, laughing, "and we live at Banagi!"

We were married in March 1956. In the intervening years I
had travelled and worked in South Africa and London, and had
met Myles again when he visited England on holiday. He was
thirty-four when we married, and although there were excep-
tions during his six years of professional hunting, he had little
patience with women on safari. They generally found the discomforts of life in the bush too great and groused about the dust,
the heat, the bumps, and the horsefly-like sting of the tsetse
flies.

Before Myles's appointment to the Serengeti we were on hon-
eymoon by the sea when a professional hunter, Eric Rundgren,

on an assignment from the Kenya Game Department, drove up in a Land Rover and invited Myles to help him shoot elephants marauding the coastal Africans' small farms. Leaping to his feet, my husband at once started making preparations to leave, and in astonishment I realized he intended going without me. After raising some objections, for we had been married only a few days, Myles reluctantly agreed to my joining them, on the condition that I brought the barest minimum of kit and made no complaints.

"This isn't a Ker & Downey safari," he warned. "The going will be rough."

Afraid he might change his mind, I made no reply. Our Land Rover, when packed, contained two African game scouts, as well as canvas beds, sleeping bags, a kettle, one saucepan, a box of food, and a kitbag each. There were no tents, chairs, or tables, and when I looked enquiringly at the half-empty pick-up, I was told that every available space was needed for the tusks we were to bring back for the government.

Eric, Myles, and I reached our destination and then walked many miles through the bush with the game scouts, returning at dusk to our camp where we slept beneath the stars. Having no servant with us, I organized our meals and washed the dishes each night. For three days the elephants eluded us. I had begun to think we would never find them when, one evening, after walking 20 miles in the humid coastal heat, a man's voice hailed us across a valley.

"The elephants are here!" he yelled. "Come quickly!"

We retraced our steps, and it was dark by the time we reached the small farm. A man stood outside his hut and gestured towards the elephants feeding amongst the crops. We could hear their stomachs rumbling, and Myles turned to me, whispering urgently: "Turn out that light!"

I quickly extinguished the hurricane lamp I had lit and stumbled noisily behind the two hunters, who moved silently through the bush as though it were broad daylight. Suddenly a powerful flashlight beamed on, and I saw the huge animals only a few yards from where we stood. While Myles shone the flashlight steadily along the heavy rifle's barrel, Eric immediately fired twice and then reloaded for another two shots. Five elephants milled round confusedly, then lumbered away in a tight group, taking their two wounded comrades with them. With all the commotion and trumpeting in the night around us, I had no idea whether we stood in their path or not, and I hurried closely on the heels of the hunters as they struck out once more into the bush, intent now on finding the animals they had hit.

This was my first experience of elephants and I had not yet grown to love them, nor to sympathize with their plight; my one concern at the time was the highly dangerous situation I imagined we were in, stumbling after the angry herd in total darkness.

Suddenly we stopped, the flashlight beamed on again, more shots were fired, and two animals crashed down. Greatly disturbed, the remainder of the herd jostled each other for a while before finally disappearing into the night.

Dazed by the excitement of those few brief minutes, I stood speechless, watching the hunters examining the carcasses and instructing our game scouts to guard the tusks till morning. We then started back to camp, a march of many miles in the dark through trackless bush. When eventually we reached the Land Rover it was very late. Exhausted, I sank thankfully on to my bed, only to hear my cheerful companions demanding to be fed. Myles's warning still rang in my ears as, stifling my protests, I prepared a hasty meal before falling into an immediate and deep sleep. Not long afterwards it began to pour with rain, and a voice asked if he could help me move my bed to the covered Land Rover. Muttering with exasperation, I buried my head deeper in the sleeping bag and slept soundly till morning, soaked to the skin. In the humidity of the coast, it was at least a warm rain.

Having survived Myles's standards by the end of that first fairly rigorous safari, he accepted my presence in the bush without further comment. For me it had been a thrilling experience and I was eager for more of this marvellous life that seemed so simple, yet satisfied some primeval longing to live close to the earth and become a part of it. I felt free as air, unencumbered by possessions, truly happy in a way I had not been before. This was the world I wanted: the sun, the space, the sky, the loneliness, and the wildness shared only with the creatures of the bush. There was a peace like that of total relief from tension, a contentment that pervaded every corner of the soul. It was life as nature intended it to be lived and I felt almost a child's wonder, a sense of being reborn into a magical world where to exist was fulfillment.

Myles still worked as a professional hunter, and was on safari with clients two months later when letters arrived simultaneously from the Tanganyika Game Department and the Tanganyika National Parks, offering him posts in their establishments. There was no way that I could contact him for several weeks and, since there were other applicants, I decided that some reply should be given as soon as possible. Making a random choice, I sent cables to both organizations, accepting the offer from the National Parks and declining the offer from the Game Department. In later years, when life in the Serengeti became too civilized for Myles's liking, my decision was sometimes questioned. The Game Department post would have taken him to Muhenge—a remote area near the vast Selous Reserve where elephants abounded and Myles would have lived the wandering life of an elephant control officer. But he never seriously regretted my choice; for the two areas he had long regarded as ideal were the Northern Frontier District in Kenya and the Serengeti in Tanganyika.

As a fitting climax to his years as a professional hunter Myles was honoured by the first award of the Shaw and Hunter Trophy in 1956, for a record Lesser Kudu shot on safari with Prince Abdorreza Pahlavi of Iran. Shortly afterwards we began our life together in the Serengeti.

The beautiful word "Serengeti" possibly derives from the Maasai *siringet*, meaning an extensive area. It was largely uninhabited country and little known for many years. Riverless plains stretch for over 60 miles to the south and east, the Great Rift mountains rise in the northeast, and numerous tsetse flies inhabit the north and west. No guide seemed anxious to lead parties there until, in 1913, the American hunter Stewart Edward White crossed from the Great Rift Valley via Loliondo to Lobo Springs, now the site of a modern hotel. Before that time the German explorer Oscar Baumann had travelled in 1892 from the coast to Lake Victoria via Ngorongoro Crater and the Serengeti. Compared with an area like Ngorongoro, which attracted many glowing reports from early explorers, the Serengeti remained largely unknown and was generally considered to be a low, hot, fever-ridden country, of limited interest in a continent then teeming with game. Until the twentieth century it was frequented only by local tribal hunters, who used poisoned arrows and game pits for snaring the animals and taking their yearly toll of the migratory game.

Stewart Edward White was one of the first to record the wildlife of the area. In a book called *The Rediscovered Country*, published in 1915,* he described the Serengeti as "the haunt of swarms of game," and added, "in this beautiful, wide, populous country, no sportsman's rifle has ever been fired." White moved among "those hordes of unsophisticated beasts as a lord of Eden would have moved," describing how,

rank after rank, they went by, each with his kind—the wildebeeste, the hartebeeste, the many topi, the eland, the impalla [sic], and all the little flanking gazelles—and so over the rise of the next hill. Each as he topped the ridge against the western sky stood out sharp-cut, a silhouetted miniature, then dipped down the other side out of sight. From the direction of the waterhole rose lazily a great cloud of dust where yet other hundreds of beasts were awaiting their turn, or rolling luxuriously after their thirst had been assuaged.

Then we followed over the rise, to witness the gradual fanning out of the procession. A little group dropped off to right or to left, and fell to grazing. Others kept on over yet more distant hills. Within the half hour the great herd had broken into hundreds of little groups, scattered over many miles, and countless hills and valleys. Again the green lawns were covered with the black wildebeeste.

Unfortunately the "virgin game country," which White claimed was the last left to man to discover "for the sportsmen of the world," did not remain so for long. At a shot from his rifle, several hundred animals trekked solemnly towards him to investigate the unusual sound. Hunting mainly around the Bologonja, Mara, and Lamai country to the north, White never actually reached Seronera or the plains.

In about 1920 another American hunter, Leslie Simpson, reached Seronera from the north and returned five years later with Stewart Edward White and two other friends. Within three months they shot fifty-one lions in the Seronera area—lions and

---

* New York: Doubleday, Page & Co.

leopards were considered vermin at that time, and it was thought that to kill them protected the game.

The route having been pioneered, hunting parties now poured into the Serengeti, until in 1929 the British Government set aside 900 square miles of country as a game sanctuary, offering protection to all wildlife, with a total ban on lion hunting. Two years later Captain "Monty" Moore, V.C., became game warden of the sanctuary, following a Captain Arundell who built the headquarters at Banagi. Captain Moore's wife, Audrey, first went to live there in 1934 and recorded her impressions in *Serengeti.**

In 1930 a huge area comprising "the Musoma district and that part of Arusha District west of the Rift Wall" was declared the Serengeti Closed Reserve, in which certain species of game were protected. These boundaries were extended two years later; by 1937 the degree of protection amounted to complete prohibition of hunting inside the Serengeti Closed Reserve of lion, cheetah, leopard, giraffe, rhinoceros, buffalo, roan antelope, hyena, and wild dog. In Schedule One of the Game Ordinance enacted in 1940 much of this country, combined with the Ngorongoro Game Reserve, was designated as the Serengeti National Park. A revival of interest after World War II culminated in the enactment of the National Parks Ordinance in 1948; but this was not brought into force until three years later, when the reconstituted and considerably reduced boundaries of the Serengeti were proclaimed on June 1, 1951. Administration of the Park then passed from the Game Department to a board of trustees appointed by the British government, the remaining country (designated in 1940) continuing to be known as a game reserve under the control of the Game Department. The total area of the Park was roughly 4,800 square miles.

By 1956 the position had not changed, although it had become evident that there was growing conflict between the Park's management and the Maasai people. After the Committee of Enquiry's investigations a year later, the boundaries were again changed so as to enclose an area of over 5,000 square miles in the western Serengeti, and to exclude the Ngorongoro Crater Highlands from the Park. For ten more years negotiations con-

* London: Country Life, 1938.

tinued for the inclusion of further small vital areas to the west and north of the Park; these were completed in 1969, giving the Park a total of approximately 5,600 square miles.

Much hard work and struggle had gone into the establishment of the Serengeti as it now stood, and it was unlikely any further changes or additions could be made. With the growing demands of an increasing human population around the boundaries, constant vigilance and toil were needed to protect the existing Park, as well as the continued will of the government to abide by its pledge to preserve the country's wildlife.

When the Serengeti was gazetted as a National Park in 1951, it was already known for its lions and for the spectacular migration of animals which filled the Serengeti Plains for six months each year. Possibly because of the custom of baiting and feeding lions when the area was a game reserve, the Seronera lions and others north of Banagi had grown exceptionally "tame," and they generally remained unperturbed when photographed from cars at close range.

In certain Park areas poaching was a constant problem. There were few African settlements along the actual boundaries of the Serengeti in 1956, and poaching meant long treks from villages several miles distant, involving the building of semipermanent camps within the game areas. These activities had continued in the past with little or no interference. Long lines of wire snares (animal traps) were spread blatantly through the bush, radiating for miles from each central camp and covering much of the country in remote areas. When poaching in these areas was curtailed, established camps became a thing of the past; but to counteract this, the poachers settled themselves along the actual boundaries of the Park and carried out hit-and-run forays across its borders. It seemed there was no way of eliminating poaching or of preventing the local hunters from continuing their tribal practices, especially when the increasing profits to be made from game trophies and skins became an added incentive. Since the actual survival of the animals depended to a large extent upon tipping the scales of the poaching war in the Park's favour, Myles's energies were primarily directed against poaching.

The Serengeti's beauty lay mainly in its golden plains, widespreading acacias, and magnificent rocky outcrops (or kopjes). During the hottest hours of day the game gathered beneath the acacias, whose matted branches offered a welcome respite from the scorching sun. Against a sapphire sky the clean outlines of granite boulders were silhouetted, sometimes in fantastic feats of balance. They harboured a profusion of shrubs and trees, their colours giving the kopjes a look almost of cultivation, like gigantic rock gardens. Composed of plains, woodlands, forest, low-lying mountain ranges, green fringed rivers, and small lakes, the Park ranged between 3,000 and 6,000 feet in altitude on a plateau stretching roughly 200 miles from the Crater Highlands in the south to the Kenya border in the north. The seasons varied between wet and dry, with the long rains occurring in March and April and the short rains in November. Although hot at times this immense rolling country, filled with nearly two million wild animals and blessed by almost constant sunshine and clear skies, enjoys one of the most equable climates in the world. At times brilliantly green, at others dry and burned, the strong contrasts and changing atmosphere of the Serengeti give it many different aspects.

Before the onset of the short rains the air would feel heavy and stifling, and the land looked more parched each day as the heat intensified. While our tempers shortened and our fears increased that the rains might fail, we watched the animals struggling pitifully to survive on the few remaining areas of un-burned grass.

And then at last it would begin, the first large drops of rain falling one by one, as if for practice, before the deluge. Our world, which previously had hung silent in anticipation of the storm, suddenly became a roaring cataclysm of sound with great bursts of thunder rolling away into the distance. Spectacular flashes of lightning lit the countryside at night and rain poured down in a continuous rush of noise; any animal we had in the house would hurry for cover to the nearest bed or chair, and there were times when I felt tempted to do the same.

On safari, wild winds preceding a downpour sometimes caused our paraphernalia to become airborne—tables and chairs taking to the bush. Afraid that our tent might not withstand the storm, we would cling to the support poles until the fury of the tempest had passed.

It was both exhilarating and a little frightening, so that I wondered at times if young animals experiencing their first storm felt their world was coming to an end. I often saw them through a tumult of water, waiting miserably with hunched backs for the force of the deluge to subside, which, abruptly, it would; not gently, with a steadily decreasing tempo, but suddenly, like a tap turned off. Only the sound of steady dripping would be left, as the sun glowed lustrously through a drowned sky and trees sparkled in their newly washed beauty. Everywhere the country would be swamped, while roads flowed like rivers and crickets shrilled loudly.

Within a day the first green shoots of grass would appear, and soon the parched ground would be replaced by an emerald carpet, dotted with blossoms like petunias called *Rhamphicarpa*. Wildflowers appeared everywhere: gladioli, yellow crotalarias, wild hibiscus, orange leonitis, lilies, daisies, blue clusters growing along the roadsides, and flowering shrubs. Animals kicked up their heels and chased one another joyously. Leaves and grass hung with jewels of moisture, fine cobwebs glistened like diamonds, the air smelled pure, and the sky shone like washed china. As if unwilling to be outdone by the wonder of the day, the evening would excel itself in brilliance, lighting the fields of grass and the solitary trees that stood like gleaming sentinels against the sky.

It was at this time, when water gathered on the plains, that the animals began their migration, moving from the woodlands at the first sign of leaden skies. Soon the plains were filled with over a million animals, and the short rains of November would keep the country habitable until the long rains began in March. During the six months that the game remained on the plains, the wildebeest dropped their young. Thousands upon thousands of endearing black-faced calves strove to remain close to their mothers' sides in the huge concentrations of game, for to become separated from their parent usually meant death. No female wildebeest would accept another's young, and once lost in the milling herds a calf could rarely find its mother again. Other wildebeest would butt the small animal away, refusing to suckle it, until eventually it left the herd to stand alone and tiny on the immense plain, a heartrending and all too common sight amongst the thousands of wildebeest born each season. For a while the bewildered creature would follow anything that moved, including a vehicle, until its end came in the form of a predator, or the vultures that waited for its collapse.

Once we watched a pack of wild dogs set off on their evening hunt, trotting towards a distant herd of wildebeest. They had not seen a forlorn calf standing nearby until it bounded joyfully towards them, attracted by their movement. A look of pained astonishment seemed to cross its small trusting black face as the pack tossed the tiny body into the air and then ripped it apart. It was over in a few seconds. Despite my efforts to accept the laws of nature, I felt sickened by the scene, which remained with me during all our years in the Serengeti as the most harrowing I ever witnessed.

A lake lying in the center of the plains held a shallow supply of saline water. Before it became a popular place for tourists to visit, we used to camp amongst the acacias surrounding Lake Lagaja and watch the flamingoes drifting across its surface. Like ballet dancers they wove patterns as they fed, trailing in pink clouds across the lake, with necks looped over and great curved beaks skimming the water. Sometimes they splashed lightly through the shallows to glide elegantly into the air, long necks and slender legs stretched out stiffly, and black-rimmed, rose-coloured wings languidly flapping as they wheeled across the water.

Down through the valleys, during these months, the animals wound their way to drink at the lake, or they waded across it, the very young calves swimming by their mothers' sides. On rare occasions, for some unexplained reason, the adults stopped halfway and returned, only to make a second or even a third attempt, ending in tragedy for their young. Hundreds of calves would be drowned or separated by exhaustion; it was pitiful to see the doomed survivors stranded and lost on the shore or running together in small herds.

Although such instances of senseless suffering appeared to me harsh and wasteful, the scene needed to be considered as a whole and the realities of life in the wild accepted. With nature so abundant, the numerous deaths among the ungulates did not seem high when compared with the mortality of rarer animals. I tried to rationalize my reactions. Even the misery caused by drought helped to weed out the old and the weak, preparing the way for sturdier, stronger animals when the rains finally brought new vigour and beauty to the landscape. In nature there were often extremes, the beauty of life counterbalancing its ugliness. My initial repugnance at the apparent cruelty of wild dogs, for instance, was in time softened by my understanding of these animals. By dispersing and moving the herds and by helping to maintain a balance between numbers and environment, they played their part in the ecology of the Park; their loyalty and gentleness towards members of their own group was touchingly affectionate.

During the migration months when the plains were populated by thousands of wildebeest, zebras, and gazelles, the predators followed in their wake: lions, hyenas, cheetahs, wild dogs, jackals, and sometimes leopards, but not man. It seemed the plains were the only safe place from poachers in the Park. Too far from the settlements, normally waterless, without firewood, shelter, or cover, and exposed to strong winds, the plains provided a true sanctuary for the animals. This might also explain their choice of the plains for calving each year at the time of the short rains. But it was not the lions' favourite habitat. We would find them lying in the sun guarding a kill without an iota of shade for miles around, panting and irritable. A lioness in season aggravated a lion's temper still further as he stalked behind her wherever she moved, ready to snarl or charge should a vehicle come too close. Hungry, tense, aggressive, and hot, by the end of a week the lion looked a sorry sight, and we could only sympathize with his temperamental behaviour.

After the long rains, in May, the country began to dry rapidly and the animals returned in vast armies to the woodlands. A strong east wind blew all day, which hastened their retreat, although there were pools of water still to be found in shallow valley catchments. Nonetheless, with backs to the wind and plodding in long lines towards the west or north, the game purposefully left the still green plains without a backward look. Sometimes they coursed through Seronera, their bleating, croaking, barking voices filling the air with sound, while at other times they avoided Seronera altogether, pouring through the Mbalageti Valley to the west. Some of them remained in the west, spilling over the boundaries of the Park into the settlement areas or into the Corridor with its large human population on both sides of the narrow sanctuary. Others moved on in thousands to the north, passing through many villages and settlements along the northwestern boundary of the Park until they reached the great Mara River bordering Kenya. There they would wander for several months, until the instinct to migrate prompted them once again to swing south to the plains.

This was the pattern of life in the Serengeti for the migratory animals—a pattern that had repeated itself for centuries and was now to be studied and analyzed. Scientific research had not come a moment too soon. With the advent of civilization in Africa time was running short for the proper conservation of her wildlife, and many people throughout the world were focusing their attention upon the welfare of the Serengeti. It was a stimulating time to be living and working in the Park.

Chapter 3

Early Days

"Two months, or six at the most, before you're back," friends had warned me.

They had talked of the difficulties of getting supplies, the lack of medical facilities, and the loneliness of life in the bush. I recalled their warnings when occasionally the silence of the Serengeti became almost oppressive and I found myself thinking aloud, humming, or singing to fill the void. Myles and I listened infrequently to the battery-operated radio and we seldom saw a newspaper.

As time passed I grew shy and feared intrusion from the out-side world, fleeing out of sight if I saw a car rounding the distant curve of Banagi Hill to approach our house.

"Let me call Kay," I would hear Myles saying to our visitors. "She was here a minute ago."

While I sat in tongue-tied misery and searched for something to say, striving to control my nervousness, I would think with amazement and envy of those people living isolated lives who found it impossible to *stop* talking when visitors called.

My dread of human contact did not extend to our encounters with Africans. Their unsophisticated lives lent them a simplicity we lacked, so that I felt relaxed in their company, admiring their customary geniality and good-natured acceptance of all things. Passing their grass-roofed villages outside the Park and seeing chickens scratching busily while children played within the swept-earth enclosures that surrounded their huts, I sometimes felt a great longing to have been born into such a life, where it seemed man's prime concern was to cultivate the land, tend the livestock, and never to think of tomorrow. What could be better, I thought, than this peaceful life with only the earth and sky as possessions, to sit with the sun on one's face and dream away the days in blissful appreciation of God's blessings?

In my heart I knew this to be a fanciful evaluation of the Africans' lives; like all human beings they suffered from many griefs and misfortunes, such as failing crops, the devastation of drought or flood, dying cattle, sickness and disease, sorcery, and destitute old age. Living in smoke-filled, overcrowded huts, their beautiful simple world hid a multitude of troubles we should find hard to endure; yet the peasants bore all their hardships with a resigned and patient docility that based itself on a philosophy of "*shauri ya Mungu*" (the will of God).

We frequently met the local people during our early wanderings around the Park, a visit to one of their villages being generally looked upon as an occasion for gladness and ceremony. The dignified elders of the community would turn out to welcome us graciously, while the women brought wooden chairs, and the children curtseyed respectfully, their round faces glowing and wreathed in smiles. Sometimes an appealing mongrel puppy scampered up, squirming with pleasure, or a hen shepherded her brood of tiny chicks past us, clucking in concern as she scuffed the dust. The gaily coloured cloths of the women and a brilliant sun would add to our feeling of well-being. With solemn formality the traditional greetings were exchanged, beginning with "*Karibuni*" (Please come in, you are welcome). How were we? How were our children? How was our work? What news? If one related bad news, such as ill-health having befallen a child, there was much sympathy expressed with sincerity and downcast faces.

Africans in their own environment treated a visitor as an honoured guest; their natural courtesy enveloped him in a warmth of good fellowship that made our own overtures of hospitality towards strangers seem almost artificial by comparison.

In those days our Banagi community comprised a clerk, a mason, a carpenter, a truck driver, eight rangers and porters, and four or five labourers. At Seronera Lodge a cook, two cabin boys, and a clerk looked after six double bedrooms, two outside bathrooms, and a dining room.

In addition to our Land Rover we had one ancient truck named Dungu (meaning the Big One), which brought monthly supplies from Musoma on the lake shore, more than 100 miles away. One day Dungu passed directly underneath a lioness lying along the branch of a tree that stretched across the road near our house. The driver had not seen her, and a deathly hush fell over the passengers in the open back of the truck as their heads cruised slowly beneath the surprised animal. She was no more than 6 feet above them and hunched herself into position to spring. Once clear, there was a great hammering on the roof of the cab, accompanied by yells of "*Simba! Simba!*" as the truck gathered speed and the lioness settled back to her slumbers.

Our house, perched atop a low hill between two rivers, had been unimaginatively designed, with a line of rooms fronted by a long verandah. The main door led to the dining alcove of a small living room; in the wall opposite was a door leading to the back of the house, with another to the side opening into a bedroom. This led in turn to a primitive bathroom beyond, to which there were two further doors—one to the back of the house and the other to the main bedroom. At some time an additional narrow room had been added alongside this bedroom which we later converted to a nursery. Two storerooms led off a small verandah at the back of the house, and a passageway extended out towards a separate kitchen with its firewood stove. The building was cool, with thick mud walls and a corrugated iron roof, painted green and faded by the sun. During the month that Myles first took over his duties at Banagi, the house had been newly whitewashed and looked more attractive than when I had first seen it eight weeks before. Twenty yards from the house stood a round thatched lavatory, with a wooden seat built over a hole dug 10 feet into the ground.

Around Banagi the bush grew thick and unchecked, overrunning any earlier attempts that had been made at gardening. Tsetse flies thrived in it, stinging us sharply at unexpected moments.

Bats inhabited the roof of the house, pervading the air with their smell. Along the verandah a huge colony of little swifts nested, spattering the walls and floor indiscriminately with their droppings. Near the house grew a fine old acacia tree in which the buffalo weavers nested, prompting Myles to remark that "as usual in life, the males do all the work, building industriously, while the females sit round looking decorative!"

To complete the picture of Banagi, a round thatched office lay to the side of our house, with another behind it for our African clerk. White ants were steadily consuming the station, and in 1959 Myles reported that it had become a race against time whether the new headquarters at Seronera would be completed before the Banagi office collapsed on our heads.

The Park's remaining staff were accommodated 400 yards from our house in a row of thatched rondavels on the banks of the Mgungu River. Two Flamboyant trees grew there, planted by a previous warden many years before, and they flowered profusely in the season, their scarlet blossoms contrasting strongly with the muted colours of the bush.

My adaptation to Banagi was made easier by having youth and the novelty of marriage to give me a sense of adventure and optimism. The absence of electricity, shops, and proper sanitation were small inconveniences compared with the thrill of hearing the lions roar at night and the exhilaration of driving amongst teeming herds of game. Nature's rich tapestry more than compensated for the isolation of our lives, and I did not miss social entertainment nor hanker for the luxuries of civilization. But there were times when I never quite knew what to do with all the quiet hours I had to myself. My previous life had been filled with people and social amusements, and I was at times a trial to Myles, intruding upon his thoughts when he preferred to read and relax, or demanding his attention and making issues out of minor disagreements. In time I learned to be more self-sufficient and to become absorbed by my own interests, discovering how to be alone without feeling lonely, and looking forward to those moments of solitude which became less frequent as the years passed.

In the beginning there was much to do, and I set my mind to making the old house as comfortable as possible. Within a short time it was home, the bush had been cleared to form a lawn, and any shortcomings in the comforts of life at Banagi seemed to us negligible. Since much of our time was spent out in the Park, the house became a base for safari operations and a warm haven from the bush.

Apart from our vegetable garden we had small means of getting fresh supplies, and we lived mainly on tinned milk, butter, and other canned food. During visits to Musoma I replenished our stocks with quantities of potatoes, onions, green bananas, oranges, and cabbages that lasted for some time. We baked our bread, kept chickens, and stored any surplus eggs in waterglass (a sodium silicate solution). Operating on a special governor's licence, Myles supplied the Banagi community every fortnight with game meat shot outside the Park. Once when kneeling in the grass to take careful aim at a kongoni (Coke's hartebeest), he discovered his foot to be within inches of a puff adder. The ranger, who drew attention to it after the animal was dropped, cheerfully admitted having seen the snake, but said he had not wanted to spoil Myles's aim by distracting his attention at such a critical moment!

Myles was an excellent shot, and at first I used to accompany him on hunting trips. But when an animal hit with a hard-nosed bullet ran for some distance before keeling over, I decided that I preferred to stay at home; Myles's dreams of teaching me to become an expert hunter dwindled to target practices on the lawn.

Soon after our arrival at Banagi we realized that a *duka* (shop) would be essential to the station, since our small community frequently asked for transport to buy food. Unable to afford large quantities of supplies, our Africans constantly ran short; and with the Park's limited funds Myles had stipulated that the truck should visit Musoma no more than once a month. The only solution was to establish our own local store, with stocks of the Africans' main requirements sold at cost price. Every day for an hour, when we were home, I would sell through the window of one of the Park's new outbuildings behind our house a variety of supplies that included *posho* (maize meal), flour, sugar, rice, tea, coffee, matches, salt, cooking oil, powdered milk, soap, paraffin, dried beans, razor blades, cigarettes, stamps, envelopes, writing paper, curry powder, corned beef, potatoes, and onions. The money to buy these stocks came from our Park's small welfare allotment, which necessitated my keeping detailed accounts.

Besides running the shop I also found myself dispensing med-

icine, my only qualification being a training course in First Aid
and Home Nursing which I had taken in my teens. Patients at
Banagi generally complained of *homa* (fever), which covered everything from malaria to the common cold; diagnosing their ailments was not always simple, since Africans have a colourful way
of explaining symptoms. "My stomach is boiling," "I am being
pinched all over," or "I'm burning up inside," were a few of
their puzzling descriptions, as they waited soulfully for the mira-
cle *dawa* (medicine) that they believed would cure them.

Faith usually helped more than the drug, but if a patient was
seriously ill or failed to respond to a malarial cure, he was sent at
once to Musoma Hospital for treatment. Although this did not
happen often, we were sometimes faced with a serious case,
such as a ranger bitten in the leg by a crocodile; another was
suspected of leprosy; and a third, to our astonishment, had had
his toes badly chewed in the night by rats without waking! A
Game Department scout once ran into a wire snare set by
poachers and nearly strangled himself before being rescued by
one of our rangers and brought to Banagi. Generally the women
had their babies without difficulty and I was only occasionally
asked for assistance.

A regular visitor to my dispensary was a character named
Bubu, who had worked for twenty-five years as caretaker of an
abandoned gold mine 7 miles away. He was a deaf-mute, but
could indicate his needs graphically in sign language. In no time
Myles became expert at this and the pair of them would hold
long conversations, gesticulating and miming to the delight of
the onlooking crowd.

"What is your news?" Myles always asked.

"Very bad," a crestfallen Bubu once replied. "Last night lions
tried to enter my house."

Touching his ears and wagging a finger in Bubu's face, Myles
retorted: "But you cannot hear them, you old rogue! How could
you know they were there?"

"I saw their great claw marks on my door this morning," Bubu
gesticulated excitedly, tearing his nails against the door, eyes
like saucers. "They wanted to eat me!"

"Nonsense!" scoffed Myles. "With all this good game meat
about, why should they want a scraggy old fellow like you?"

Bubu loved a joke and was consistently good-humoured. He

lived in total isolation at Kilimafeza (Hill of Gold) in a flimsy corrugated iron shack. Regularly, on his visits to Banagi, an outraged ranger accused him of philandering with his wife, which he roguishly admitted to be true. Myles would be obliged to reprimand him although we all sympathized with Bubu, and he certainly seemed irresistible to the ladies.

Each time he came to Banagi he asked to count his savings, which Myles kept locked in the office safe. Bubu knew to a cent how much should be there and he would count the mildewed coins on the floor in studied concentration. Then, nodding vigorously, he would produce further savings from his ragged pockets to add to the pile and pour the grimy money back into the bag. His visits were always accompanied by a gift of eggs, pawpaw (fruit), or a chicken; in return I would give him tea, matches, and anything else he needed, particularly *dawa* for his illnesses. I suspect he suffered from rheumatism, especially during the rains, for he was not young. With his eyes rolling in his head and using dramatic gestures, he would describe to me the excrutiating agonies inflicted upon him.

Sometimes tourists arrived at Banagi, incoherent in their descriptions of a madman encountered at Kilimafeza who had raced downhill at them, screeching and waving his arms. Wild and ferocious, he carried a *panga* (wide flat blade), and, the visitors would claim, they had only just managed to keep ahead of him. We explained that this was our friend Bubu, trying to direct them onto the right road to Banagi, for the other track led to the old mine with its dangerous unmarked shafts plummeting hundreds of feet into the earth. In his kindly efforts to help Bubu eventually erected a blank signboard at the junction, pointing in the right direction. But, wagging his head from side to side, he continued to bemoan the foolishness of some tourists in taking the wrong turning, and he was puzzled further by their reactions to his frenzied attempts to put them onto the correct track.

One day Bubu walked in from Kilimafeza looking very ill. For once he was unable to raise a smile and, at Myles's insistence, he was taken to Musoma Hospital much against his will. A week later he was back, having discharged himself and hitched lifts to Banagi. He looked miserable, lying pathetically on a friend's bed.

"Why has he returned when he is not better?" Myles demanded.

"He had to return, Effendi," answered a ranger, "because he knows he will die tonight and he wants to be amongst his friends."

"What nonsense!" Myles retorted. "Why should he die tonight?"

"He will die," repeated the ranger.

After a few moments with the old man Myles returned to the house, strangely downhearted. That night, in the early hours, there was a call at our door. Bubu had died. He was given a simple burial at Kilimafeza the next day. We never again doubted the strange perception which some Africans have of knowing in advance the moment death will overtake them.

One of Bubu's best friends at Banagi was our house servant Murumbi, or Fundi, as we called him. Frail and untrained, Fundi's only previous work had been as a stoker for the furnaces of a gold mine near Musoma, but we employed him during our first weeks at Banagi for his gentle manners and honest face. We were not wrong; Fundi proved a faithful friend and remained with us during all our years in the Serengeti.

We were not so fortunate in finding a suitable cook. Our first candidate had a habit of shouting at the top of his voice, which he lowered only when he was asked to talk quietly. Since we seldom heard a break in the din that penetrated from the kitchen 20 yards away, I suspect he bellowed to himself when there was no one in the immediate vicinity. Our next cook had a weakness for *pombe*, the local beer, and he would weave into the house breathing strong fumes and smiling happily. Staggering in one evening with a tray of coffee, he carefully approached the small table near me with glazed eyes fixed upon the wall above my head. Slowly he lowered himself and dropped the tray with a clang to the table. Then, beaming round in relief at our guests, he turned and lurched from the room.

Eventually we engaged a general labourer, whom I trained to cook, and who accompanied us on safari. His name was Paulo, and he worked with us for twelve years, contending with the ever-increasing flow of guests in the years that followed.

At the end of a day's work Myles and I would sit on the verandah in the cool of the evening and watch the animals converging on the river to drink. Occasionally a resident herd of twelve roan antelopes appeared, their masked faces and sweeping horns providing a rare thrill in a Park where roan were uncommon. Although Chandlers reedbuck were also scarce, they too could be glimpsed between the trees on the Banagi hillside. Buffaloes, giraffes, impalas, and waterbuck abounded, and during migratory seasons, zebras and wildebeest sometimes poured through the valley. Rarely were elephants or rhinos seen; but from the verandah we frequently watched lions stalking through the bush or lying in the shade of a tree.

The view from our house was a constantly changing pattern of life, with birds and animals of all descriptions. On some evenings we walked to the rivers on either side of the house or climbed to the top of Banagi Hill, where we scanned the country through field glasses. Although we were intruders into this tranquil scene, our small settlement seemed to have become absorbed into the environment and to have been accepted by the animals. Lions padded regularly along the verandah at night, buffaloes lay up under trees close by, impalas and waterbuck appeared on the lawn to drink at the small pool, and a porcupine visited us nightly until a lioness killed it near the house.

We generally spent our evenings reading to a background of music from our small battery-powered record player. I had hoped to have a piano at Banagi, but the difficulties of distance, bad roads, and tuning were too great, and we collected records instead, alternating the programme between Myles's preference for light music and mine for classical.

One evening our attention was diverted by a strange sound above our heads, like a stream of pebbles rolling across the hardboard ceiling. Climbing through a trapdoor into the roof of the main house, Myles shone his flashlight all around; the area was empty but looked suspiciously clear of bats and other small creatures. The next morning Fundi told us he had seen a large snake two days before, emerging from the eaves to lunge at the passing swifts as they flew in and out of their nests; we had been on safari at the time. Each day, and especially at night, the noises continued. I became increasingly convinced there was a snake living in the house. After searching the main roof several times, Myles finally decided to remove the corrugated iron roof partitions of the added section to the house. There he found the almost perfect skin of a very large black mamba, only recently sloughed, together with the remains of many little swifts. Our lethal guest must have left the premises after shedding its skin, for we never again heard the ghostly sounds of its passage across the ceiling.

Although the Serengeti harbours a great variety of snakes, we seldom encountered them at Banagi. Driving home from safari one day, we were slowly crossing a narrow tributary of the Orangi River a few miles from the house, when a 10-foot black mamba reared up from the road and whiplashed past the window of our Land Rover. The bite of this sometimes aggressive snake can kill within twenty minutes, and there was a wild scramble on the open back of our pick-up as the rangers sprang to life and tried to abandon ship. By the time Myles brought the Land Rover to a stop, the mamba had slithered into the branches of a nearby tree.

On another occasion I awoke abruptly from a deep sleep to feel my foot lying against a reptile in my bed. Thinking it was a snake, I lay completely immobile and felt my skin crawl with horror. This was a situation that I knew was a possibility in the Serengeti, and one that others living in the bush had experienced. The problem now was how to move my foot and escape unharmed. Without thinking, my body suddenly leaped from the bed to the floor in one tight movement. The disturbance awakened Myles and he helped me uncover the snake, stripping the bed while I held the flashlight. To our surprise we found a very large palpitating toad squatting nervously beneath the covers! Picking it up tenderly, I carried it outside to the bush.

We sometimes discovered young cobras about the house; but the place which harboured the greatest number of snakes at Banagi was our outside lavatory. Although Myles identified them as harmless hissing sand snakes feeding on the geckos (lizards) that lived there, it was nonetheless disconcerting to see one staring beadily down through the thatch of the roof. The doorway of the little building was screened by a curtain, and I hoped a cobra would not glide in one day, which, I had been told, was a common experience in such places.

One night as I neared the curtained doorway at about ten o'clock, I heard an ominous series of low growls. They sounded close, but in the limited light shed by my flickering lamp I could not see any lions nor judge where they lay. The lavatory was a few feet away and I sped into it, hearing with alarm the lions' warnings growing louder and more menacing. They were just outside, and there was nothing between us but a cloth. Half an hour passed. Since Myles usually fell asleep the moment his head touched the pillow, I could not count on his investigating my absence. Thinking I would have to spend the night in the lavatory, I was wondering how to fasten the curtain more securely when, to my immense relief, I saw a flashlight beaming outside. The lions growled as Myles approached; he saw several pairs of eyes glowing in the darkness 12 feet beyond the little building. Flashing lights make lions nervous and Myles quickly snapped off his torch before reaching the doorway.

"How long are you intending to stay in here?" he enquired innocently.

"There are lions outside," I replied with feeling. "I'm not coming out while they're still there."

"Okay," said Myles. "Well, goodnight! I'm off to bed."

He turned to go, and in a trice I was at his side, scurrying along and expecting at any moment to be leaped on from behind. Myles liked to believe the Banagi lions were gentlemen, and in this instance they behaved perfectly, with only a few parting growls to speed us on our way.

Incidents involving lions and the African members of our community were frequent. On one occasion a ranger bicycling to Seronera met a pride of eight on the road. He accelerated and tore through the lions, losing in the process a load of millet tied in a *kikoi* (sarong). He did not stop to retrieve it. Later a tourist reported seeing the torn cloth amongst the lions, which he thought looked most ominous.

A pair of mating lions once spent a week in residence opposite the cement works at Banagi, where the labourers made blocks for constructing new buildings. Their playful growling disturbed the block-makers considerably, and they invariably downed tools and fled whenever the lions walked to the river and stared across at them.

In 1957 we were joined by Gordon Poolman, a Park ranger sent to assist Myles in the development of the Serengeti. Gentle and strong, Gordon had been born in Kenya and was skilled in mechanics, roadmaking, and building, as well as being an experienced game-catcher. He and Connie, his warmhearted wife, lived in a mud structure consisting of two rooms, a storeroom, and an outside kitchen situated on the Seronera River, a mile from the visitors' lodge. It had been built beneath the most beautiful acacia in the Serengeti, which was later burned by the careless workforce sent to demolish the old building when the Poolmans' new house at Seronera was completed.

For nearly two years Gordon and Connie lived in their miniature house, called "Cobra Cottage" by Myles after their many encounters with snakes. One day when Connie opened the door of their storeroom and stepped in from the rain, she saw a strange circular object on the floor at her feet. The storeroom had no window and, being shortsighted, Connie peered about, accustoming her eyes to the gloom. Mystified by what she thought was a bicycle tire on the floor, she raised her voice to call for the cook; at that moment the tire rose up in front of her and spread its hood. Connie hurriedly withdrew.

On another occasion their cook heard an uproar outside the kitchen one night, and opened the door and confronted at close quarters a lion in combat with a hyena. He slammed the door and immediately scaled the high vertical wall dividing the kitchen from his living quarters. Dinner was not served that evening. The following day large tufts of hyena fur and lion pug marks were found by the kitchen door.

In those early days, apart from supervising the dispensary and shop, my tasks included keeping a record of all the animals we saw on safari, which I entered each month on a chart. This was a crude start at making a game census in the Serengeti and was later carried out with far greater efficiency by annual aerial counts. In the office I helped with typing and bookkeeping, returning each month from safari to wrestle with the accounts while Myles wrote his monthly report. Flies buzzed round the hot, sparsely furnished building where we worked, and outside a buffalo occasionally bellowed or lions killed an impala. It seemed incongruous in such a place to be sitting in an office at all, but the monthly returns were mandatory, and we sometimes had our problems. The sight of Myles busy at his desk, the clerk entering figures into a ledger, and a secretary hammering a typewriter, was activity enough to impress any casual passer-by. As time went on, greater skill and equipment were acquired, along

with an increase in the number of files, a gleaming filing cabi-
net, and a row of ledgers.

Through an asthmatic radio transmitter, twice a day at 8:00
A.M and 2:00 P.M. we shouted in communication with the outside world amidst fearful atmospheric noise. Additional sets
were used in the field, which inspired our small son in later
years to delight in revving his toy Land Rover through miniature
muddy rivers, bawling to his sister on a make-believe radio for
reinforcements to be sent in, and rendering his own sound effects of crackles and explosions in a most realistic manner.

One morning when Myles and Gordon went out to work in
the bush, they left their wives at Banagi without transport. I had
just given Connie two soluble aspirins for a headache when she
suddenly became giddy, turned deathly pale, and fainted. Not
knowing the reason for Connie's collapse, I rushed to the radio
and sent out an emergency call for help. No one answered. We
had no transport, no means of communication (except during
scheduled hours), and my knowledge of nursing was elementary.
Although Connie revived shortly afterwards from her allergic reaction to the aspirin, it impressed upon me our predicament
should we ever be faced with a dire emergency.

In a lighter vein Edith Harvey, wife of our Park warden at
Ngorongoro Crater, enquired one morning if she could bring me
anything from Nairobi.

"Yes, please," I bawled. "I need a bra. Over."

As I released the button, a visitor entered the office behind
me, followed by others.

"A what?" Edith shouted, amidst loud reports. "Please say
again. Over."

The colour rose to my cheeks. "A brassiere, size thirty-six.
Over."

But Edith still could not hear. In desperation I gave up and
wished her a good journey, ending the conversation with "Over
and out." Myles then gleefully introduced me to the Com-
mander-in-Chief of the British Armed Forces in East Africa, on
a short visit to the Park. My face was crimson.

In 1959 a new house was built at Seronera for Gordon Har-
vey, our new Chief Park Warden, who had been living at
Ngorongoro as warden in charge of the eastern Serengeti.
Engaged by Parks a month before Myles, and senior in age,

Gordon had had long experience of both administrative and field work during his years of government service. He was a charming, humorous man, and a born naturalist. His artistic wife, Edith, was the daughter of one of the first Europeans to settle in Kenya. We had spent many happy weekends with them at Ngorongoro when they lived there, and in turn they visited us at Banagi, bringing baskets of flowers and vegetables from their abundant garden. While Gordon concentrated on the administrative side of running the Park, Myles's duties as Deputy Chief Park Warden now became mainly concerned with the fieldwork of the Serengeti, which included preventing poaching.

At Banagi, the isolation of our lives and dependence upon one another created a family atmosphere amongst our small community and we knew each person individually. Myles found his job both rewarding and fulfilling, and he encouraged those under him to work with the same wholehearted enthusiasm. The respect and loyalty built during those three halcyon years stood him in good stead in the difficult times which were to come. Many members of the Field Force, which increased over the years to seventy-five rangers, remained in the Park for all of our time in the Serengeti, and there were some fine men amongst them. In later years each one of these long-serving veterans of the Park delighted in reminiscing about the early days at Banagi.

The era of the Serengeti's early development and of the Park's infancy was drawing to an end, and the peace of Banagi was soon to become a thing of the past. At the time we little knew what changes lay ahead.

Chapter 4

Poaching

In July 1959, Myles wrote in his diary:

We carried out a sweep along our southern boundary, which resulted in the arrest of fourteen poachers, the destruction of three camps, and the capture of eighty-five wire snares, with large quantities of meat. About thirty snares were removed round the water of the upper Miaga River; and in a camp nearby the carcasses of eleven Thomson's gazelle, just removed from snares, were lying in a heap. There was something incredibly pathetic about those Tommy, all completely unmarked except for the puffy head and neck denoting death by strangulation, and all killed without a poacher stirring a yard from camp, because the animals *had* to visit the only water in the entire area, which was covered from every direction by wire snares.

Such incidents were tragically common in the Serengeti, where poaching had been continuing largely unchecked for many years. Myles's main task when we arrived was to combat poaching as effectively as possible. With the resources at hand this meant almost constant journeying around the Park, creating a disturbance amongst the poaching fraternity and the illusion of greater pressure against them. In effect, it was more like psychological warfare in those early days, with less than a dozen rangers against hundreds of poachers; but it was also the beginning of a most successful campaign to bring poaching within the Park to a virtual standstill.

At that time much of the Serengeti was still unexplored, and there were no roads into vast tracts of country inhabited by permanent poachers' camps. In order to reach these areas we had to hack our way through the bush and cross countless river beds and tributaries. Without roadmaking machinery, every available hand was put to the task of making tracks. We walked many miles, cutting the bush and marking trees along the routes to be followed by the Land Rover. If large numbers of wire snares and poachers were captured on patrol, the prisoners occasionally walked to camp, handcuffed and escorted by armed rangers, and we sometimes accompanied them to relieve the burdened Land Rover.

Into the limited space of this small, battered, but tough vehicle which we called the Banana we piled our tent and provisions, as well as five rangers, a cook, and their belongings. Our luxuries were few. At strategic positions in the Park Myles erected temporary guardposts, constructed of old army prefabricated huts, to be used on our safaris or as cabins for rangers patrolling on foot.

Once in camp the Land Rover was stripped to a minimum for anti-poaching forays into the bush, so that we bumped across country with little showing above the general level of grass and shrubs. When poachers were spotted carrying their bundles of dried meat, snares, and weapons, Myles would race upwind towards them to lessen our chances of being heard. Then, turning in astonishment, the poachers would see us at the last moment, drop their loads, and dive into the nearest thicket. While Myles and the rangers leaped out in pursuit, my job was to drive round to the opposite side of the thicket and deter any attempts at escape. Since I was dressed in jeans and a bush hat, the poachers were not to know that an unarmed woman sat at the wheel, and in any case the Land Rover always proved a sufficient deterrent to the poachers breaking cover. They preferred to hide, sometimes vanishing completely into a patch of bush that the rangers scoured from end to end. Occasionally a disturbed buffalo broke from cover, snorting indignantly and scattering the rangers.

The Africans firmly believed that some poachers possessed the power to transform themselves into animals, thus escaping capture in the guise of buffaloes, hyenas, or even lions. They told us of a patrol that surrounded a small thicket into which two poachers had fled. The rangers confidently entered the bush and were put to flight by two buffaloes. After a short time the rangers reentered the bush, where not even a rabbit could have concealed itself effectively, but they could find no trace of the poachers. Had these men attempted to escape, the rangers would undoubtedly have seen them on the plain, for it was open grassland with little cover. The immediate interpretation put on this disappearance was that the poachers had transformed themselves into buffaloes, and in a country prone to superstition such beliefs could not be shaken.

On one occasion Myles reported having followed eight human footprints to a gully where he found a pair of recumbent figures lying on their stomachs in thick grass. Just as he and the rangers were about to close in, two angry lions exploded from the bush and passed within 3 feet of the two motionless poachers. Convinced that they had been following four men, the rangers believed the lions to be the missing two poachers. If this were not so, why were the captured men not afraid of the lions, and why were they not attacked when the lions could not have failed to see them lying so close?

The poachers carried a powder made for them by their witch-doctors, and this the rangers burned in terror whenever it was found, for they believed the powder gave poachers the power to change into animals. The people of Sukumaland in particular, to the southwest of the Park, were greatly influenced by sorcery. One of their witchdoctors even tried his skills on Myles, when the effects of the anti-poaching campaign began to be felt. Returning from safari one day, we found a trail of spent matches and several small burnt offerings laid throughout our house. Nothing had been touched or removed, but each room appeared to have been visited and a spell cast.

During those first two years in the Park we travelled all over it and spent most of our time in the bush, settling at Banagi only for the long rains from March to May, when the rivers on either side of the house rose in flood and isolated us from the outside world. A rickety bamboo and rope bridge had been slung across the Mgungu River which ran between Banagi and Seronera, and a vehicle would be left on the opposite bank to enable us to get out. Crossing the river could be disconcerting, as the frail structure swayed over the swirling flood waters, where I imagined crocodiles to be lying in wait. If the water was not too high, I preferred to wade through it along the concrete causeway, forgetting crocodiles in my efforts to withstand being swept downstream. Later, when our first baby was born, it became even more alarming to watch the rangers carrying her basket over the swollen river, lurching and struggling against the strong current as they tried not to stumble.

Crossing the flooded Grumeti River, I once lost my footing and crashed into the foaming water. After hurriedly managing to right myself, I saw Myles gesticulating wildly on the opposite bank, and thought he was agitated by my predicament. Surging about, I waved reassuringly and laughed as I tried to maintain my balance amongst the rocks. Then suddenly I remembered his precious Bausch and Lomb binoculars slung around my neck, which were now underwater. By this time Myles's face was contorted, his shouts drowned in the roaring torrent. It was some time before he forgave me.

On the first day of an anti-poaching patrol we would drive slowly through the bush searching for vultures overhead or for human footprints on the game trails. These signs sometimes led to a line of wire snares or a poachers' camp hidden in a thicket. Word soon spread that rangers were in the area, and the poachers either lay low or retreated; but once a prisoner was captured he usually informed on his compatriots, making the search for the others easier. Their camps would be destroyed and their meat, trophies, and hunting weapons confiscated. Occasionally an ambush was laid to await the poachers' return, which caused pandemonium when they walked unsuspectingly into the trap and someone yelled an alarm. Taking to their heels with the rangers in hot pursuit, some poachers fought savagely when capture was imminent, and it could be dangerous work.

Myles once shouted a warning to a ranger about to catch hold of a running poacher, as another poacher behind him raised his *panga* to bring it down on the ranger's skull. Hearing the warning as he heard the swish of the long wide blade, the ranger raised his rifle in both hands above his head and received the full force of the blow across the rifle stock, which broke in two. There were instances of rangers being slashed in hand-to-hand combat and of near-misses by poisoned arrows; but in no circumstances were the rangers allowed to shoot at a man except as a last resort. One poacher, shot through the forehead with a 14-gauge riot gun after firing several poisoned arrows at the rangers, suffered no ill effects whatsoever. He ate a hearty breakfast the following morning, was taken to hospital, and recovered completely.

Rifles were carried mainly as protection against wild animals, and were sometimes dangerous in the hands of the rangers. One of our best men was shot through the thigh by accident when his companion fired to frighten a gang of poachers into submission. This incident took place before we had an aircraft, and the ranger lay in the bush for several days until by chance Myles found him. He was taken to hospital immediately, spent many months recovering from gangrene, and was never strong enough to work again as a ranger. He became instead a tourist guide at Seronera Lodge.

When patrolling the Park we were sometimes faced with unexpectedly exciting situations. On one occasion Myles stopped the Land Rover and pointed to a number of vultures perched in the trees by a dry riverbed. Their presence frequently betrayed a poachers' hideout with its racks of drying meat; scrambling out, we all marched silently towards the area. After walking a mile or two, we reached the gully and started down its bank. A series of loud grunts immediately protested this intrusion, followed by the precipitate retreat of Myles ahead of two furious lionesses. It was every man for himself as we all ran for our lives, leaving Myles perilously near to the lionesses, who chased him for a short distance before returning to their kill. When the immediate danger was over, he was amused to see his wife in blue jeans still galloping across country without a backward look. In the trees the vultures continued to wait patiently for their share of the feast.

One of the hazards of searching for poachers' camps along gullies and riverbeds was the possibility of walking into dangerous game. Hidden from view by the dense cover, a disturbed buffalo or lion could on occasion put a patrol to flight; but it was a risk run by the poachers too, some of whom were found by the patrolling rangers gored to death by a buffalo and abandoned by their fleeing companions. In Myles's office lay the skull of one such victim, amongst a display of snares, with an inscription in Latin borrowed from a Sicilian cemetery that read: "I was once like you, and you will be like me."

During those early years we were appalled by the extent of the killing and by the cruelty of the methods used. The fight to curb poaching was an unending battle to protect wild animals from decimation. Myles enlisted as much assistance as possible from neighbouring organizations, such as the Game Department and the police. By keeping up the pressure against established gangs, his relentless campaign ended in their eventual disappearance from within the Park. Such combined anti-poaching operations sometimes had their funnier moments. Once when we joined forces with the Game Department in the Sumiji area, northwest of the Serengeti, two honorary game rangers enthusiastically stalked and arrested a solitary African by the river.

"Where is your camp?" they demanded roughly.

"Over there!" answered the surprised man, pointing in the direction of our tent through the trees.

To the game rangers' embarrassment, they had unwittingly arrived back at camp in that wooded and confusing terrain, and had arrested our indignant cook as he washed his clothes! During those three days, however, thirteen poachers were arrested, three hundred wire snares captured, and two large camps destroyed. The camps contained the meat and skins of nearly sixty animals, including two lions.

On another occasion while investigating the telltale sign of vultures, I came on a freshly killed zebra in the riverine forest of a sandy riverbed. The nearest ranger answered my call, took one look at the dead animal, and murmured "Simba!" Peering into the undergrowth where he pointed, I saw the shadowy figure of a crouched lion anxiously watching our activities from only a few yards away. We did not stay to find out how many other lions might have been in the vicinity.

One of our anti-poaching operations helped put an end to the wholesale slaughter of animals in the Duma region, southwest of the Park. Myles remembered this country from his hunting days as a favourite poaching ground, and he determined to make a track through to it. The previous warden warned him of the difficulties he had encountered, hindered by rivers and deep gullies which had rendered his own efforts unsuccessful. But by dint of hard work and perseverance, 30 miles of track were cut and our Land Rover arrived at the Duma River within two months.

A sweep through the area confirmed Myles's worst fears. Poaching was completely out of hand and had continued undisturbed for many years. The country looked utterly desolate, and few animals were to be seen. Long lines of cut thorn bush radiated for miles from camps built into rocky kopjes, holding snares at intervals to trap the animals as they stepped through the gaps. We came on some of the victims, still alive and struggling to free their legs or heads from the tightening steel nooses that held them to a tree or heavy log. Those we could release we set free, including a rare roan antelope; but more often than not the animals had to be shot. Once the rangers came on a zebra being eaten alive by two hyenas whilst it struggled to escape. Whitened bones were scattered everywhere, and a smell of putrefying meat filled the air. With so many carcasses for the vultures and scavengers to devour, even nature's method of keeping the wilderness clean had failed. Little game was left. I sadly watched a solitary kongoni walking carefully along a line of snares, looking for a safe way through; but wisely it decided not to risk any of the deadly gaps until it reached the end of a line and bounded away. Seeing the kongoni trotting jauntily into the distance, I thought gloomily that it would be just a matter of time before this animal too was trapped.

Although on that first occasion we saw few animals, we discovered later that the Duma lay on a route followed by the vast migratory herds, and this accounted for its popularity with the poachers. We were seeing it just after the migration had passed through, when it was virtually devoid of game.

In five days we covered some 400 square miles, burning to the ground every poacher's camp we found and removing every snare from the thorn bush fences. By the end, over 1,000 steel cables had been collected, which represented an average of 100 for each man captured. Untying the 9-foot nooses knotted to trees and logs was hot and tiring work in the tsetse-infested bush; but we continued without a break from dawn till nightfall until all traces of poaching activity had been removed. Only eleven poachers were captured in the initial surprise attack by our small band, for news travels fast in the bush and the gangs had fled to their settlements, 15 miles away. They left behind most of their belongings, which were destroyed along with the camps, filled to overflowing with racks of drying meat, great mounds of skins, and trophies from buffalo, roan, zebra, waterbuck, topi, giraffe, wildebeest, Thomson's gazelle, kongoni, reedbuck, and ostrich.

Billowing clouds of smoke filled the air as we progressed, giving warning to poachers further afield. Finally, our resources at an end, we turned for home and despatched the truck from Banagi to collect the prisoners and vast piles of snares and weapons. Steel cables are virtually impossible to destroy. Myles decided the best way to dispose of them was to throw them down the Kilimafeza mineshafts, which descended hundreds of feet into the ground. Even in those days snares cost between 1 and 5 shillings apiece, a large sum to an African earning an average of 2 shillings a day. Yet there always seemed to be an unlimited supply of steel cable, stolen from mines around the province. As pressure increased from the anti-poaching drive, the price of a snare rose to 10 shillings or more; and when Myles introduced a scheme whereby the rangers were paid a shilling for each snare brought in, this again resulted in the capture of many more. However, despite the thousands collected each year, the surrounding diamond and gold mines provided an inexhaustible supply of replacements, and it was impossible to eliminate snares completely.

Our efforts to help trapped animals sometimes made matters worse. Coming on a bull eland one day, we thought it unusual that the animal did not run as wild eland normally do when hearing a vehicle. This animal's fearless behaviour struck us as odd, and Myles stopped the Land Rover to look at it more closely. At once the eland moved. To our dismay we saw it struggling to pull an enormous log to which it was tied. Still strong and healthy, it was obvious the eland had only recently been caught. The stricken animal struggled across a deep gully, dragging the heavy weight, and we were desperate in our anxiety to release it before the noose tightened. But it took a few minutes to find the eland again after we had crossed the riverbed, and by that time we were too late. A short distance from the gully the eland already lay dead, strangled by the tightened cable around its neck.

Such incidents aroused our anger and pity and made us more determined than ever to eliminate poaching from the Park. The campaign became almost a crusade and Myles's prime concern. Apart from the unlawful destruction of game, the cruelty involved intensified our efforts to put an end to it. Saving the game can become an obsession. When I was away from the Serengeti, I would find myself thinking of the migration's passage through certain poaching areas at that particular time of year, and imagining animals being shot by poisoned arrows or dying in snares. Strong animals—such as buffaloes or rhinos—sometimes broke the steel cable in their Herculean struggles to pull free, and they survived with the noose embedded deeply around neck, head, or leg. Occasionally the bone grew over and encased the steel inside, causing unimaginable suffering.

We once came upon a buffalo with an enormous gaping wound around its neck. It was lying in a mud wallow, endeavouring to relieve the pain of this horrifying mutilation nearly a foot wide. The stench of rotting flesh was indescribable and flies buzzed around in swarms. I could not bring myself to watch as Myles ended the animal's misery with a bullet. Examining it afterwards, he discovered an old and broken snare which had sawn through the tough skin and flesh to the bone. From its condition and the extent of the wound, it was clear that the buffalo had suffered weeks of agony.

No one who has seen the results of wire snaring can remain indifferent to its use. Each time we came on a zebra struggling to free itself, or a topi wound tight around a tree, I became incensed anew at the cruelty of man. We once tried to release a wild-eyed topi by throwing a coat over its head whilst rangers worked at the noose, but it died from shock. The poachers sometimes hamstrung their snared animals to keep the meat fresh, and also to avoid having them eaten by vultures before they could be collected. This was the most sickening sight of all.

The worst case of mass slaughter we ever saw was after a gang of some fifty poachers herded a large number of buffaloes into a thick patch of bush which they had previously set with snares; forty-two buffaloes of all ages were killed in that one operation. Before the poachers escaped with the spoils of their successful drive, three of them had been apprehended by the rangers and the rest fled. Myles and I were on safari at the time, and the rangers led us to the gruesome scene.

There was, however, the satisfaction of knowing that some progress was being made against the poachers. Towards the end of 1958 Myles wrote in his diary:

An attempt was made to trace the Tabora River, our future eastern boundary, to its junction with the Mara. The country was extremely difficult to navigate, being a maze of gullies and rivers. One new poachers' camp was destroyed, several snares captured, and many old camps found. Some interesting points emerge from this first phase of Operation Overdrive:

1. Poachers in this area are no longer using the long fences for snaring game. The snares when found are now in clusters of ten or twenty in thick patches of acacia thorn. This must be to avoid heavy losses as, when one runs into a fence, all snares are automatically captured by following up the line. Now, unless one actually runs into one of these clusters, they are not noticed, as there is no sign of cut trees or fence.

2. The poachers' camps in this area are very well concealed. In one instance, the entrance to the camp was 150 yards upstream. The poachers entered a small path and followed the river bed to the camp.

3. In one camp the roofs of the huts were covered with fresh wildebeest skins. Easier to kill wildebeest than cut grass?

4. When poachers were pursued in this area, absolutely the last articles to be dropped were the steel snares, which indicates the value they set on them.

5. This area showed signs of heavy poaching and had been long undisturbed. It will need constant attention, and a well-organized system of foot patrols to cover the broken country.

Myles added that the price of wildebeest tails, used as fly whisks, had increased in 1958 from 20 shillings to 35, a small indication that the fight against poaching was beginning to show results.

One outcome of the Duma operation was an official's estimate that 150,000 animals were being killed each year in the Serengeti. Among other factors, his calculations had been based upon Myles's report of the number of snares captured on that safari. This was evidently given some publicity and enlarged upon in the local press. At Banagi we were unaware of the report until we listened one night to the overseas news and to our amazement heard a familiar voice announce that "Myles Turner, warden of the Serengeti National Park in Tanganyika, estimates that two hundred thousand wild animals a year are being killed by poachers in that area."

With the pressure lamps hissing and the little swifts twittering in their nests outside, we could hardly believe our ears. Two hundred thousand animals was one-tenth of the Serengeti's entire game population. At such a rate of destruction the Park would stand small chance of survival! Nevertheless it was good propaganda, for interest in wildlife conservation had not yet been sufficiently aroused and we greatly needed the support of the public.

Our early safaris were especially interesting in that we often camped in remote and undisturbed areas, and moved on after only one night. If we were late in reaching camp, we would sleep in the open with our mosquito nets hitched to a tree to save ourselves the trouble of putting up a tent. This, Myles believed, was adequate protection against inquisitive lions or other wild animals venturing too close; I had no alternative but to take his word for it. By affording a measure of concealment and by raising doubts as to whether the occupants were actually asleep, it was possible that the gently blowing white net *did* deter the animals, for we were not disturbed. On one occasion, however, we discovered pug marks in the sandy ground of two lions that had circled our beds in the night.

One evening when Myles and I were camped by ourselves near Lobo Springs, many years before it was chosen as the site of a modern hotel, I carried a hurricane lamp down to the stream to wash the dishes. As I bent towards the water, I became aware of loud lapping sounds. Expecting to see a hyena, I peered into the night and saw the outline of a lion crouched drinking a few yards from me. While I listened in trepidation to his long unhurried laps, he appeared quite unperturbed by my presence. At last the lion rose to his feet. Glancing lazily in my direction, he turned and vanished into the night on great silent paws.

Under a sky filled with stars, Myles watched this same lion stalk majestically past our tent, his mane gleaming in the silvery light. Shortly afterwards, a series of roars reverberated through

the night, rolling on and on, as one lion and then another joined
in the chorus, their mighty voices gradually diminishing to a suc-
cession of deep coughing grunts before fading away altogether.
Not a sound disturbed the stillness for several minutes, until at
last the spell was broken by a nervous whistle, followed by high
cackles of hyena laughter. From time to time the hyenas' voices
were interspersed with the panicky bark of a zebra, a rush of
hooves, scuffles and sudden silences. Tension hung heavy in the
atmosphere. The next morning we saw vultures circling over the
remains of a wildebeest killed in the night. No trace could be
found of the lions, who had eaten their fill and retired to some
shady retreat for the day.

Lions seemed to favour Lobo, as we discovered on another
safari to that area. This time we stayed at Klein's Camp, named
after Al Klein, an American hunter who camped there during
the 1920s. Our cook at the time was a very large but timid man,
liable to jump at his own shadow when in the bush; so we were
not surprised when he rushed to our tent one evening and announced that there was something breathing heavily in the camp
kitchen. By the glow of his hurricane lamp he could see nothing,
but he insisted, in a slightly hysterical voice, that whatever was
breathing must be very large and very dangerous. Myles
soothed him with assurances that he was being unduly nervous,
and after a while the cook returned reluctantly to his fire. A few
minutes later he reappeared at the run, in a state of such agita-
tion that Myles resignedly left the table to accompany him and
set his fears at rest. Shining his flashlight around, to his astonishment he picked out the gleaming eyes of a lion in thick bush, 10
feet from the fire. It had been watching the cook's activities and
possibly enjoying the smell of our simmering stew. The cook almost fainted with shock as the huge beast bounded away with a
grunt after Myles hurled a burning ember in its direction. He
left our service shortly afterwards. In years to come when visiting his friends in the Park, our erstwhile cook enjoyed retelling
this story many times, reliving his terror with characteristic gig-
gles and excited gestures.

We had not been long at Banagi when we discovered that our
mild-mannered house servant was on excellent terms with the
most notorious of the poachers, many of whom lived in his village at Mugumu on the western outskirts of the Park. Through

him Myles sent messages to these men, informing them that he had knowledge of their latest escapades and that it would not be long before the Field Force caught up with them. In reply Fundi would relay his friends' salutations to Myles, adding with barely concealed mirth that the poachers were undeterred in their pursuits and were looking forward to the coming season, when the migratory animals spilled over the Park boundaries into their settlements.

Liked by everyone, Fundi was a devoted family man with an enormously fat wife, twice his size, and an adored daughter named Sarah, whom he continually asked Myles to photograph. We found it difficult to imagine his having such rough associates as the poachers, for he disliked the hardships of safari life and was the gentlest of men. Dignified and sensitive, with a strong sense of humour, he and Myles often exchanged jokes and I would hear Fundi chuckling quietly to himself for hours afterwards as he laboriously went about his duties. Although he was conscientious and willing, he worked slowly; it required much patience and tact to hustle him along without causing offense. But I found it impossible to scold him, for he gave of his best without ever overextending himself. After a time Fundi decided to make his fortune as a shopkeeper in Mugumu. Too trusting, he gave credit to his customers and was back with us within a year, having lost all his money. He then resumed work in our house and rewarded us with his steadfast and faithful service until we left the Serengeti.

Over the years Mugumu village spread and grew from a few huts to more than four hundred along the boundary of the Park. Since virgin bush lay uncultivated and devoid of wildlife for miles west of the settlement, it was evident that poaching had attracted many of these inhabitants. During the seasonal visits of the migratory animals the villagers turned out in force; every man, woman, and child engaged in the profitable business of slaughtering the teeming herds. When game was scarcer the poachers set their snares across the Park boundary at nightfall and removed them before dawn, to avoid being seen by the rangers on their regular patrols.

Although Myles fought the poachers with thoroughness and determination, he felt sympathy for the local hunter who killed to eat. His real war was with the commercial poachers, those who shot and snared animals wholesale for material gain; for it was these men who posed the greatest threat to wildlife. When it became too dangerous to hunt by day, the poachers grew more cunning and could sometimes be heard driving at night without lights. Motorized poaching increased over the years, with more and more animals falling victim to the rifle and muzzle loader; it was often those officials employed by other responsible organizations in the province who were the worst offenders.

As the years went by, a mutual respect seemed to grow between Myles and some of the legendary poaching figures who had gained honour amongst their peasant kinsmen for exceptional courage and skill in the field. These men would be captured, imprisoned, and eventually released, only to be caught again and brought before Myles. Every prisoner was photographed, his details recorded, and charged for indictment at court. Many of them became accustomed to the procedure and did not seem to mind being imprisoned at the Kingi Georgie Hotel, as they called their jail. They were well fed and their main worry was that their wives might run away in their absence—a fear that was frequently justified.

The usual sentence for poaching in those days was six months' imprisonment for a first offense. This acted as a fair deterrent, since the poachers disliked being away from their homes for long. From the Parks' point of view, taking prisoners 100 miles to court was a great waste of time and money if the sentences given were too light; and in the early days the magistrates were ardent conservationists, giving the Parks all the support they could. In later years, however, sentences fell to as little as two weeks' imprisonment, or even an official pardon from a magistrate sympathetic to the poachers, whom he regarded as impoverished citizens. Myles eventually succeeded in influencing this attitude, so that the sentences were again increased to three months by the time we left the Serengeti.

Before Tanzania became an independent state in 1961, one of the last District Commissioners in our province would astound Myles and horrify the poachers by pronouncing sentences of two years or more in ringing tones. Since these sentences were always appealed against and reduced to six months, Myles enquired why such long sentences were given in the first place.

The District Commissioner retorted: "It's the psychological effect I'm after. If the poachers think they'll not be seeing their wives, children, and friends for two years, it might make them and the others think twice about poaching."

An administrator who ruled his district with a rod of iron, the Commissioner was a fine ally to Parks. At the time the new Park boundaries were being demarcated, his fiery outbursts would subdue all those around him and astonish Myles by their effectiveness. Walking up and down hills in the scorching sun and arguing for hours with various chieftains about where the line should go, the Commissioner once drew himself up to his full 6 feet and announced sternly: "I have *not* come here to be dictated to about where, or where not, the boundary should go. It will go where *I* say it should go, and it will go here!" With that, he jabbed his stick into the ground, and the line went where he decreed, without further ado.

Our safaris in those early days often took us to the Grumeti, a river running from where it joined the Orangi River west of Banagi to Lake Victoria. During a visit to this area Myles stopped late one afternoon to show me one of his old hunting camps along the river. It was an idyllic site, cool and secluded in the riverine forest, carpeted with fallen leaves. There was a flat open space amongst the trees, shaded from the sun, with the deep sand of the Grumeti a short distance away harbouring small pools of water remaining after the long dry season. Although the light was fading, patches of clear turquoise sky shone through the branches of the trees. Leaves shimmered and whispered in the slight breeze, and birds sang as they flitted above our heads.

We wandered about in silence, my steps leading me down into the riverbed where I noticed the track of some broad object winding its way through the sand. Thinking a snake had passed that way, I called to Myles, who identified the track as being that of a large log dragged by a buffalo. All too plainly the story lay written in the sand, and the spell of that magical place was broken by yet another instance of man's cruelty. It was dreadful to contemplate the agony suffered by this animal dragging its burden to the fast-drying pools of water each day, the steel noose cutting deeper into its neck with every step. I could only hope it had not suffered for too long. Sitting gloomily by the river, I watched Myles and a ranger climb the opposite bank to find the wretched creature and put it out of its misery. Night was falling when I suddenly became aware of the buffalo standing silently across the river in dense bush. I called softly to the men. Myles answered and instantly the animal took fright. Crashing through the forest, it vanished from view, and the men only managed to catch a glimpse of it. By then it was too dark to follow.

Returning next morning, we continued the search. This time there were vultures in the trees and Myles thought the buffalo might have died in the night. Wondering if perhaps the same thing had happened as when we frightened the eland, I suddenly heard an uproar in the forest, followed by a helter-skelter of rangers and warden tumbling down into the riverbed. Behind them stood a lioness angrily lashing her tail at the top of the steep bank as the men sped to safety. For a spectator, and with no immediate danger to the men, it was impossible not to laugh. Shortly afterwards, to my dismay, the rangers and Myles circled back for a second attempt at finding the buffalo. Inching carefully towards the kill, they were again put to flight without a chance of seeing the dead animal. There seemed no way of discovering whether the buffalo had died from strangulation or had been killed by the lions. At least its suffering was at an end, for there were no further log tracks in the sand.

One of the curious aspects of anti-poaching was the fact that captured poachers invariably led the way to the hideouts and camps of their compatriots. It was also difficult to understand their absence of pity for the suffering of animals. It may be that compassion is not a natural emotion; that it needs nurturing from infancy by example and teaching. On the other hand compassion for animals may be a luxury which only the materially secure can afford, the very poor enduring hardships that leave little scope for sympathy with other creatures. For human suffering, particularly that of a child, these same people sometimes showed a concern that surpassed our own. Even so, I still found myself outraged when I heard laughter at the acute suffering of an animal, and wondered how such completely opposite reactions could have evolved: total indifference on the one hand, and overinvolvement on the other. In our civilized society, with its social stresses and fears of increasing human population, there was perhaps a danger of letting our compassion for animals become greater than that for our fellow men.

At times I would bathe in the rivers around the Park. Myles disapproved, warning me of crocodiles. Since the Grumeti River in particular harboured a great number of them, Myles would sit on the bank with a loaded rifle across his knee whilst I swam. I thought this an unnecessary precaution, until one day a poacher disappeared into the jaws of a monstrous crocodile after leaping into the Grumeti to escape his pursuers. The rangers, close on his heels, witnessed the reptile erupting from the water to grab the unfortunate man, who was not seen again. Some months later their story was verified when his belt and shoes were recovered from the riverbed during the dry season.

It was difficult not to yield to the temptation of a cool bathe after a day's safari in the sun; but after this incident I was more careful about choosing shallower pools shielded by boulders and rocks. In years to come, when our children spent hours splashing round and playing in sheltered pools, I always kept close watch from a nearby shore. There was usually a risk in such waters, including, I learned later, the danger of infection from bilharziasis, the snail-borne disease common to most rivers in Africa.

Lynda, our first baby, was a few months old when we camped southwest of the Park in a desolate area called the Simiyu, an unattractive featureless country. Swarms of tsetses stung me to distraction whenever I used both hands to feed the baby and protect her from the flies. Dry riverbeds and tributaries crisscrossed the scrub bush that stretched away to a flat horizon, and the sun burned hotter there than in other parts of the Serengeti. At that time of year much of the vegetation had been burned by poachers.

The morning after we arrived, Myles and his rangers left early for an anti-poaching sweep through the region, leaving an armed ranger to guard the camp. Our tent stood under a small tree, providing scant shade in a depressing landscape of black ash. Smouldering tree stumps sent up spirals of smoke, and country which had not been burned was tinder dry, with hardly a green leaf or blade of grass to be seen. In a cloudless sky the sun seared one's body, the wind blew unmercifully, and the air quivered with heat. While Lynda slept in her basket and the cook and I busied ourselves with our chores, the ranger wisely took himself off to a nearby stream to try his luck at hooking a catfish.

Suddenly, out of the torrid silence I heard voices. Through the bush appeared a group of six men, dressed in tattered rags, armed with bows and arrows, and carrying leaf-wrapped bundles tied with strips of bark. They seemed in high spirits and chattered gaily as they loped towards us. The cook stared openmouthed at their approach. After exchanging greetings, they told us of their successful hunt.

"What animals have *you* killed?" they asked.

I realized then that the poachers thought we were a hunting party, albeit a poor one. My defensive demeanour changed, and I glanced towards the cook, inclining my head slightly in the direction of the stream. He took the hint and slipped away while the poachers and I walked towards Lynda's basket to admire the baby. All at once a voice boomed: "*Simama!*" (Halt!). At the sight of our guard with rifle at the ready, the poachers were too astonished to do anything but comply, and the ranger swiftly clapped handcuffs on them. Feeling a ridiculous sense of guilt at betraying their friendship, I watched uneasily as realization dawned on their faces. Suddenly the poachers burst out laughing, and the cook and ranger joined in their hoots of mirth. Once again I was impressed by their ability to laugh in the face of misfortune.

That afternoon Myles and his men returned to camp in a Land Rover filled with wire snares, but no prisoners. He was surprised to see our six handcuffed poachers squatting by the kitchen fire, and his green eyes stared moodily at them from under his battered old hat.

"Where have *they* come from?" Myles asked, scowling. His face was covered in dust and ash and he looked an intimidating sight.

"We arrested them," I answered lightly, nodding towards the cook as if it were an everyday occurrence for the two of us to capture poachers. Myles was skeptical and I doubt he believed my story; but he was pleased when our prisoners led the rangers to other camps and more poachers were caught.

On another occasion we were en route to a camp in the north when we spotted the heads of a long line of poachers bobbing

above the tall grass some distance from the road. With our two
rangers and cook Myles took off in pursuit, while I stayed behind to protect the heavily laden Land Rover from other
poachers who might attempt to set it alight. Although I was
unarmed, the presence of a guard would be enough to deter the
poachers from sabotage.

After a time I heard a shot, followed by another, then silence.
An hour passed and the bush seemed unusually quiet. Having
seen at least twelve poachers, I was fearful that our small band
might have been overwhelmed, and I began walking in the direction Myles had taken; but there were none of the usual
shouts in the distance to guide me. After covering nearly a mile,
I paused in uncertainty. Should I continue and risk losing my
way? My sense of direction in the bush was not good and I
decided it was wiser to drive to the nearest ranger post for assistance. But before retracing my steps I stood quietly for a moment and listened intently. To my relief, a cheerful voice
sounded far away and I headed towards it. Myles and the
rangers were on their way back and appeared in high spirits,
having captured four poachers.

It had been a long chase. After following the poachers for
some way as quietly as possible, to shorten the distance between
them, the rangers had been about to strike when one of the
poachers turned and saw them. He shouted and immediately
the loads of meat and weapons were dropped while the poachers
took to their heels, running like the wind across a gully and up
the other side. Realizing they could not escape with the rangers
so close behind them, one man stopped and aimed a poisoned
arrow, which fell just short of Myles. The man started to fit
another arrow to his bow when a bullet from Myles's rifle struck
the tree a few inches from him and a second threw the dust up
at his feet. The poacher quickly turned and vanished into the
bush. Those of his compatriots who were not so fleet of foot
hurled themselves to the ground when the shooting began, and
the rangers grabbed as many of them as they could before the
remainder got away. Two weeks later, through Fundi, we received a message from Tega, the gang leader, expressing deep
regret at having fired at Myles, whom he had thought was one of
the rangers.

To be hit by a poisoned arrow means certain death, for there is no known antidote. The poison is made from the Acokanthera tree, which grows wild in the bush. The bark and leaves are boiled until a tarlike substance remains, and this the poachers pack into small wooden containers to shield its potency from rain and sun. The poison must be introduced into the bloodstream and can kill in less than five minutes, although it may take several days. It has no ill effects on the edibility of the meat. The potency of the poison varies according to the freshness of the poisonous agent in the plant, called ouabain. Once a poacher fleeing from the rangers stumbled onto one of his own poisoned arrows, which pierced his leg. Although the rangers did their best to help him, the man calmly composed himself and died within the hour.

Myles tried for years to have possession of poisoned arrows prohibited by law, but he never succeeded. This was because the authorities considered it an effective weapon against carnivora and vermin in defense of human lives and property. In effect it could not prevent the charge of a determined buffalo or lion and was used mainly for killing animals and sometimes people.

One of the worst poaching areas of the Serengeti was around Ikoma, a small settlement 20 miles northwest of Banagi. We had often camped there by an old German fort, built more than half a century before, its crumbling crenellated walls pockmarked with cannon shot from World War I. These walls remain to this day as part of the structure of an attractively designed modern hotel.

Another heavily poached area lay to the north of the Park, in the Lamai Wedge Game Reserve, which was incorporated into the Serengeti in 1967. Before this event, anti-poaching operations were carried out with the help of Army Air Corps helicopters. The reserve was situated across the wide Mara River, and the army used these operations as training exercises, thereby enabling the Parks to patrol an otherwise inaccessible area. As Myles had long suspected, poaching activity in the Lamai was appalling, but without ground support not many of the prisoners captured could be carried out. It was unlikely that the poachers had ever seen a helicopter before, yet those who were arrested would wave nonchalantly to their more fortunate comrades as they lifted off vertically. The noise and strong currents of air generated by the rotor blades sometimes alarmed the guinea fowl, which scuttled out of the bush and took flight hurriedly, turning upside down in their struggle for control. Rhino and buffalo would charge around bushes, hooking everything in their confusion at the clattering uproar above them.

A splendid causeway was eventually built across the Mara River, enabling us to drive into the Lamai. People living along the Isuria escarpment boundary resented being evicted from their former grazing grounds and they caused a great deal of trouble. Lining the escarpment ridge, they would hurl rocks and abuse at us from 1,000 feet above whenever we patrolled the area. To withstand reprisals, the Parks' ranger post was especially reinforced and barricaded. In the end, after a number of explosive meetings between the administration and the local people, a compromise was reached whereby the former inhabitants were allowed only grazing rights in the Lamai.

The anti-poaching campaign continued ceaselessly throughout our years in the Serengeti, and it soon became highly organized. A well-equipped ranger force, radios, permanent patrol posts, Land Rovers, and a grader for roadmaking were largely made possible by generous support from America and elsewhere. These donations were stimulated by the brilliant fund-raising efforts of our director, John Owen, and to a lesser extent by Myles on visits to conferences. Some of them were contributed by friends from his hunting days. The most valuable asset to the Serengeti was a light airplane, which Myles learned to fly in 1961. He used it for searching out the poachers, for game reconnaissance, and for maintaining quick and close contact between guardposts and headquarters at Seronera. Airstrips were made all over the Park, and a thorough check kept on operations in the field. Discipline was of a high order in the armed ranger force. With strict control exerted over the use of ammunition, there had to be a good reason for every round expended, and each man took his responsibilities seriously. Amongst the rangers there was a sense of pride which stemmed from Myles's own belief in his work, and throughout all the upheavals and troubles which came in later years, the rangers remained a close-knit band of men. In the inevitable shake-up in authority due to transition from British to African rule, Myles would have been in a precarious position had not the men respected his command. Decisions regarding disciplinary action and dismissal were now made by a local workers' committee appointed by the community, and Myles was left with little means of controlling an armed force of seventy-five men other than the mutual trust and common ideals so carefully built together over the years. Yet despite his reduced authority, only minor disturbances ruffled the smooth running of the Field Force, which functioned efficiently to the end.

Notwithstanding all the efforts of Myles and his rangers, poaching continued (and even increased) over the years, on account of the growing market for game trophies. Within the Park itself, however, poaching was minimal, being mainly confined to its periphery. At peak times of the year, when the migratory animals spilled out into the settlement areas, poaching intensified.

Each year Myles kept a graph showing the numbers of steel snares collected and of poachers captured. By 1972 when we left the Serengeti, the totals stood at over 22,000 snares collected, and more than 1,000 prisoners convicted at court. With the high profits to be made from killing animals, and the light punishment meted out for poaching offenses, there was no hope of eliminating the practice. Yet, under the protection of the well-organized Field Force, the Serengeti continued to survive the annual poaching of game during the years we were there. By 1972 the migratory population had almost doubled, to 900,000 wildebeest, 600,000 zebras, and approximately 1 million gazelles.

Chapter 5

Jason

Less than a year after our arrival at Banagi a tiny Siamese kitten came to live with us, and we named him Jason. He was a gift from the Provincial Commissioner of our province, who bred these cats and was to spend the next fifteen years with us in the Serengeti.

As we drove with the kitten from the commissioner's house, I turned and saw his mother standing forlornly in the roadway, her mouth opening and shutting in sad protest until we were out of sight; Jason was the last of her litter. He already behaved with dignity, sitting composedly on the middle seat of the Land Rover and gazing round with hazy blue eyes. For his size (he was no more than 6 inches long) he was a most self-possessed animal, and showed no fear or emotion at being taken from his mother. Myles and I were impressed by his personality.

At Banagi I decided to train our kitten to a collar and lead, so that he could be fastened when necessary on safari, and kept indoors at home until the doors were closed for the night. Wardens who came later to the Serengeti allowed their cats to roam freely after dark; one survived by becoming wild itself, another failed to return after less than a month's freedom, and a third was carried off by a leopard an hour after sundown in full view of the household staff. To the best of our knowledge our cat had every one of his nine lives, but we witnessed only a few of his many narrow escapes.

Until our son was born in 1959 Jason accompanied us on all

our safaris, soon adjusting to the nomadic life we led and to the routine we followed. He enjoyed travelling and needed no encouragement to get into the Land Rover, sometimes jumping onto the front seat and waiting while we packed the car. On reaching camp he would be tied to a chair until the tent was pitched and then released and deposited onto my bed. Sniffing all around the tent, at his box of sand and his dishes of food and water, Jason first liked to establish himself in his new surroundings before moving cautiously out into the bush. He often disappeared for hours on end, exploring the country and never deigning to answer when called. But he was a friendly cat and enjoyed company, and he always returned before dusk, to sit across my knees by the campfire and join in the general conversation.

One night when we were camped under a large tamarind tree on the banks of the Grumeti River, Myles warned me that *siafu* (driver ants) might invade our tent. These ants marched in armies during the rains, attacking anything that lay in their path and biting fiercely as they swarmed over their prey. Helpless young animals, birds, and insects would be eaten alive, adult people could be driven from their beds, and even elephants gave way to them. After the ants' bodies had been torn off, their jaws remained locked in the flesh; it was said that some Africans used them as a crude method of stitching wounds. On many occasions we were obliged to strip off our clothing in order to rid ourselves of hundreds of *siafu* which had crept upon us unawares, biting all together as if at a given signal. It was amusing to see a victim of the ants' attack suddenly leap into the air, cursing as he shed garments in a frenzied attempt to get at the vicious creatures.

We would have been prudent on that safari to have surrounded our tent with hot ash or a line of diesel fuel, for *siafu* generally moved from nest to nest at night during the wet season. But we were tired and planned to travel on the next day, and we took a chance; the three of us, including our two-month-old baby, Lynda, squeezed into a small tent with Jason asleep under my mosquito net. Lynda's basket, covered also by a net, lay alongside our camp beds.

As the hours passed Jason became more and more restless, mewing softly and twisting about at my feet. "Do be quiet," I kept murmuring, drugged with sleep and kicking at him through the blankets. But he refused to lie still, until eventually I was wide awake. Shining the flashlight on him in exasperation, I saw to my dismay that the mosquito net was alive with *siafu* struggling to get through the fine mesh. Even more alarming, they were swarming over our baby's small basket. A number of them had already worked their way inside and in a matter of minutes they would have been all over Lynda, biting her in their hundreds before her cries would have woken me. Scooping her out of her cot I hurried to the Land Rover, while Myles sprayed the ants with insecticide and scattered hot ash around the tent to prevent thousands more from pouring in. I never again ignored Jason's distress signals.

One night not long after our Siamese kitten came to Banagi, Myles heard a sudden noise on the verandah and opened his eyes to see the back of some animal passing beneath the window. It was during the hot, dry weather, and a bright moon added to Myles's sleeplessness. Assuming that a hyena had disturbed him, he bounded across the room, flung open the door, and shouted: "*Wandoka!*" (go away!).

His irritation at being awakened changed to consternation when he found himself confronting a lion at three paces. The huge animal looked at him in surprise before turning and padding silently away. Further along the verandah was another lion, looking through a window of the sitting room with its front paws resting on the sill, and a third stood by the front steps. When they were all together, the three great beasts moved away into the night as if subdued by Myles's outburst. We then discovered Jason, his eyes rounder and more crossed than ever, staring through the thin pane that had separated him from the biggest cat he had ever seen. For days afterwards he was unusually quiet.

A few months after this incident our inquisitive cat made the acquaintance of a spitting cobra. Jason was a guest of the Poolmans at the time, and they followed our system of keeping him indoors at night, allowing him to wander in daylight. Each morning Jason would spend hours searching for field mice, and for a while all went well. Then one day Connie heard the cat mewing pathetically, and she rushed out to see him stumbling towards the house on his knees, crying in bewilderment and fear. Jason was blind. Guessing the cause, Connie bathed his eyes with milk, and within a few days his sight was restored.

There were times when our cat managed to escape at night after being freed from his lead, and these adventures were usually planned when we had guests for dinner. Hiding under the sofa, Jason would streak through the door the moment it was opened for our departing guests. He would then sit quietly in the bush until the search for him was abandoned. This did not happen very often, and I was usually able to find him again by glimpsing his eyes glowing in the beam from my flashlight before he quickly turned his head away. Jason loved being out when there was a full moon. On one bright night, after seeing that he was safely indoors, I went to bed without checking that the door was properly fastened. Our cat was an expert at opening doors. Whenever he heard us moving about in the early hours before dawn, he would leap at the door handle, banging it up and down to an accompaniment of frustrated cries as he struggled to join us. Sometimes he succeeded.

That night I awoke to a loud rasping grunt, and raised myself on one elbow to see a leopard gliding noiselessly past my window in the moonlight, so close I could almost have touched it. Leopards frequently grunted at night outside our bedroom, first one series of sawing coughs, a short silence, then another. I had tried often to tape-record this call, extending my arm very quietly towards the machine on hearing the first grunt; but when the following call came, it was always from a great distance. The leopard had apparently heard the faint click of the recording switch and moved silently away.

Although this leopard must have been aware of my presence (they have acute hearing), it padded unhurriedly past until it reached the corner of the house and disappeared from view. The animal's sleek perfection in the moonlight had made the breath catch in my throat, and I relished the thrill of it, feeling again a sense of privilege at such a splendid sight. After a while my thoughts turned to Jason. Was he safely in? Feeling sure he must be, I went back to sleep. The next morning there was a knock at the door and Fundi came in with the morning tea. His first words were: *"Paka haiko"* (The cat is not here).

Instantly remembering the leopard, I leaped from my bed. Jason had always returned for breakfast from previous escapades, but on this occasion we looked everywhere and could not find him. He was still missing at midday, and some of the rangers joined in the search through the kopjes and across the plains. There was no sign of him. Sitting down to a late lunch, I remarked gloomily that I did not think Jason would return. At that moment the door burst open and Fundi rushed in, shouting excitedly: *"Paka amerudi!"* (The cat has returned).

We hurried out, and relief swept over me when I saw Jason racing towards the house across the open plain. With fur standing on end and eyes wild with fright, he sped straight into his fireplace chair and remained speechless for several days, refusing to purr or even to leave the house. There could be little doubt that he had encountered the leopard I had seen the previous night. Since leopards also climb trees, the cat's only means of escape must have been to squeeze into a crevice of the rocks or inside a hollow tree trunk, possibly within a whisker of the leopard's searching claws. Certainly he had been through an unnerving experience, and it was some time before he ventured into the bush again.

Some months later while breakfasting on the verandah, Myles saw Jason trotting down the driveway a short distance from the house. Converging on him through the tall grass were two black-backed jackals, one on each side of the road. After it seemed clear that they were intent on attacking the unsuspecting cat, Myles intervened and drove them off.

Jason was seven years old when we went on our first overseas vacation, and Myles's mother in Kenya looked after him. It was Jason's first taste of life outside the Serengeti. Since domestic dogs were not allowed in the Park, he had never met them. A neighbour who regularly visited my mother-in-law had two Dobermans that were notorious for killing cats, and each time she called she would tie them to the garden gate while Myles's mother checked that our cat was shut safely indoors. One day Jason escaped through a window at the same moment as the dogs were released. Seeing the cat wandering across the lawn, they flew at him and would have torn him to pieces had Jason not stood his ground. He showed not the slightest fear, bristled to twice his normal size, and spat viciously while the barking dogs danced round him. Myles's mother could only think he must have faced far more intimidating beasts at close range.

Those dogs little realized how mild an adversary they faced, for Jason had the gentlest manners of any cat we knew. There was only one occasion on which he scratched our two-year-old son: Jason was in the open and more apprehensive than usual, and Michael tried to grab his tail. In the house the children could do anything with him and he would suffer their attentions with a pained expression and low complaints. Jason's voice held many variations of tone to indicate his moods. A long and drawn-out yowl with an unsteady note at the end meant that he was exasperated beyond endurance. Deep and sustained moans, when on his lead, signified an immediate need for his sandbox or he could not be held responsible for the consequences; this last desperate warning was delivered very quietly without moving a fraction from his chair. To be certain no one overlooked him, Jason conversed almost continuously when awake, the monologue ending on a quavery note if he felt ignored. When we packed for safari and he thought he was to be left behind, he would prowl round complaining loudly until my distracted yell sent him flouncing from the house, quivering indignantly with tail twitching on high, his grumbles fading into the distance. Our cat could seldom be silent, except when asleep, and even then he would frequently chitter in his dreams.

Whether in the house, the Land Rover, or the tent, Jason always secured the most comfortable seat. If, later, someone removed him, he would sit on the floor and gaze with cross-eyed disapproval at the usurper, reminding him that he was there until he was restored to his original position or to the lap of the person sitting in it.

Although the children were not always gentle in their games with Jason, he seemed to know they were very young and he never hurt them. I think he enjoyed the attention they lavished upon him, but sometimes I would step in to rescue the cat from torment or to save the toddlers from Jason's possible retaliation when I saw his tail lashing from side to side as the children sat astride his back and held his ears. There were also times when they carted him round in a loving but inadequate embrace, held too tightly or even upside down. One day, thinking the cat looked a little odd, I discovered on closer inspection that the whiskers on one side of his face had been cut while those on the other remained long and luxurious. Jason acknowledged my scrutiny with a long-suffering moan, as if to say I was not seeing things and this was indeed the plight to which he had been reduced. In time the whiskers grew again.

Our evening walks across the plains were usually accompanied by our sociable cat, who would frequently stop to investigate the tantalizing smells in the grass and then rush to catch up when we called. Sometimes he lost track of us and would stop and voice a special yowl, standing forlornly till we came back for him. But he also enjoyed explorations on his own and was often away for hours, returning on occasions in the car of a driver who had found him a mile or more from home.

One morning Jason was out hunting and I watched him stalk a guinea fowl in the grass. He was crouched and inching towards the bird when another guinea fowl appeared, and then another. Soon there were twenty, all advancing noisily on the surprised cat. It was too much for Jason. At the last moment he turned and fled, his tail like a bottle brush, and the flock at his heels. They chased him all the way to the house, which greatly offended his sense of dignity. Seeing me on the verandah as he rushed in, he immediately launched into a long and indignant tale of woe.

In the beginning Jason's hunting about our house included small birds; but he soon learned that feathered kills were frowned upon and would make himself scarce at such times. When remains were found scattered on the verandah or by the back door, I would call sternly for the culprit and listen for his answering call. But he always remained mute in his hiding place, eventually appearing with ears laid back and loud vocal protests at the scolding he knew was forthcoming. In time he stopped stalking birds and would allow wagtails and shrikes to hop within inches of his concentrated gaze, making no move towards them.

During the years Jason lived with us, he was called upon to adjust to the invasion of his house by our orphaned wild pets. Each in turn would be greeted with a stiff rebuff, which softened in time to tolerance and sometimes even to affection. From the start Jason always made clear who was master, and he allowed no liberties such as playing with his tail or creeping up on him whilst he slept. A cross-eyed glare and a hiss usually served its purpose in cowing the newcomer and discouraging such behaviour; only our bat-eared fox refused to be put in his place, and he tried the old cat's patience to the limit.

When Jason was nearly fourteen, we acquired a long-haired Siamese kitten that we named Amos. He loved to sit on my shoulder and would run straight up my dress to cling precariously with his sharp claws until I caught him. Fearless and charming, Amos purred thunderously, and he quickly overcame Jason's hostility. We found it touching to see our venerable old gentleman lying in ambush for his small companion and pouncing out at him in passing. With his beauty and personality Amos would have made a worthy successor to Jason.

One day a visitor and her small son called at the house and the boy played delightedly with our kitten, who was then seven months old. After walking to their car and seeing them drive away, I returned at once to the pile of typing that was awaiting me. Fifteen minutes later Myles walked through the front door and asked: "Who has killed Amos?"

I stared blankly at him, then said: "What do you mean?"

"Someone has run over our kitten," Myles explained. "He's on the road just outside."

Rushing out, I found Amos lying in the spot where the car had stood: he had been killed instantly by a blow on the head. For several days afterwards Jason looked for his small friend, puzzled by his sudden disappearance.

Shortly after this depressing incident, when Jason was almost fifteen years of age, he stopped eating. Within a few days his backbone had become visible and his stomach swelled with fluid. Although he seemed in no pain and purred whenever we gave him attention, he appeared to be in great discomfort and his voice had become much softer. Except for an illness at a Nairobi cats' home two years before, where he had been left for the first time during one of our overseas vacations, Jason had never been sick in his life. I was frantic with worry. He had eaten nothing for more than a week and was being kept alive on cod liver oil and vitamin drops.

After receiving my radio message, our resident vet, Bernd Schiemann, returned late one night from Nairobi, and he decided to operate on Jason the following morning. Confident that the cat's illness was curable, I drove in high spirits to the Research Institute, while Jason mewed and purred constantly. He complained mildly at the first unsuccessful anaesthetizing injection, but was put to sleep at once by the second. I then waited outside for news that all was well.

After several minutes a serious Bernd came to the door of the laboratory and told me that a large tumour was strangling Jason's intestine. At his age he could not survive the operation, and, if the vet did not operate, Jason's remaining life of possibly six weeks would end in pain. Stunned by the unexpectedness and finality of this statement, I walked into the laboratory to see for myself the hopelessness of trying to keep Jason alive. At the same time I saw how peacefully he breathed under the anaesthetic, and the serene expression on his lovable face. There was no question about the decision I had to make. I turned and stumbled into the sunshine, leaving Bernd to end Jason's life with a painless injection.

The next day, in answer to my request, our kind friend returned Jason's body to me in a box. I was grateful to him for not throwing it into the bush for the scavengers; and I was touched, too, by the sadness of our faithful Fundi, who had looked after Jason all his life and enjoyed his companionship in the empty house when we were on safari. With his help I buried the box in a deep hole, on which we placed a heavy granite rock. Around the grave we planted aloes.

Some weeks later the hyenas devoured Jason, their demoniacal cackles filling the night. By burying him inside a box, where air was trapped, I had betrayed him to the scavengers; but I felt no bitterness. In Africa, where nature removes all trace of death and decay, the laws of the wild must prevail. This was our old friend's final resting place, and our memories of him extended only as far as that. Replanting the aloes, I replaced the granite rock, and looked for the last time at his simple monument inscribed with the words: "Jason—beloved cat."

Chapter 6

Bushbabies

"Where will you go to have the baby?" Myles asked one day early in 1958.

His question took me by surprise. Having helped some of the African mothers on the station, I could foresee no difficulties to our child being born at Banagi, and I rarely thought about it. My main concerns were with such things as a layette, or whatever one called baby clothes.

"Why, nowhere," I replied. "The baby will be born in the Serengeti."

I had visited a doctor only once, was healthy and strong, and felt sure a midwife would be all we needed. But Myles was not persuaded; he insisted that the child should be born in a hospital. In the end I decided it was unfair to put him in a position of responsibility and anxiety should things go wrong, and I made arrangements to go to Dar es Salaam, the capital of Tanzania, where my sister lived.

A week before the baby was due, Michael Grzimek flew me to Arusha in his zebra-striped Dornier plane, and from there I took the scheduled flight. Michael had recently arrived with his father from Germany to begin a research programme in the Serengeti.

During our journey we circled over L'engai Crater, the Maasai's Mountain of God, a still active volcano east of Ngorongoro. As we looked into the fiery depths of this sinister mountain that rises to a symmetrical cone-shaped peak of 10,000 feet, I felt a

sense of awe and fear. There was a brooding, almost threatening
atmosphere about L'engai, standing alone and slightly apart from
its dormant cousins in the highlands. The mountain's dramatic
beauty, devoid of vegetation, contrasted strongly with the softer
mountains of Ngorongoro nearby and distant snow-capped Kilimanjaro. Eight years later it erupted spasmodically, a strong
wind carrying the volcanic ash over Seronera, 70 miles away,
while in the distance L'engai shone high and silvery above abandoned Maasai huts in a lunar landscape of grey dust.

In Dar es Salaam I had no warning of the complications that
were to follow, and it came as a shock to know that Myles had
been right in urging me to leave the Serengeti for Lynda's birth.
She was three weeks late in arriving and was born after three
anxious days in hospital with every modern help. For a further
two days she was kept from me under intensive care; but she
weighed almost 8 pounds and soon recovered from her ordeal.

Lynda was seven weeks old when we returned to the
Serengeti. From the first she loved the bush, accompanying us
wherever we went and adapting to our nomadic life with little
fuss or disruption. We placed her small cot on a board stretching
from the window seat of the Land Rover to the dashboard shelf,
and I travelled in the middle seat between her and Myles.
Across the rear window of the cab we fitted a curtain to screen
us from the rangers when Lynda needed feeding en route.
Later, when she was weaned to a bottle, I would pre-measure
milk powder into sterilized bottles and add lukewarm boiled
water as required from a Thermos flask, to avoid breaking our
journey. Lynda enjoyed being fed while in motion, and if there
was difficulty in getting her to suck her bottle at home, I would
ask Myles to take us for a ride. The moment the jolting began,
our baby drank contentedly to the last drop.

On safari I was no longer able to accompany Myles on his
daily expeditions into the bush, and he would set off very early
each day with his rangers, leaving one of them to guard the
camp. Having a baby to look after made this no hardship, and
from the first Lynda thrived. A healthy and beaming baby, she
grew up surrounded by nature in the clean open air with the sky
for her roof. She spent many of her waking hours naked on a rug
in the sun, kicking her chubby legs vigorously. The heat, the
tsetse flies, and the dust did not seem to affect her; she cried

only for good reason and never whined. Mostly she lay in her basket under the trees, smiling and cooing for hours as she watched the changing pattern of the leaves and the brightly coloured birds singing and flitting through the branches. Her eyes missed little, and from her earliest days Lynda loved nature, remaining absorbed by it as she grew up.

With small children it seemed that the simpler life was the happier they were. For the first year of her life Lynda lived mainly in a tent on safari, and was largely uninterested in manmade toys. Her favourite playthings were the small creatures of the bush, which she handled gently from the first and found fascinating. Later on, when asked if she would like a baby brother or sister for her birthday, she answered: "I would like a terrapin, a frog, or a monkey."

On that birthday Connie Poolman gave her a tin filled with small insects, some of them brightly coloured, others shining like jewels. It was by far her nicest present that year. Her other great interest was books. Like Myles, she would spend hours poring over them, even before she could read. The only toy upon which she lavished affection was a teddy bear her father had given her as a baby.

Our small daughter's curiosity about anything that moved caused us consternation on more than one occasion, for the Serengeti abounds with poisonous snakes, scorpions, and centipedes. Hearing her crooning over a *dudu* (insect) for minutes on end, I once found a large black spider crouched on the verandah parapet, ready to spring forward if Lynda touched it. Some primordial instinct had stopped her curious hand from reaching out, for she was only two years old at the time and knew no fear. As I covered the spider with Myles's cyanide jar, used for collecting specimens in the Park, it sprang to attack, opening its large pink mouth and bunching its hairy legs before succumbing to the poisonous fumes.

Scorpions were more common, and on several occasions Lynda narrowly escaped being stung by them. Usually I saw them first, in the toy cupboard, under flowerpots, or in our tent on safari. Once, when camping at Ndabaka Gate near Lake Victoria, I heard sounds coming from her canvas bag, and shook out a nest of six scorpions from inside her clothing. During wet seasons we found scorpions in greater quantities about the house—inside cups, in the bathtub, under newspapers, or even climbing the mosquito nets. There were two species that abounded in the Serengeti: the more common orange type, and a less poisonous variety, larger and black. We took great pains to warn Lynda against them, and prayed she would not be tempted to grasp one.

My concern grew when the warden of another park was rushed to Arusha Hospital, delirious with pain after being stung by a scorpion of the same venomous type as our smaller species. Two weeks passed before he recovered. I asked the doctor at Arusha what action we should take in the event of our daughter being stung, and he gave me small comfort. In his opinion the poison could kill a young child, but he suggested that an injection of local anaesthetic might help to reduce the extreme pain. This was added to our stock of medical supplies and we hoped for the best.

One day when Lynda was seven months old, she became seriously ill. At first there seemed little reason to think she was in danger, for she continued to behave normally, gurgling, and smiling happily. But she was unable to eat, and even glucose water could be given only in small quantities. My immediate fear was gastroenteritis, although, other than a slight fever on the first evening, she showed no signs of listlessness or dehydration. Perhaps she had suffered a mild stomach upset. Each day I thought she would recover, but when she continued to refuse food my anxiety mounted. I stopped two vehicles passing through Banagi during this time, and in one of them was a nurse, who told me I had no cause to worry as she watched our baby playing contentedly on a rug.

On the fifth day a teaspoon of Vitamin C was added to her glucose water, and immediately she vomited. But this time, instead of recovering quickly, she lay exhausted and pale in her cot. Thoroughly frightened, I collapsed into tears. At that moment Connie and Gordon arrived at our house. They hurried to the office, just as Myles switched off the radio after a routine two o'clock transmission. The next contact would normally have been at eight the following morning; but fortunately he had not been able to receive Arusha clearly and there were important messages to relay, so a special call had been arranged for 4:00 P.M. that day.

As soon as Myles called Arusha again, he asked that they telephone Nairobi for an aircraft to be flown to Seronera immediately. At first there was some doubt as to whether it could reach us and return to Nairobi before nightfall, but in the circumstances the charter company official agreed to try. The plane arrived and we bundled into it, Lynda still semiconscious and I numb with shock. Hastily shutting my door, the pilot took off; ten minutes later the door blew open and my hat sailed out. We returned to Seronera in order to close the door again, and were finally airborne by six o'clock. The pilot appeared nervous about the approaching dusk; when we landed at Nairobi an hour later, there was just enough light to see the runway. Myles's sister cancelled a dinner engagement to rush us to hospital, where to my dismay I discovered that Lynda's weight had dropped from 18 to 15 pounds during the previous five days. The specialist told me to call her the next morning at eight o'clock.

I hated leaving Lynda, but my hopes were raised by her sudden beaming smile just as I prepared to go. The following morning, after a sleepless night, the specialist reported that our baby had suffered some kind of virus infection, and that this had reached a climax at Banagi the previous day. Lynda was now on the road to recovery. However, I was very glad to have her safely in hospital, where it took two weeks of skilled care and feeding by tube to cure her.

After life had returned to normal, we were faced with bills for the chartered aircraft, private hospital and specialist fees, all of which amounted to two months of Myles's salary. Although our medical attention in Tanganyika was free, we had chosen to fly Lynda to Nairobi in Kenya, where specialized facilities were available; the onus was ours. For the first time we realized the dangers and disadvantages of our isolated lives. My theories that babies were strong and resilient, and that nature was the best healer, had indeed been put to the test. Later, the trustees of the Parks kindly came to our assistance by meeting the cost of the flight to Nairobi, which in any case would have been no further than to Arusha. They also agreed that any future flights to transport critically ill staff or their families to hospital should be met by the Parks. This concession did not in fact justify the fears raised by some that young families might prove an expensive liability, for luckily we were never again faced with such an emergency. Our optimism soon reasserted itself and we felt no wish to live nearer civilization.

A short time after our return to the Serengeti we camped on the Duma River in a round, prefabricated uniport erected there as a patrol base. So as not to disturb Lynda by our movements through this metal building, I put her temporarily along the front seat of the Land Rover parked across a game path leading to the river. Myles and I were sitting at our evening meal with a hurricane lamp flickering on the table between us when all at once we heard a large animal galloping nearer and nearer. My one thought was for Lynda's safety, as I imagined a rhino bearing down upon the Land Rover from the thick bush that surrounded our camp. Leaping to his feet, Myles yelled at the approaching beast, which apparently wheeled suddenly and thundered away. Hardly had we resumed eating than we were again startled by the drumming of hooves. This time, before we could think what action to take, a huge and crazed-looking wildebeest loomed into our small circle of light just beyond the table. Myles promptly hurled his jacket at its head, whereupon it swerved away and crashed over the bank into the muddy river 20 feet below. There was a loud splashing before it clambered out onto the opposite bank and vanished into the night. To see the wild-eyed creature bearing down upon us as if intent upon our destruction had been an unnerving experience. We could only surmise that the animal was blind, following its usual route to water, and that we had alarmed it by our voices.

About a year later, when Lynda was two, she had her first encounter with a cobra. By this time we had moved to our new house at Seronera. Situated between two rocky outcrops, it appeared the house had been built on a public thoroughfare for snakes, which lived in the kopjes; puff adders and cobras were especially common. Later they realized their unpopularity and withdrew almost entirely from the area.

We had recently hired an African ayah, or nanny, the wife of one of our rangers, to help with the work when our second baby was born, and to watch over Lynda when I was busy elsewhere. The ayah's name was Tibrandi, and she was a listless woman with huge protruding teeth and a kind heart. After Lynda had played as usual on the verandah, I put her to bed for her morning rest, and the ayah tiptoed back into her room to tidy it. In the meantime a large cobra had entered the room from the verandah, and was moving towards the passage door through which the ayah walked. It lunged towards her, startled by her sudden appearance, and she slammed the door with a terrified scream. The next thing I heard was Lynda whimpering.

When a hysterical Tibrandi said there was an enormous snake in the nursery, I rushed in and saw Lynda standing up in her cot, upset by the noise. I could see the snake behind the dressing table where it had tried to hide, and I sent someone to call Myles while I gathered up the child and hurried from the room.

That day I decided I would try to teach Lynda to be wary of snakes. It had shaken me to think of her playing on the verandah seconds before the cobra appeared, for had she seen it she would undoubtedly have gone up close to admire it. The snake might then have become frightened and struck at her. Lynda was not yet able to talk, so the lesson had to be in pantomime. While she rested, I carefully arranged the dead cobra on the verandah steps and waited till we were playing together some hours later. Suddenly I pretended to see the snake, and dragged Lynda away, pointing at it and shouting: "*Nyoka! Nyoka!*" (Snake! Snake!). She burst into tears, and I comforted her, re-iterating again and again, both in Swahili and English, that snakes were bad. After a while her tears turned to smiles, and I believed the warning had sunk home; but to be sure, I thought it wise to put the lesson to a test.

While Lynda slept that afternoon I placed the same dead cobra on the verandah at the back of the house. Later, walking directly past the snake with Lynda toddling behind me, I pretended not to see it and listened for her cry of horror. Instead, her steps slowed, there was a pause in her baby chatter, and after a short silence I heard a delighted cry followed by coos of wonderment. She repeated her new word again and again, and called to me to come and look. My tiny daughter was crouched on the floor, face bent lovingly towards the cobra as she tried to get it to respond to her.

I did not try again to instill a fear of snakes into Lynda until she was older and more able to understand. For one thing I could not bear to see her terrified by the pantomime I had acted for her benefit; and for another it seemed a waste of time, since her love of nature excluded all timidity. Lynda's cries of alarm when I dragged her away from the cobra had been at my own terror, for she herself had never shown fear of any living creature. There was nothing more I could do.

Unlike the wild animals we raised, children have no real awareness of peril, nor that sixth sense which warns even domestic animals. But as the children grew they learned of the dangers they must avoid, and there was some comfort in knowing that they would not now try to touch or pick up poisonous creatures.

In our early days of safari the tent we used had laces instead of zips, with the doorway flaps tied back for ventilation. There was no ground sheet. Some effort was needed to fit our three beds into the small interior, and this left no space to move, except around the legs of the stool that held Lynda's sleeping basket.

One night I lay looking out at the brilliant stars crowding through the open doorway of our tent, until eventually I fell asleep. A few hours later I awoke suddenly with every sense alert. Some instinct kept me silent while I listened to Myles's quiet breathing and strained to pick up any unusual noise or movement. There was nothing, and after a few seconds my tension relaxed. At that moment a leopard coughed gratingly outside. The sound was so loud that it woke Myles, whose deep breathing stopped as he heaved over in bed.

"That leopard's close," he murmured.

"You're right," I answered. "It was inside the tent a moment ago."

Myles laughed; but I knew there could be no other reason for my sudden awakening from a deep sleep. Lions roaring outside, or hyenas snickering, usually failed to rouse me; yet on this occasion a leopard had brought me to total consciousness without making a sound. The leopard had probably entered the tent and circled the stool holding Lynda's small cot, and some subconscious instinct had warned me of danger to my child. I thanked our good fortune that we did not live in an area where leopards carry off children, which in other parts of Tanzania was not uncommon.

Lynda was sixteen months old when our second baby, Michael, was born in 1959. Again Myles would not agree to Banagi as a suitable birthplace and, after my former experience in Dar es

Salaam, I was not quite so eager as before. We compromised and decided on Musoma, our nearest hospital, 100 miles away.

Just before Michael's birth Myles's doctor advised him to have a minor operation and I returned with Lynda to Banagi, leaving a disgruntled husband in Musoma. The following day a radio message from Arusha instructed us to move at once to the Poolmans' house at Seronera, site of the new administrative center for the Serengeti. Connie and Gordon Poolman were on overseas vacation and it was considered imperative that we live in their house until a new one for us had been built, to avoid the 11-mile journey from Banagi to Myles's office at Seronera. The task of moving house began, until eventually Lynda and I were installed in our temporary home. The curtains then had to be altered to fit the windows and the house made as convenient as possible for Myles's mother, who would be coming to look after Lynda while I was in hospital. The one storeroom in the house had been locked by Connie and Gordon, so that our large supplies of food had to be fitted into the linen cupboard and labelled for easy reference.

I was exhausted by all this activity when a Land Rover drove up with Myles and his harassed doctor, who had been unable to keep him in hospital a moment longer. The doctor, a volatile Irishman with merry blue eyes, looked at my ashen face and promptly switched patients, insisting that I accompany him. After some protest I meekly agreed and took Lynda with me to Musoma, where I spent the next two weeks in hospital, recovering from a threatened case of toxemia.

In the end all was well and Michael arrived safely. At the time there were no European patients in the hospital, and a cook was especially taken on to prepare my meals. The African patients were fed mainly on *posho* (maize meal), the country's staple diet.

"What would you like for lunch today, Mama?" the cook would enquire politely each morning, before setting off on foot with a *kikapu* (basket) to buy the food I had ordered. There was no one to wash the baby or his clothes, so I did these tasks from the beginning. Visitors leaning over the cot to admire the new arrival gave no thought to germs and infection, and everything was splendidly informal.

Michael was ten days old when he began his life of safari in the bush. Unlike Lynda, our son did not grow up with any spontaneous affinity to nature and the wilds; but he loved everything connected with life on safari and took a lively interest in Land Rovers, rifles, fishing, airplanes, and the activities of the Field Force. From the first he was a friend of the rangers, joining as much as possible in their work and way of life. They in return showed him great kindness, for Africans have a deep affection for children, especially boys. Less critical and impatient than we are, they were rarely heard to scold or correct their children; yet I never saw an African child throw a tantrum or deliberately disobey his elders. The children were seldom rowdy or obnoxious and seemed to develop in an atmosphere of tranquillity, accepting their way of life without discontent or envy. There are few more appealing sights than that of an African *toto* (child), with his chubby good looks and innocent face entirely devoid of guile or ill-temper.

Birthday parties for our children were attended by many of these *totos* each year. It was touching to see their shy anxiety to behave correctly, and I would go to great lengths to encourage them to relax and enjoy themselves. Treasure hunts proved unsuccessful—they always ended with me digging up the toys hidden in the garden and distributing them amongst our small guests. Food which had taken such hours to prepare would remain untouched. But if Myles and I left the scene, it miraculously disappeared within a few seconds, probably tucked within the voluminous bosoms of the children's mothers, who sat silently by with the youngest of their *totos*. Bags of sweets tied in coloured paper, and balloons, were always popular once the children grew accustomed to the loud bangs when they burst. As each year went by, our parties became noisier and more spontaneous.

Michael's first two years in the Serengeti were not entirely free from anxiety. He was three months old when he had his first convulsion, brought on by a high fever he developed. It was the prelude to others that he suffered whenever he was ill, or fell and hit his head on the hard ground. Each time I found it a terrifying experience, and would hold his small, rigid body in my arms until he resumed breathing. He was also afflicted with digestive troubles that caused him to be underweight until he was a year old. Changing his diet, and leaving him for a week in Musoma Hospital, had no effect. Finally, on a chance recommendation, I discovered the cure to lie in daily doses of yeast tablets; from that moment Michael's digestive problems were at an end, and he gained weight. He was always a bright and active child.

Until 1966 no other European children lived in the Serengeti. Anticipating the loneliness a child might feel in such isolation, we planned on having our two children born within the shortest possible interval. From the first they were friends, although there were the usual disagreements and differences of opinion from time to time. Of the two Lynda was the more independent, able to play for hours alone and sometimes impatient of Michael's interruptions. He, on the other hand, needed companionship and insisted on entering into Lynda's solitary preoccupations with caterpillars, tadpoles, ant farms, and the like. When bored with this, he would do his utmost to persuade her to join in the safari game, with his make-believe rangers and poachers, toy Land Rovers, intricate roads, and rivers carved into the dust. Although totally uninterested, Lynda always humoured her small brother for as long as she could stand his constant repetition of the zoom-zooming sound made by Land Rovers bogged down, cryptic radio messages, and being relegated to the role of the "baddie" poacher. In the rains they took great delight in finding the deepest mudhole they could, and would spend hours playing in it, sometimes emerging muddy from head to toe.

Although Myles's work was concerned with anti-poaching and field duties and we still continued to camp out occasionally, our lives in the Serengeti had become less roving. Office administration was growing with an increase in personnel, tourists, important visitors, and Lodge accommodation. Much of Myles's fieldwork was now done by airplane, which cut down still further on ground safaris. Roads were improved, water supplies increased, transport enlarged, staff recruited, and houses built. The Lodge had been enlarged to accommodate forty visitors instead of twelve, and the Serengeti was attracting an increasing number of people. As we became involved in the rapid development of the Park, the small family atmosphere of the early days began to fade. Scientists started working in the Park, which was no longer the remote, largely unexplored area it had been when we first knew it. Charter airplanes brought tourists regularly, and there was a weekly scheduled service by DC-3 from Nairobi. Seronera had become a spreading village, and Banagi was now of little importance except as the site for the first research laboratory, built in memory of Michael Grzimek who was tragically killed in his Dornier in 1959.

As our son Michael grew up, he experienced only the last of our nomadic years. Nevertheless he too came in for his share of adventure. One day I was not surprised to hear him telling Lynda that there was a *nyoka* on the verandah; he was almost two at the time, and had recently learned this Swahili word for snake. Thinking perhaps he was practicing his vocabulary, I went to investigate and saw a huge puff adder, more than 4 feet long, climbing the verandah steps towards the fascinated children. With the help of the servants it was killed. I was always afraid the children might unwittingly step on one in the grass. Puff adders tend to be sluggish and to rely on their concealing markings to escape notice; in spite of their inert appearance, they are capable of striking with amazing rapidity and are reputed to be responsible for more serious cases of snakebite than any other species.

A few hours after we killed the puff adder, Michael came into the kitchen and announced importantly that he had found yet more snakes. Unable to believe it, I went to where he and Lynda had lifted a large stone at the side of the driveway. Under it lay two perfectly marked puff adders, each less than 6 inches long. In all probability they were the young of the adult we had just killed. Small as they were their poison was equally deadly, and I told the children very emphatically that they were not to touch any snakes they found, however little and harmless they looked. Puff adders are viviparous, and as about thirty to forty are born at a time, I knew there would be many more in the vicinity.

Two years after this incident I was giving Lynda her lessons on the verandah when Michael came in cradling a baby hyrax (rock rabbit) in his hands. It could not have been more than a few days old, and we were enchanted. Telling Michael we must return the baby to its mother, we all trooped to the place where he had found it, and prepared to set it down on the road. While the children bent over the small animal, a slight movement in the grass nearby caught my eye, and I turned to see a large cobra with outstretched hood rearing up a few feet from where we stood. Realizing at once why Michael had so easily captured the petrified hyrax, I pulled the children away and shouted to some labourers, who were building our guesthouse, to come quickly. For what seemed a long time the cobra remained erect, weaving from side to side, before sliding away through the undergrowth into the kopjes. It was out of sight by the time the labourers sauntered to the scene. I shuddered at the thought of Michael grasping the hyrax at the very moment when the snake was prepared to strike.

Myles told this story in his monthly report, and it was picked up by the press and published in the British newspapers. But it did not end there. We were now faced with the prospect of caring for our small hyrax. The rest of the colony had obviously bolted when they spotted the cobra and there seemed little chance of the mother looking for her baby. In any case it would be one of a litter and unlikely to be missed.

Having already tried unsuccessfully to raise hyraxes, I decided this time to wait twenty-four hours before feeding it with any milk formula. Instead I gave it lukewarm glucose water and deposited the tiny creature inside my shirt for warmth. It protested vigorously in a continuous and piercing shriek, the volume of sound out of all proportion to its size. By the end of the day, nine hours later, I had had enough, and decided to enjoy a walk without my small vociferous guest. No sooner had I left the verandah after placing the hyrax in a cardboard box on the table, with a cushion on top to prevent it getting out, than I heard a strange low sound punctuating the high-pitched screams. Looking out, I saw a full-grown hyrax perched on top of the box, making distressed sounds in answer to the frantic yells from inside. I crept up and opened the box, and the adult hyrax (a species which is normally timid) jumped to the ground at my feet and waited to escort her baby away. When it tried in vain to follow her up onto the parapet, the mother ran round to the verandah steps and called from there, a peculiar guttural cry. Then together they raced to the kopjes, the baby still screeching.

Some years later we were camped at a saltlick called Larelemangi, on one of the many tributaries of the Bologonja River in the north of the Park. Below our tent lay the stream, with fresh water and shady trees, where we bathed and fished. It was an idyllic place for the children, who played on the sandy shore and spent hours trying hopefully to hook a tilapia, the delicious fish that lived in such waters. At night elephants came down to drink after eating the salt, and occasionally herds of zebra, wildebeest, or buffalo woke us by stampeding past on scenting lions in the vicinity. I always expected them to crash into our tent, but somehow they avoided it, although on one occasion a rhino did blunder in and carry away our canvas washbasin with much huffing and snorting.

We were enjoying a morning by the river when Myles returned from patrol and repeated his warning to the children to watch for snakes when playing by water. After a late lunch he went to his tent to rest, while Lynda decided to go fishing. Michael and I remained in camp.

It was a hot, lazy afternoon, with flies buzzing and birds calling in the trees. Suddenly a scream of terror from the direction of the stream shattered the drowsy atmosphere. All my fears for the children rose to the surface as I imagined Lynda being attacked by some animal she had walked into. I rushed out, and saw her stumbling towards the tent with what looked like a ratel behind her. Calling "What is it?" I ran towards her, at the same time thinking how aggressive these badgers could be with their strong claws and teeth. Lynda gasped: "Snake!", and at once the impression of a honey badger at her heels vanished. It had been produced entirely by my imagination; later, Michael told me that he too thought he had seen an animal chasing Lynda. She was so frightened that at first I could get nothing out of her; while I tried to discover whether she had been bitten by a snake, Myles appeared.

"What's going on?" he asked calmly. "You all sound like a troop of baboons."

I expect we did, jabbering and crying, with the memory of that scream still chilling my blood. After Myles heard Lynda's story and made certain she was all right, we walked to the river. Within 3 feet of where she had been standing by the water's edge was a cobra in the reeds. It was still reared up with hood spread wide and tongue flickering. Lynda had noticed it only on remembering her father's advice, and her horror at finding herself staring at a snake about to strike had sparked off her screams as her fat little legs propelled her away.

This experience did not lessen our daughter's interest in wildlife; in fact, a few years later she became fascinated by snakes and began collecting the less dangerous specimens while on holiday, including an 8-foot python she named Delilah. She released them at the end of each holiday and new ones would be caught when she came home again, for I did not share her enthusiasm in caring for them.

Owing to their isolation the children were very shy, and they sometimes went to ground if strangers called. On one occasion during a visit by our old friend Syd Downey, the well-known professional hunter who was godfather to Lynda, he kept asking: "Where's Lynda?"

Michael, no more than 2 feet high, grew tired of hearing this oft-repeated phrase, and finally muttered: "Under the sofa." And there indeed she was.

During another afternoon's conversation with unexpected visitors, a mysteriously moving curtain revealed our small son, who had grown fidgety in his hiding place. But this stage passed when, at the age of seven, they went to boarding school in Kenya and learned to play with other children. Lynda's passion for poking about in hedges and flowerbeds, looking for wild creatures, was soon noticed; later she took charge of some of the animals kept in the biology department of her English school. Michael, on the other hand, left much of his bush background behind him and joined enthusiastically in social activities and sports.

By the time the children started school, they had learned to read, write, and do arithmetic at home with the help of a correspondence course. At first they looked forward eagerly to the adventure ahead, but their enthusiasm waned with each holiday that they spent in the Serengeti. To make the long terms less tedious I would drive 500 miles to their school in Kenya for half-term weekends. Such visits were not possible after they transferred to schools in England three years later, and we saw them only for their holidays at Easter, Christmas, and in the summer.

After Michael joined his sister at school I missed their laughter, voices, and personalities dreadfully, and wondered how best to fill the hours that I had spent with them. The question asked so many times by visitors to the Park seemed now to have a new significance: "What do you *do* with yourself all day?" The future looked empty and suddenly the house was too quiet. For a while I occupied myself with office work and our increasing social life at Seronera. Yet with the children gone I felt little enthusiasm for what I was doing.

This period of lonely aimlessness ended a few weeks later when Myles brought me a fox cub, whose lively personality took up much of my time and attention.

Chapter 7

Seronera

In 1959 the headquarters for the Serengeti were changed from Banagi to Seronera, 11 miles away, which was to be our home until we left the Park in 1972. We had known about the proposed move for some time, and in those months I was able to adjust to the sadness of leaving Banagi by turning my thoughts to the choice of a site for our new house.

The location we chose was between two rocky outcrops that were enlivened by flowering shrubs and trees. Huge granite boulders concealed the house on both sides and tall acacias shaded the level ground between them. Looking west we faced a hill called Nyaraswiga across sparse woodlands and a line of trees that marked the river; and to the east we looked upon open grasslands that verged onto the Serengeti Plains. Sometimes a pair of dikdiks darted away like delicate fawns, or giraffes browsed in the kopjes, their long necks merging into the foliage of the bush. Birds of all description sang and flitted about, and tree hyraxes balanced on the acacia branches overhead.

For as long as we lived there I never ceased to be impressed by Seronera's beauty. The sweeping plains were cropped short by grazing animals, and jutting rock outcrops lay scattered about the countryside, their sculptured shapes outlined against the sky. Flat-topped umbrella acacias and lime green thorn trees shaded the herds of gazelles and wildebeest. There was a quality of light that made the landscape glow, while the boundless sky shone with a blue vitality that seemed to crown the unique wonder of Seronera.

In the 1960s the development of the Park headquarters partially spoiled Seronera's magic; but in those early days there was nothing to mar its splendour. Each day dawned with a purity that suggested the beginning of time, and each day brought its variations of light, colour, and mood. When evening turned the grass to gold and threw the vivid green acacias into brilliant focus against a stormy sky, or shining clouds cast purple shadows across the sunlit hills and plains, I was struck by Seronera's perfection with a force that took my breath away.

Designing our house within certain specified dimensions greatly interested me, and I kept close watch on its progress, making minor alterations during construction. Gordon Poolman, a kind and patient man, was in charge of building operations in the Park, and the house was exactly as I had envisaged it when completed in 1960. It had a wide verandah, a large sitting room with dining alcove, three bedrooms, and bathroom leading off a central passageway, a pantry, a storeroom, and a small verandah at the back. Several yards away was a kitchen with firewood stove, connected to the house by a covered way. Myles once came on a cheetah sitting atop a half-built wall; it was unusually tame for those days and seemed reluctant to leave, gazing out across the plains with sphinxlike concentration.

During the construction we lived in the Poolmans' house, and each day I walked a mile to the site of our building, pushing Michael's pram while the ayah wheeled Lynda in her pushchair and our cat Jason scampered beside us. He soon grew to know the route so well that he would sometimes set off by himself and be brought back later by one of the workers. Although buffaloes lived in the patches of bush around our settlement, they were not common and there was little risk in walking unless we were unlucky enough to meet a lion. However, life in this area could be unpredictable. A few years later an African was knocked from his bicycle by a rhino and fatally gored—an unusual disaster since rhinos were rare at Seronera, whereas buffaloes had become an increasing hazard.

At Seronera, before we moved to our new house, my time was largely taken up with the children and housekeeping. But there were still times when we met a creature from the bush to remind us of our wild environment. One of these took place in the Poolmans' pantry, a room that contained an aluminum sink with draining boards along one wall and a china cupboard along another. Into the empty corner space where these two units met I deposited spare paper bags, and from time to time I heard a rustling amongst them. Thinking this was a field mouse, I ignored the sound, for the cupboard was too large and too heavy to move in the confined room. One evening while Fundi served dinner, he announced there was a snake in the pantry, a part of which could still be seen protruding into the room. After fetching his rifle, Myles fired at it, and pulled a 7-foot cobra out from under the china cupboard. There were no further rustlings amongst the paper bags. Remembering the many times we had stood close to this snake when working in the pantry, I felt a certain sense of remorse at killing a creature that had done us no harm.

Shortly after we settled into our house, I pushed open the door to the verandah one night and heard a loud hiss. I also felt a slight obstruction against the door. "Singing" ants make a high-pitched buzz when disturbed, and I expected to see these insects when I stepped behind the door to switch on the light. Instead I saw the tail end of a cobra slipping out of sight beneath a cane sofa 2 yards away. It had been lying against the door, and I had apparently stepped over it while reaching for the light switch.

Snakes were common about the house in those first years at Seronera, and the birds constantly gave them away, twittering and squawking as they hopped beside them in the grass. Speckle-fronted weavers, starlings, and d'Arnaud's barbets usually raised the alarm, betraying the presence of a snake or, more often, a slender mongoose which also robbed their nests. Once I saw two snakes lying on top of each other. They were puff adders, the one underneath being long and fat with a short thin tail, and the one on top much smaller. At first I thought this was the larger puff adder's baby, but it was more likely that the two had been mating.

On another occasion we found a puff adder entangled in the chicken wire that surrounded a patch of parsley growing by our back door. It had squeezed through a hole in the wire, stuck halfway, and tried to get out again through another hole. The wretched creature lay helplessly entwined and could not move. Myles shot it.

We were away on safari when our house servant heard the chickens squawking hysterically one night. Fundi's sole means of defense was a Maasai spear we had given him, several feet long. Grasping his spear, he hurried out and flung open the door of the chickens' house. To Fundi's consternation the interior was filled with a huge cobra writhing amongst the seething hens. He gamely lunged into the darkness with his spear and managed to kill the snake. But he was too late to save the chickens, nine of which had died instantly, the rest dying over a period of three days from smaller doses of poison.

After this incident Myles boarded up the henhouse so tightly that not even a lizard could have squeezed through; but he was unable to prevent yet another wild creature from getting in only a few weeks later.

We had gone to bed after entertaining the District Commissioner and his wife from Musoma, who were our first guests in the new house. Moonlight streamed through the windows, sprawling long shadows from the trees and picking out a pair of dikdiks that stood like miniature statues on the lawn. As I drifted into sleep a lonely hyrax called plaintively from atop a sentry post high in the rocks. Suddenly there was a loud knocking at the door, and I heard the cook's voice urging us to hurry; the chickens were in trouble. Shaking Myles awake, I leaped from my bed, for this time our hens were pedigree birds from Nairobi recently flown to Seronera at no mean expense. We hurried out and saw Fundi, the cook, Myles's orderly, their wives and children all standing silently in the moonlight watching our chickens being chased around their wire enclosure by two honey badgers.

"Do something!" I shouted, adding my voice to the chickens' squawks. Myles fired a shot into the air, and the badgers promptly broke through the enclosure and came straight for us. Completely fearless, they will even attack a Land Rover if provoked, biting and tearing at the tires with their formidable claws. We took to our heels, Fundi's enormous spouse discovering a hitherto unknown turn of speed as she trundled into the distance in her gaudy draperies. Myles fired several times, rocking with laughter at the sight of his wife sprinting in bright orange pajamas across the moonlit plain, and of us all fleeing for our lives. When the badgers disappeared, we returned in disarray to assess the damage. It was worse than I feared. All the chickens had been attacked and all died within minutes. The badgers had got at them by ripping open the planks of the henhouse—tearing the 4-inch nails loose with their powerful claws.

Once when the cook got up at dawn, sleepy-eyed and yawning, to let the chickens out, he saw them emerge and then stop dead in their tracks. Instantly alert, the cook looked about and found himself face to face with a pride of lions staring intently through the wire of the hen run. He immediately returned to his quarters and left the chickens to their fate; none was harmed.

My efforts to provide eggs in the Serengeti ended with the chickens' annihilation by the badgers. There was now no longer the same need, since weekly trips to Arusha for building materials had replaced the monthly journeys to Musoma. A regular order with an Arusha grocer made housekeeping much easier, although the condition in which the supplies arrived, at the end of a bone-rattling journey of 200 miles, sometimes made me wonder if the new system was an improvement. Burst bags of sugar, shattered eggs, broken bottles of gin, and vegetables reeking of paraffin from a leaking drum, were all too common. We salvaged what we could, wrote complaints to the grocer about his packing, and hoped for the best.

Although Myles grumbled about the large amount of food kept in my double-sized storeroom, experience had taught me to keep reserves to meet such setbacks as flooded rivers, bogged-down trucks, smashed or ruined consignments, and an increasing number of guests, some of whom arrived unexpectedly. It was not possible, in such circumstances, to rush to a nearby shop and replenish stocks, although we did have a *duka* of sorts. Until this became a full-time job for an Asian shopkeeper, recruited by Parks from Ngorongoro, I continued to run my small shop for the Africans. But their numbers were rapidly increasing and my voice was lost in the clamour of a dozen insistent and simultaneous demands, while a forest of outstretched arms waved crumpled notes through the window. Since our weekly supplies from Arusha were quickly exhausted, I did not blame the customers for wanting to be served first. On paydays Myles would detail his Field Force sergeant to maintain order in the long queue outside the shop window, and this ex-army sergeant major would bawl impressively at the customers to keep in line and not scramble to be served all at once.

The Asian shopkeeper built up a thriving trade at Seronera. After Independence in 1961, it was handed over to the Africans themselves to be run as a cooperative store; but with growing shortages and complaints about inefficiency, the food situation steadily worsened and became a major problem. Another difficulty was our inadequate water supply. When attempts to provide water by damming valleys and digging boreholes had proved unsuccessful, a pipeline was eventually laid to the Bologonja River, 50 miles away. This had been Myles's recommendation from the beginning and it should have solved our water problems; but due to the inadequate and faulty piping and frequent bursts in the pipeline caused by elephants, the supply was never sufficient for the settlement's growing needs.

Shortly after we moved to Seronera, our small dispensary was taken over by a trained medical worker and a midwife, who coped with endless ailments and new babies as the population expanded. By 1972 when we left the Park, some two thousand people were living in the Serengeti, compared with about twenty in 1956. These included the numerous dependents of the men employed in the Park and a labour force recruited for building a large modern hotel at Seronera, which had not been completed when we left. A school was opened with four teachers and up to one hundred children of all ages. There were suggestions for a church, a mosque, and even a cemetery, although none of these actually materialized. Educational films and soccer provided entertainment, and occasionally a match was played between an African team and such European wardens and scientists as could be rounded up. Despite the enthusiastic support of the crowd, and many a goal being saved by our director, John Owen, the European team invariably lost. Over 6 feet tall, John made an imposing figure in the goal, his pipe clenched firmly between his teeth and a deep meditative look in his eyes.

John Owen joined the Tanzania National Parks administration in 1960. His appointment had a greater impact on their development than any other single event in all the years we lived in the Serengeti. During the ten years that John led Parks, he propelled the organization into the twentieth century with inspired zeal, drawing upon his remarkable reserves of energy and vision to reach the goal he had set. With the resources available to him, it seemed an impossible task at the time. When talking of his schemes and policies for Parks, our director liked to use the analogy of a juggler keeping several balls in the air without letting any of them drop. Myles quickly came to appreciate his outstanding qualities, and he felt a sense of pride and privilege in working for him. John Owen's notable achievements for conservation and wildlife research were later recognized by the award of an honorary doctorate from Oxford University, and of the rare Order of the Golden Ark by the World Wildlife Fund. An important contribution to John's work and to conservation in general was also made by his self-effacing wife Patricia, who, through her devoted support, did so much to help her husband.

Until John Owen's arrival little progress had been made in the development of the Park since it was established in 1951. Owing mainly to lack of funds and political insecurity, it had remained almost a forgotten land with few tourists. Then, in 1957, Colonel Peter Molloy, a previous director and a most able administrator, interested Professor Grzimek in the Serengeti, which proved a turning point in drawing it to the attention of the world. As a result of the publicity the Serengeti received from television and books by Grzimek and others, tourists began to flock to the Park. A special kind of person was needed to make the most of this opportunity, and from the first John Owen "grasped the nettle," devoting himself to his task with single-minded enthusiasm and far-sightedness.

Most people who have seen the Serengeti consider it the finest wildlife sanctuary left on earth; yet those of us involved in its protection felt an almost aching sadness, for there seemed small hope of preserving it for posterity. People could not be allowed to starve if there were wild animals about, rich in protein and utilizing large areas of viable land, and it was realized that the needs of Africa's increasing human population must ultimately prevail. Conservationists were overwhelmingly outnumbered and to a large extent helpless against growing difficulties and pressures from all sides. We hoped that for a while at least there would still be room in Africa for wild animals; yet to survive, the animals needed to justify their existence, and they could only do this by attracting tourist revenue and foreign currency.

With the uncertainties that lay ahead, John Owen rapidly came to a decision. Speed was essential, so rather than tackle each day's problems as they came, he anticipated a Serengeti which, by proving viable, might endure into the future for years to come. His plan was threefold: the promotion of tourism, to ensure the economic success and independence of Parks, assisted by grants from conservationists and appreciative visitors; increased wildlife research, internationally based, as a factor towards creating greater political stability, and also in order to advise on better methods of game management by producing a deeper knowledge and understanding of the animals in relation to their habitat; and education of the local people, through films and the written word, instilling into the minds of the citizens of the country an appreciation and desire to preserve their wildlife.

All of these aims needed large sums of money, to provide hotels, roads, research offices, laboratories, hostels, vehicles, airplanes, staff, film units, and much else. In addition to the Serengeti, other wildlife areas in Tanzania also fell within our director's master plan and required protection and development. The task of raising money for those schemes was shouldered by John Owen, who went to anyone who would listen. His quiet charm and dedication to conservation, together with a tough determination, were largely responsible for the brilliant success of his campaign to establish and extend the Parks. In his pamphlet *The Friends of the Serengeti,* he wrote:

We are oppressed by a sense of urgency. Events move quickly in Africa; we must keep ahead of them. We must train those who will have to carry the responsibility in the future. It is our aim to leave in competent dedicated hands an indestructible system of National Parks. We have plans worked out which give us a firm prospect of doing this. We have experienced and devoted staff on the spot. But we need the help of men and women of goodwill all over the world, those who are as convinced as we are that the Serengeti and the less famous Parks are unique—magnificent, ancient yet perishable, natural works of art—and they belong to us all.

John Owen felt a great responsibility towards ensuring the continued survival of the Serengeti. The obvious danger was poaching, and that was already being tackled by Myles. In appreciating the necessity for understanding the interaction of the plants and animals in National Parks, and in following carefully the trends and changes which might be deleterious, John Owen was ahead of his time.

The ecological degradation of the East African grasslands was most apparent in 1961, when there was a major drought. The questions that ecologists began asking, and which John Owen took very seriously, were: Could the Serengeti sustain a million or so grazing animals without becoming overgrazed and eroded like the surrounding country? Was it already overstocked with animals? Should we be cropping them? These questions led in turn to others which were being asked for the first time in East Africa, such as: What is a National Park for?

In order to answer some of these very pressing questions and, in particular, to learn whether the Park was deteriorating in any way, John Owen set up a small research unit in 1961, under Dr. Jacques Verschuren, famous for his work in the Congo. It was important to know whether there was any *natural* control of wildlife numbers and, if so, whether it was operating effectively to maintain the population within the carrying capacity of the country. The most obvious controlling factor was predation; but were the lions, hyenas, and leopards killing enough animals to keep the numbers in balance? Dr. George Schaller and Dr. Hans Kruuk wrote two outstanding books on their research aimed at answering this and related questions, and they said essentially that predation was responsible only for a small part of the mortality that was roughly balancing the births. Something else was much more effective in controlling population; and this was later shown, mainly by Dr. Tony Sinclair, to be a regulation of numbers by the availability of food.

There were also the dangers of overgrazing to be considered, although there was little sign of this in the Serengeti. The growing destruction of trees by elephants, and the gradual changing of the tree communities through the loss of mature trees, was proving a more serious problem, inasmuch as the replacement of the older trees by regeneration was simultaneously being hindered by grass fires. Could the destructive effects of the elephants be counterbalanced by a reduction in burning, so that more young trees developed to replace those pushed over by elephants? The scientists felt that natural regeneration could do so, but that there would be a time lag before the new trees matured. Perhaps the most important conclusion reached by the researchers was that the grasslands and the grazing animals were in equilibrium, and that the grasslands remained undamaged by the wildebeest, even though their numbers grew steadily from possibly 250,000, when we first arrived in the Serengeti, to about 900,000 when we left.

From 1960 the years seemed to speed by as the Serengeti developed at an ever-increasing rate. As part of the educational programme a large hostel was built to accommodate African school parties brought to the Serengeti, who were driven round in a Parks' truck. Films by professional photographers were shown in the evenings and lectures delivered by Myles and the other wardens. To make room for increasing numbers of tourists, the Lodge was temporarily enlarged by the addition of tented accommodation, and hotels were planned. Airplanes were donated or purchased from funds raised abroad, and John and Myles learned to fly; first a Cessna 150, then a Piper Super Cub, and finally a Cessna 180 for the Serengeti and a Cessna 182 for John's use in Arusha. Additional scientists arrived and the Serengeti Research Institute was established in 1966, with Dr. Hugh Lamprey as its first director.

Hugh had lived for many years in Africa as the wildlife biologist in the Tanganyika Game Department, and he was greatly respected for his achievements both in the field and as the first principal of the Mweka College of Wildlife Management in Tanzania, which had been started to train wardens from all parts of Africa. Under his able direction a number of revolutionary and fundamental discoveries were made in the Serengeti, and many interesting studies carried out on lions, hyenas, buffaloes, elephants, topis, impalas, vultures, wildebeest, zebras, and Thomson's gazelles. In addition studies were conducted on soil analysis, vegetation changes, grassland productivity, botany, geology, population dynamics, the destruction of habitat, veterinary problems, and parasitical work. The ecological monitoring programme and analysis of increasing amounts, varieties, and complexities of data collected by the scientists were coordinated by the senior ecologist of the Institute, Dr. Mike Norton-Griffiths.

The first few years of the Institute were not entirely free of problems and stress. Unreasonably but perhaps naturally, we felt resentful at this violation of the wildness as for research purposes animals were immobilized, tagged, collared, and shot. From time to time some scientists showed a happy disregard for Park rules and discipline, and Land Rovers could occasionally be seen careering recklessly through the bush. Disagreements and misunderstandings inevitably arose, and the wardens' actions were frequently challenged by the scientists, by whom they were outnumbered nine to one. Myles held strong views on wildlife management, and long experience had given him an instinctive sureness in making policy decisions. He found it frustrating to have to argue with researchers, some of whom had spent only a few months in Africa and were guided solely by their academic training.

However we realized that the old-fashioned game warden had had his day, and that the future lay with ecologists and their like. It seemed inevitable that the methods of men, however dedicated, dating from days before most people had heard of ecology, should be looked into and brought up to date as a result of detailed studies being made of the complete ecosystem. Time was running out for the preservation of wildlife on our crowded planet, and we needed every bit of knowledge to protect what remained. Ecology may in the long run have arrived too late, but the facts had to be assembled for the best management of the limited wildlife sanctuaries left to mankind.

Acknowledging these facts, my faith in the judgment of Myles and other experienced wardens remained unshaken, for I believed them to be of a select band of conservationists whose natural wisdom had been gained from many years spent in the field.

Any differences of opinion on policy within the Park did not affect our social relations with the scientists and we made a number of friends amongst them. After ten years in the Serengeti I now lived a community life, with tennis evenings at the Research Institute and neighbourly visits with Ros Lamprey, Anne Sinclair, Kay Schaller, Jane Kruuk, Ann Norton-Griffiths, and many other wives living on the station. Lynda and Michael had other young playmates at Seronera; although a few years older, the two Lamprey children became their special friends. During school holidays we organized safaris together, enjoying these sometimes adventurous excursions into the bush as much as did our children.

As time passed, the number of tourists visiting the Park reached about 52,000 in 1972, compared with less than 400 in 1956. Within a few years of joining Parks, John Owen had won many distinguished friends for the Serengeti, and a rest house was built at Seronera to accommodate official Park guests. This modest building was christened "the Taj" by Myles, and a number of well-known names filled the pages of its guestbook. A large part of our time was now taken up by entertaining and looking after these visitors, and our active social lives made it hard to believe we still lived in the same Park as in 1956, when we rarely saw a visitor.

With more and more tourists flying to Seronera, the air traffic was at times so heavy that Myles returned one morning from a routine patrol to find himself circling the airfield for fifteen minutes while three other charter planes landed ahead of him. Aircraft now played an important part in our lives, and two hangars were built for them. One housed the Parks' Cessna 180, and the other was occupied by a Cessna 150 privately owned by Sandy Field, who replaced Gordon Harvey as Chief Park Warden in 1963. An ex-Provincial Commissioner from Uganda, and a bachelor, Sandy's two great passions were flying and elephant hunting. More than anyone we knew, Sandy always had the right word in any situation, and his personality and wit enlivened many a social gathering.

Although life at Seronera was very different from Banagi, our increasing involvement with people still represented only one aspect of our lives. The animals were close at hand, and it was always possible to go among them even during the most hectic times. A short walk behind our house, with the sky curving high and wide over golden plains stretching to the horizon, and I would feel a sense of infinity that made my head spin. Clouds sailing overhead in fascinating splendour and colours streaking the western sky at sunset competed for attention with the landscape and animals. Here, for a while, I could recapture the peace of mind I had always known in the bush. Awareness of sound, smell, and sight are heightened by silence and solitude; I would breathe deeply of the warm clean air, conscious of birds calling to one another, and of the wind building up in soaring waves, dying away, rustling through the grass, or sighing in the trees. Sometimes a flash of colour caught my eye as red and blue agama lizards scuttled across a rock, or vitelline masked weavers clustered round their nests like bright yellow flowers. Reassured by my stillness, the animals would soon resume their normal activities, and I would watch a topi high-stepping behind its mate with nose lifted and tail high, or Tommies sparring together and chasing off rivals. Seeing them helped to lift my spirits, before I returned once more to the chores and concerns of civilization.

There were times when leopards and rhinos were brought from outlying areas for release at Seronera. Mwanza township, on the shores of Lake Victoria, and the surrounding rocky kopjes, had a large population of leopards that lived on chickens, dogs, and goats. Periodically the game warden would trap these animals and bring them to the Park in a cage, mounted on a truck. A wire would then be taken from a sliding door over the cab of the truck to a Land Rover, and the crate opened from the safety of the smaller vehicle. It was best to lie low when releasing these animals, for their behaviour was always unpredictable, and in their nervous state they were liable to attack anything. Sometimes they would rush straight out and make for the nearest cover; at others they would sulk for half an hour or more and refuse to leave the cage. Once, we watched a young leopard leave her cage and roll delightedly in the grass before moving quietly away; another attacked the truck on being released.

Around some areas in the Musoma district, increasing settlement meant that the few surviving wild animals there were in danger of extermination. Thirty miles southwest of Musoma, in the Kibakari area, an isolated pocket of rhinos remained, and Carr Hartley, a professional game trapper, was given permission to catch and remove them on the condition that for every two caught he gave one to the National Parks or Game Department. After a few days of captivity these huge animals usually became very placid, contentedly munching the food provided. One day, while Carr did his best to coax a rhino to reverse out of the crate, slapping its flank from the side of the truck, the annoyed beast jerked its head up through the roof on which a friend and I were sitting. A large piece of horn suddenly appeared between us, splintering the wood and sending my aluminum camera box flying through the air. My companion was so unnerved that she was unable to photograph the following sequence as the rhino backed out and then charged the truck.

In 1963 our children began building a treehouse in the branches of a large acacia at the end of our lawn. Helped by the local carpenter, Lynda and Michael eventually built a platform which stood 15 feet from the ground, surrounded by a low fence of saplings, with a roof of palm fronds. There was room for only two to sleep in the treehouse, and I would sometimes take the children in turns to spend a night there. The entrance was through a hole in the floor, at the top of a rough ladder nailed to the tree. Hauling up the mattresses, blankets, and lamps on a rope, we would shut the trapdoor, make the beds, and wait for Myles to shut down the electricity generator. Then, in the silence that followed, we would listen and watch for the animals.

One night the young son of an American scientist who lived at Seronera asked if he could stay with Michael in the treehouse. Not wanting the boys to be on their own, I squeezed in with them. It was a beautiful night, the stars gleamed in profusion, and a bright moon lit the country around us. Three buffaloes grazed a short distance away, a hyrax croaked its lonely call from the kopjes, zebras barked, and at intervals a hyena whooped. The excited boys talked late into the night, whispering and leaping up every now and then to look out, until eventually they fell asleep. Later I woke to hear a leopard's rasping cough close by, and hoped it would not decide to spend the night in our particular tree. When dawn began to break, our small guest suddenly yelled: "Hey, *Mike!* There's a *lion!*"

Michael and I sat up with a jerk and watched a lioness walking towards us across the plain some distance away. She passed out of sight behind the kopjes and reappeared again, still moving in our direction, until she was directly beneath our tree. Sensing our presence, she looked up suddenly with startled eyes, tensed her muscles, and sank into a half-crouch. For a moment I wondered if she might jump. Instead she bounded away in long loping strides, glancing back at us in surprise as the sun rose slowly over the horizon. It was the start of another new day at Seronera.

Chapter 8

Wild Pets

One hot afternoon at Seronera I heard Myles's Land Rover draw up outside the house. Calling to me, he reached into his pocket and held out one of the smallest animals I had ever seen. It lay in the palm of his hand with eyes shut and an enchanting expression upon its tiny face.

"A present for you," Myles said. "Know what it is?"

"A mongrel dog?"

He shook his head.

"A wild dog?"

"No," Myles answered. "Try again."

"Jackal?" I was beginning to run out of ideas.

"Wrong again." Myles laughed. "It's a bat-eared fox."

I wondered how he could possibly tell. The cub's ears, normally the most noticeable feature of its species, were so small as to be virtually nonexistent. Myles told me he had found it abandoned on Lamai airstrip, in the north of the Park. To enable the mother to retrieve it, he had left it for an hour while he went about his work. But the small creature was still there on his return and, rather than risk having it killed by jackals or birds of prey, he decided to bring it home. Foxes are normally concealed by their parents until several weeks old; it was rare to find a cub so young in the open, and Myles wondered if in fact the baby was a runt, rejected by its mother.

I was delighted to have it and immediately set about choosing a name. Finally we decided on Mchutu (pronounced

Mmchootu), the Waikoma word for bat-eared fox. Our cub quickly came to know his name, for he was never called by any other.

To begin with it was not easy looking after the little animal, who weighed less than 5 ounces. Within two days of his arrival I travelled by road to Kenya to visit the children at half-term and Chutu came with me, cradled inside my shirt for warmth. Unhappy with the milk formula I was feeding him, he looked exhausted and weak by the time we reached Nairobi, nearly 300 miles away, and I drove directly to see Tony Harthoorn, a leading veterinarian experienced in wildlife work. In Tony's opinion the cub's only hope of survival would be to find a nursing cat or dog. As this was not possible, the fox and I spent another miserable night.

The following day, while lunching with friends, Chutu lay still and lifeless against my skin. Each time I thought about him the tears rolled down my cheeks, which was embarrassing at a popular Nairobi hotel. In desperation I phoned the Wildlife Orphanage for advice. They said they could not help, their only experience at the time being with young jackals; but they suggested that I strengthen the milk formula and that I provide a hot water bottle at all times for extra warmth.

This proved the turning point for Chutu. Within a few days he had gained in strength and was a frisky ball of mischief. I added baby cereal, egg, and insects to his diet, and his weight soon doubled. In six weeks he had gained 2 pounds; by the time he reached maturity, he weighed 8 pounds, the average weight of a male fox. We never discovered his sex, and even our Serengeti Research vet was perplexed; but judging by Chutu's subsequent behaviour when he lived wild, I believed him to be male.

From the start Chutu was an enchanting pet, rushing about like an animated toy, fluffy tail in the air. Whenever he greeted us he would wriggle his body with pleasure and roll over to be tickled. His most marked characteristic was joyfulness, which gave him a particularly attractive personality. Exhausted from playing, Chutu loved to sleep in my lap, lying on his back with front legs limply bent over, back legs stretched straight out, and a blissful expression on his tiny face.

During his first two weeks the little fox tried each morning to leap from the floor to my bed which seemed an impossible feat at the time, for he was no more than 6 inches long. His gymnastics would begin before dawn when I was only drowsily aware of the jump-thump sounds Chutu made as he leaped up and fell back again. Having been roused several times in the night by his piercing yells for food, I generally turned a deaf ear, trusting hopefully he would come to no harm. But one morning I heard the familiar jump followed by silence instead of the usual thud as he hit the rug. My eyes flew open in alarm. To my surprise I saw Chutu standing on the pillow with his head on one side, looking the picture of impish mischief as he gazed triumphantly down at me. From then on he lived on my bed.

Although as a very small cub he hated being in the open, Chutu followed me on walks, calling constantly in a nervous birdlike chirrup. It seemed to be the only sound he could make, apart from furious snorts and growls when playing or feeding. He was a glutton, so that we all worked ourselves to a frazzle each day collecting grasshoppers and other insects to keep him going. On rainy nights I thankfully filled up as many jars as I could lay my hands on with flying ants. But these lasted for only a day or two, and he would again be seen hanging about at mealtimes, looking pathetic and hungry. One day, to appease the little animal, Myles handed him a piece of steamed pudding. To our astonishment, Chutu seized and devoured it instantly, his bright eyes looking up eagerly for more. Our feeding difficulties were at an end, for we soon discovered our ravenous small fox would accept anything that came his way, snarling and growling continuously like a kettle on the boil. Amongst other things his diet eventually included eggs, bacon, pork, chocolate cake, biscuits, sausages, chicken, and fresh toast, preferably buttered with a touch of Marmite (yeast extract). Later, small snakes and mice were added to his menu, and these he loved most of all.

The instinctive fight for survival must surely be strong in bat-eared foxes, for Chutu's table manners were appalling and he was best left alone when feeding. With ears laid back and vicious snarls he lashed out, even if offered a second morsel whilst still engaged on the first.

Chutu sometimes displayed this same aggressive behaviour when playing, particularly with Myles's smelly tennis shoes. He loved to chew on them, grunting and growling, and usually ended the game by urinating on them, much to Myles's displeasure. But woe betide anyone who tried to interfere or take the shoes away! Another of Chutu's favourite games was to have a dressing gown or towel waved in front of him, at which he promptly charged. With ears flat, plumed tail waving, and an expression of ecstasy on his small face, he would leap straight off the ground and go down fighting savagely inside an entanglement of cloth.

Apart from this frenzy whilst feeding or playing, Chutu showed us great affection and was a most lovable pet. Before reaching maturity, he could be picked up and cuddled, and would make soft mewing sounds of pleasure, burying his wet nose into my neck or hand.

As the weeks went by our fox grew more and more beautiful, his main features being the huge ears and luxuriant black-streaked tail that swept the ground. His coat changed from rough and woolly to silky, with an unusual patch of short fur in the middle of his back. His ears swivelled constantly at every sound and he would react violently to any sudden noise, such as a sneeze, dashing beneath my bed from the depths of sleep above it. He also disliked rain, again cowering under the bed until the storm had passed. Once when he was caught outside in a downpour, he rushed to the fireplace of the unlit bathwater heater and emerged in a hurry with paws and fur slightly singed from the live coals that were covered by a layer of ash. It took a few hours to soothe the perturbed little cub, who had just taken to spending a lot of time outdoors.

Chutu was now about six months old and we were beginning to feel dubious about the nocturnal habits of bat-eared foxes; we were also skeptical about their mainly insectivorous diet and ability to locate beetles and mice inches underground with their enormous ears. Our fox still slept soundly all night; the noise his ears located best was the clatter of our meals being brought in, when he would come skidding along the slippery floor, plumed tail aloft and round black eyes gleaming. By this time he was hunting for about two hours each morning, digging shallow holes in short bursts and pouncing ineffectively into the grass. During long periods of immobility after a digging frenzy, he would listen intently, nose to ground, immense ears cocked, and one delicately shaded paw folded backwards. Even in the house he sometimes began digging frantically: under the door, the sofa, or the boot of someone sitting in a chair. As at feeding times, it was best not to interfere.

Time passed and Chutu became increasingly restless at night. He would now keep us awake by scratching at the door and chewing on anything he could find, and Myles urged me to set him free. But with leopards prowling round our house at night I was nervous and doubtful about his ability to fend for himself. For a while we banished him to the spare room, where he promptly ruined my best rug and was miserable at being left on his own. Finally, in some trepidation, I released him into the night. Chutu was eight months old.

The next morning, to my relief, I saw our cub curled up asleep in the sand outside the bedroom. He had by then taken to sleeping in the open at all times and I missed not seeing his familiar figure on my bed.

For a few days we had no problems. During the day Chutu slept outside, tucked into a corner of the house where I could see him; at dusk he vanished in search of adventure. On his second night of freedom, Bobby Kennedy (son of the late Senator Robert Kennedy) saw Chutu outside "the Taj" guesthouse where he was staying, and brought him back to our house, thinking the fox had escaped. Bobby was fourteen years old at the time, and he had grown fond of our little fox while on a visit to the Park.

A week after Chutu's return to the wild he disappeared. Noticing he was not in his usual "burrow" one morning, I set out across the plains to look for him.

"Have you lost your fox?" Bobby asked, when I passed the guesthouse where he was breakfasting. I nodded and at once he joined me. But our search proved fruitless. For eight more days I walked morning and evening, calling Chutu's name, until I decided he was dead. My loss of hope filled me with sadness.

Exhausted from days of anxiety, I slept soundly that night for the first time since Chutu's disappearance, no longer listening for a scratching at the door nor getting up to investigate any obscure noises. All at once a sharp bark outside our window woke me instantly. I leaped from my bed, knowing it was Chutu, although I had never before heard him bark. Rushing out, I saw three bat-eared foxes racing round and round the house. Each time they circled one of them barked as it passed our window. I called Chutu's name, but the foxes raced on, until in the end I began to doubt our fox was amongst them. Suddenly one of the little animals broke away from his companions and shot through our bedroom door in a state of high excitement. It was Chutu.

Beside myself with joy, I hurried to defrost some pork, his favourite food. The delicious smell of cooking pork made Chutu frantic, and he scrabbled at my legs, more ravenous than usual, while I murmured consolingly to forestall his impatience. To add to the turmoil, a disgruntled voice called from the bedroom: "If I came in at one o'clock in the morning, you wouldn't make all this fuss!"

Although he sounded indignant, I knew that Myles too was delighted at Chutu's safe return. But his exasperation increased when the ecstatic animal insisted on joining us in bed, after he had wolfed his meal. With Chutu's small wet nose tucked into my neck, we did our best to doze peacefully together. He was covered with fleas and his increasing restlessness made sleep impossible. After twenty minutes we could stand it no longer. I opened the door, regretting that Chutu's nocturnal habits had prevented us from enjoying his company any longer. He raced out, and stood for a moment on the top step with every sense alert. Finally he stepped into the night. At once his two companions bounded towards him out of the darkness, apparently amazed at his safe deliverance from the house. They raced after one another in a game of tag, their long tails sweeping out as they sped around the lawn, until eventually they disappeared from sight and did not return. I felt elated at Chutu's return, and relieved that he had learned to take care of himself and was accepted by the wild foxes.

After that first visit Chutu returned many times to the house; sometimes he scratched at the door with his sharp claws, while at others he appeared suddenly in our midst during the early part of an evening. I never again heard him bark. He now hated to be picked up, and if people attempted to stroke him he was liable to bite them, being always in an excitable state. Eventually no one dared to pet him, with the exception of Myles and myself. Even Myles could not lift him, and when I did so Chutu sometimes turned and sank his teeth into my arm, but without drawing blood. Then he would gradually relax in my arms for a short time before struggling to be put down. In a world populated by predators, he had learned to be both defensive and aggressive, and his immediate reaction to being touched was to resist.

Each time Chutu returned he seemed wilder, and it would take him longer to remember us. But I always greeted him affectionately and never once did he bite me in earnest. Friends warned me of the possibility of rabies in foxes and I was told of a woman in the Amboseli Game Reserve in Kenya, who had looked after a bat-eared fox rescued by the rangers from a hyena. When the animal died, a postmortem revealed rabies; those people who had handled it were given injections in Nairobi, and the woman reacted strongly to the treatment, indicating she might already have contracted the disease. Nevertheless I continued to give our fox an enthusiastic welcome each time he visited us, and turned a deaf ear to the warning of visiting veterinarians and friends.

One night I awoke to the familiar sound of digging at our door, and hurried to let Chutu in. There was the usual fuss of preparing a midnight feast for the ravenous little animal, who devoured an enormous meal and then made a token attempt at settling down for a snooze with us. After a few moments he grew fidgety and I let him out again, standing for several minutes on the verandah while Chutu listened intently. After he felt it safe to venture outside I returned to bed; but hardly had I closed my eyes than a terrified scream from Chutu brought me to the door. I threw it open and two bodies flung past me into the bedroom. With my bare feet in a sticky mess on the floor (which I took to be Chutu's blood) I stumbled desperately around in the darkness, calling his name and trying to find him. An irate Myles joined in the uproar by bellowing: "What the hell's going on? You'll have a leopard in here one of these days."

It suddenly occurred to me that maybe a leopard *had* followed Chutu into the room. In the confusion I had been unable to identify the animals when they hurtled through the door; but as my eyes adapted to the darkness, I soon picked out a small fox standing close by. Approaching it, I stretched out my hand; immediately it raced past me and out of the room. Chutu then emerged sheepishly from under the bed. He had had a bad fright, not realizing what had pounced so unexpectedly at him out of the darkness; this caused him to defecate, which I had thought to be blood. Now having rapidly regained his nerve,

Chutu sailed out into the night to continue his new relationship on a surer footing.

We had not seen our fox for two weeks when a Land Rover arrived at seven o'clock one morning and deposited him at our front door. Chutu had been found 4 miles away by a visiting hunter who knew him well. His party were driving past when they noticed a fox happily waving its tail beside a burrow down which another fox had hurriedly disappeared. The hunter stopped to call Chutu, and the delighted animal allowed our friend to carry him to the Land Rover. For once Chutu did not bite. This may have been because the hunter had last seen him as a half-grown cub and was unaware of this new tendency, which lent confidence to his handling of the excitable little fox. Chutu was overjoyed to be home after this long spell away, and for the first time in many weeks he slept the rest of the day on my bed. The next day, knowing he had to travel 4 miles to return to his mate, I drove to the burrow to see if Chutu was safely back. There was no sign of him. Worried by his disappearance, I kept check on the burrow for several days. However, all was well, and our fox soon called at the house again with two friends.

It was on this occasion I decided Chutu was male. After eating his meal, he trotted a short distance across the lawn and waited expectantly. Suddenly two foxes raced up to him and one of them engaged Chutu in a seemingly fierce battle. At times the two bodies struggled at my feet, locked in combat, and I wondered whether to step in and separate them. But Chutu seemed to be enjoying the fight tremendously, racing away with tail arched and closing again with his opponent, while the third fox looked on with interest. In the end I decided the two combatants were old friends, enjoying a mock battle for the favours of their lady friend. They seemed to be having so much fun that I left them to it and went back to bed.

The last time I saw Chutu was the night before I flew to England to settle the children at their new schools. Knowing I was to be away for several weeks, it was particularly gratifying to be visited by my erstwhile pet, after a fortnight's absence. At the time we were entertaining friends to dinner, and our cook noticed two bat-eared foxes trotting past the kitchen. He called Chutu's name and immediately one of the foxes swerved from its companion and hurried behind Fundi into the dining room. By good fortune we were eating pork. Scooping Chutu into my lap, I suffered the threatening half-bite as he readjusted to his other world. Everybody offered him scraps from their plates, which he gulped down eagerly before struggling to be released. He looked sleek and well and waved his tail ecstatically while he rushed about the room. When finally he left to rejoin his friend, I watched him go with a feeling of sadness, wondering if we should meet again.

During my absence in England Myles wrote from time to time to say that Chutu had called. He came often at first, searching the house and wandering in and out of all the rooms, which he had not done before. Each time Myles showed him affection and fed him heartily; but after a while Chutu's visits ceased altogether. I returned a month after his last visit to the house and tramped the plains calling his name to let him know I was home. But he never came back. I liked to think he had moved out of the area altogether and that he lived to a normal old age.

Until Chutu's arrival I had had little experience of wild pets. Other than mongooses for the children, tortoises, mice, and hyraxes, the only wild animals we had looked after were a pair of young zorillas (striped polecats). They were the size of kittens, with beautiful black and white coats and fluffy tails. Zorillas are nocturnal animals, and ours were found by the Lodge staff at the bottom of a deep, disused rubbish pit. They could not have been more than a few weeks old. We named the handsome creatures Dee and Dum, for they followed each other everywhere, one behind the other, and refused to be parted. It was fascinating to watch them playing together in the evening; even Jason gazed with cross-eyed amazement at their antics as they scooted round and round the room, arching their small backs, charging and tumbling together for hours before settling down to sleep in blissful companionship all through the day. Like skunks they are capable of ejecting an appalling stench from their perineal glands when alarmed, and it was impossible to rid oneself of the smell for several days; we were fortunately spared a demonstration.

Being carnivorous, the zorillas proved easy to feed. At night they slept in a long wired cage, covered by a heavy tarpaulin and quantities of thorn bush. The little animals flourished, until

one morning I found a hole chewed through the wire and no
sign of our two pets. Although Myles feared a hyena had killed
them, I hopefully put out food each night and it always disappeared. Several weeks later I caught sight of the now almost full-
grown zorillas. I called to them, and Dee and Dum scuttled up
to their meat, but they would not allow me to touch them. We
were delighted that they had survived the hyena (possibly by
ejecting their powerful scent), and that they continued to live
around our house. Shortly afterwards we sadly discovered the
hindquarters of one of the little animals in the kopjes, presum-
ably killed by a leopard which had left the section containing the
musk glands. We never saw its companion again.

Our mongooses started with one of the dwarf variety, acquired at the coast; we named him Kitu, meaning "Small
Thing." Weighing little more than a pound, he fitted comfort-
ably into Myles's pocket, and we carried him wherever we went.
On safari Kitu had his own tiny box with his name painted over
it. He loved nothing more than to sit at my feet, untying the
laces of my shoes as fast as I tied them up again. Affectionate
and intelligent, Kitu's downfall was caused by his fearlessness.
Unafraid of vehicles, he was eventually run over, his size
making him difficult to see. It was a tragic end for an endearing
pet.

Some time later we were given two banded mongooses. They
delighted in puzzling our guests by creeping up and stealing
food from their plates while we talked. This always amused our
children, who loved to see the visitors' astonished faces when
they reached for their cake and found it mysteriously missing.
The children fed their pets at mealtimes, and this had made the
mongooses incorrigible thieves. On one of our three months'
overseas vacations, we finally released them far from home
within the vicinity of a colony of banded mongooses. By this
time they were well accustomed to foraging for themselves and
had often spent nights out in the bush.

Among our children's favourite pets were a pair of dormice
they named Engelbert and Humperdinck. Myles had found
their mother inside a pile of rangers' clothing while reorganizing
the Field Force store, and he had brought her home for the
children. She was a ferocious little animal, vibrating with rage
and biting savagely when touched. The reason for her behaviour

became evident a few days later when she produced four babies. We nurtured them until they were fully grown, and then kept two of the youngsters for the children. The remaining two, with their mother, we gave to Professor Grzimek, who looked after them in a specially heated box in his Frankfurt office.

Bertie and Humpie were charming animals with black beady eyes, fluffy tails, and grey furry bodies. Nocturnal in their habits, they slept all day in a bedroom of soft rags and emerged at night into their living room of sand, grass, and sticks on which to climb about. They were completely tame, although they sometimes demonstrated their aggressiveness by chittering and trembling with anger if roused from sleep by an admiring visitor.

The children took turns at cleaning out the mousebox and providing titbits for the dormice to eat. Their diet consisted mainly of bananas, biscuits, and cheese, and they thrived. Occasionally they would gnaw holes through the wire mesh of their box and escape; but they always returned to sleep during the day in their comfortable beds. Although I repaired the holes each time, I discovered one morning that Bertie and Humpie were no longer in their box. They had finally disappeared after living with us for five years. Since the average lifespan of a wild dormouse is about two years, our mice had done very well to have survived for so long.

During his time in the Kenya Game Department, Myles looked after a cheetah and two wild dogs. The cheetah was lost when it jumped out of his Land Rover unnoticed, in pursuit of a hare or some other wild creature, and it could not be found again in the expanse of country they had covered. The wild dogs were reared together with Myles's pack of Airedales and foxhounds (a mixed breed), used for tracking buffaloes in the forests. Always independent, they preferred to keep to themselves and to follow their own trails; but in the evenings they would return to Myles's camp for meat. The wild dogs never lost their strange, unpleasant smell, and the other dogs disliked them. Finally the two unfortunate animals were set upon and killed by the domestic dogs before Myles could intervene.

When we first joined Parks, the authorities made it clear that they wished to discourage private zoos, animal orphanages, or any other attempts at keeping wild pets. The policy of allowing nature to take its course meant that no assistance would be forthcoming for the upkeep of abandoned or sick animals, and it was virtually impossible for us to start any kind of private sanctuary. Apart from needing staff to help with the animals' upbringing, it would have been difficult to finance their maintenance on Myles's salary alone. Fortunately we were seldom faced with the problem of making a choice between caring for an animal or abandoning it to its fate. Lost wildebeest calves were too numerous to cope with and the occasional sick animal we tended usually failed to rally because of its weakened condition.

During hard times we sometimes shot a buck to feed a pride of starving lion cubs; but this was later criticized by scientists, who felt that the Parks' general policy should be to let animals and plants find their own equilibrium with as little interference as possible. In the scientists' opinion a more suitable means of helping the lions would be to control bush fires from spreading along rivers so that lions could hunt more easily. Feeding them, the scientists reasoned, only added to their problems by creating a lion population larger than the area could support. According to the renowned ecologist George Schaller, the Serengeti lions had reached an equilibrium with their environment and tended to remain stable. There was also the question of ethics in shooting a healthy prey animal to feed lions which in the natural course of events would die; and to shoot emaciated cubs meant removing many that would ultimately survive, since most lions go through a bad time at some stage of their lives. When there were protests from visitors encountering suffering cubs, it was explained that about 50 percent of most large mammals die before reaching maturity in the wilds, one cause of mortality in lions being starvation. Visitors were reminded that they were viewing the lions in their natural habitat; if they insisted on seeing only well-fed animals, they should visit a zoo, not a National Park.

In those early days, however, we had little understanding of nature's means of keeping a balance between predators and prey animals, and we did occasionally allow our sympathies to hold sway when we were confronted by the pathetic sight of starving cubs. This instance of man's compulsion to help his fellow creatures led me to ponder the complexity of human nature. On the one hand there was man's need to help animals in distress (whereas wild animals felt no such urge to help human beings), and on the other hand there was his desire to kill animals, sometimes by appallingly cruel methods and often for no other reason than that he enjoyed the "sport" of killing. Animals felt no such wish to kill man, unless they were afraid, provoked, or driven by hunger. Most behaviour within species was characteristic, whereas it seemed man behaved in a totally individual and unpredictable manner.

With the high rate of predation in the Serengeti, lost or sick animals rarely survived for any length of time. Hyenas, vultures, wild dogs, cheetahs, lions, leopards, and the smaller predators such as jackals and birds of prey, were all on the lookout for a meal, and a weakened animal was easy prey. Other than lost wildebeest calves, we seldom came across an abandoned young animal. However, with increasing numbers of visitors roaming the countryside and watching for game, more instances of animal distress came to our attention.

One such instance was Gussie (or Augusta as we first named her), a Grant's gazelle left on our doorstep by a visitor. The animal had been found, newly born, a short distance from a leopard the tourists were photographing in a tree. They concluded that the gazelle on which the leopard fed was the mother of the fawn lying curled in the grass. In all probability they were right, for some scientists believe an antelope has no odour during the first few hours of its life, to protect it from detection until it can run swiftly. Emerging from my bath, I found the tiny, wet creature abandoned in a cardboard box on our verandah, the umbilical cord still hanging from her navel. She could not have been more than an hour or two old, and it was difficult to see how such a frail creature could survive. But Gussie proved strong and determined to live; within a few days she had accustomed herself to her canned milk diet and was following me everywhere, her delicate hooves skidding on the concrete floor.

We built a small enclosure for her, though Gussie seldom stayed in it, preferring to walk behind me whenever possible. She would even run behind the car, knowing I was in it, if she saw me leave the house. Generally she stepped daintily along at my heels and ran to me when I called; but on the occasions she decided to play truant during our evening walks, there was no stopping her. She delighted then in keeping just out of reach, bouncing stiff-legged with all four feet off the ground at once.

I decided to tie a long rope to her neck, the only way of catching her being to step on the trailing end. This would bring Gussie up with a jerk and it always surprised her, since she evidently thought she had a good lead on me as she danced across the plains, turning her head imperceptibly from side to side to keep me in view.

There can be few animals more elegant than Grant's gazelles, with their large velvety eyes, tidy white rumps, and broad dark stripe along pale rufus-coloured flanks. Short tails tucked out of sight add to their svelte look, and they move in an almost springy fashion, their back legs giving an impression of being longer than their front, as if built for speed.

At first our young gazelle slept in the house, but later we transferred her to an old generator barn, where she stood less chance of breaking a limb by slipping on the concrete floor. One day when Gussie was six weeks old, a companion was found for her whilst we drove with our official guests amongst the migratory animals on the plains. Investigating vultures dropping from the sky in large numbers, we came across a dead female Thomson's gazelle, as yet untouched by the scavengers. She was an old animal with a much swollen belly, which made Myles wonder whether she might be pregnant. He opened her abdomen and found no fetus, but she had evidently died giving birth, for she was heavily in milk and was completely unmarked.

We then looked about for her fawn. After a brief search the party concluded that the attendant vultures must already have devoured it. Unconvinced, I continued to walk in widening circles around the dead gazelle until I stumbled suddenly upon a tiny animal lying hidden in the grass. It was the old gazelle's baby, still wet and glistening from its recent birth.

We carried the fawn home and put it with Gussie for warmth and comfort. This proved a mistake, since a newborn animal tends to focus on the nearest being it sees as its mother, which is termed "imprinting." In the same way that Gussie imprinted on me, so the baby Tommy imprinted on Gussie, and in consequence would go to no one else, butting the older gazelle in the belly whenever it felt hungry. Although I could feed the fawn by holding out the milk bottle (which it soon realized was its only means of sustenance), the little gazelle refused to go to anyone else, preferring to starve than be fed by the servants. This meant that Fundi had to capture and forcibly feed the tiny animal if I was away. Most of Gussie's time was now spent in the enclosure with her young companion; when she was let out for her evening walks, the Tommy would plunge at the wire in desperate efforts to follow.

Weeks later while Myles and I were on safari, Fundi entered the enclosure in order to shut the gazelles in their barn for the night. As usual the Tommy flung itself against the wire meshing, this time hitting the one place where it was hooked around nails to form a rough doorway. The wire separated, the animal hurtled through, and then made off in stiff-legged bounds across the plains. Fundi tried every means he could think of to lure it back, as a last resort rounding up the available rangers to help. This only terrified the gazelle further, with the result that it was soon lost for good. Had Fundi not driven the fawn so far from home, I felt sure it would have returned to Gussie as its foster parent. But it was some comfort to know that the little animal was now old enough to graze and, being no longer solely dependent on milk, it had a reasonable chance of survival amongst the large herds of Thomson's gazelles around our house at the time.

Apparently unaffected by the Tommy's disappearance, Gussie continued to roam about, losing none of her tameness. By this time I had removed the rope from her neck, since she could now fend for herself if she escaped. In order that we should be able to recognize her when she joined a herd, we pasted a strip of adhesive tape around the base of one of her horns. Over the weeks I noticed that Gussie was growing increasingly reluctant about being shut in for the night, although she remained docile and would run to me when I called. There were few gazelles around Seronera at the time, most of them having moved to the plains; Gussie, immature and alone, would have stood small chance at night amongst the many predators. She no longer cared for milk, but the bottle was still a lure. By using it I was able to grasp her leg and carry her in for the night. She now weighed nearly 100 pounds, and I knew that I would soon not be able to lift her.

In the end our gazelle solved the problem herself. A small herd of Thomson's gazelles had moved into the area and Gussie enjoyed mingling with them during the day. Even with Grant's gazelles about, she still preferred to join the Tommies, and we wondered if this might have some relation to her early association with one of their species. Grant's gazelles are larger than their cousins, and Gussie was easily distinguishable in a herd of Thomson's gazelles, despite her immaturity. Going out as usual one evening with her bottle, I called to her; a gazelle immediately detached itself from the herd and bounded towards me. She looked very young as she ran, for Gussie had not yet adopted the adult gait and still used the stiff-legged bounces known as "stotting." When she was within a few feet of me, she stopped abruptly and would come no closer. I coaxed and cajoled, trying every trick to get her within catching distance, but she kept just out of reach. Finally it grew dark and I returned with misgivings to the house. Although it was what I had wanted, this was Gussie's first night in the bush and I was afraid for her.

The following day she was still there and I breathed a sigh of relief; but at the back of my mind I still intended to catch her if I could. Walking out amongst the gazelles on the plain for the next three evenings, I was each time accompanied by Gussie, who always kept at arm's length. She refused to come to the bottle although she gazed longingly at it, and she would not permit me to rub her head around the growing horns, which normally she loved.

On the fourth day I decided our gazelle could take care of herself. No animal survived for three nights around Seronera without learning to avoid predation by hyenas, lions, or leopards; having achieved this wisdom, Gussie should now be allowed to take her chance. With this in mind I set out to find her.

"Gus-sie!" My voice rang across the plain as I walked towards a large herd of Thomson's gazelles half a mile away. At once a head raised itself from the grass and she trotted joyfully towards me; when she got to within a few feet she stopped as usual and looked at me uncertainly. Hesitating for just a moment, she then stepped briskly up to the bottle and sucked vigorously at it. Astonished by her confidence and complete trust in me, I wondered about the telepathic powers of animals. Could she have read my thoughts and known there was now no danger of being captured and shut inside for the night? After four days of wariness, it seemed uncanny that she should lose her fear of being caught the moment I had made up my mind to free her.

Gussie drank her fill, then pushed her bony head up against my hand. Together we walked across the plain for a short distance and she made no attempt to move out of touching range. Finally deciding to rejoin the herd, she trotted away in her high-rumped gait and I watched her until she mingled into the herd and was lost to sight.

From that day Gussie visited the house daily. She sometimes climbed the verandah steps, her slender legs sliding from under her in all directions, and she showed no nervousness of strangers. Having long since indicated her distaste for milk, she now drank only water from the beloved bottle.

By the time Gussie reached maturity a few weeks later, the gazelle herds were beginning to return to the central plains, which started some 10 miles from our house. As their numbers dwindled my apprehensions grew, and I urged Gussie to go with them.

"Go on, Gussie, go *on!*" I kept repeating, shooing her in the direction of the few remaining gazelles. She would trot a few paces with me behind her and, when I stopped, turn and look at me with large questioning eyes. But she kept returning to the house until finally she was the only gazelle left in our area. Each morning I would look out and see her still there, peacefully grazing on the lawn. If anything, she had become tamer than ever, missing her gazelle companions; I worried that her herd instincts might have been partially lost in her early upbringing by human beings.

As the days passed I became more and more anxious for Gussie's safety, even though Myles continually assured me that she would soon rejoin the gazelle herds. He may have been right, for one morning I awoke to find that Gussie had gone. Although I wanted to believe she had migrated at last to the plains, I was also afraid she might be dead. After looking and calling for her on foot, I searched in the Land Rover. Every vulture seen dropping from the sky was investigated and every tourist driver asked for information. I checked every kill and looked at it with relief after seeing that it was not Gussie. Eventually a message arrived that cheetahs had killed a gazelle near the Lodge. The African could not say whether it was a Thomson's or Grant's gazelle. Since the kill had been close to human habitation, I set out with a heavy heart, expecting to find my gazelle. Stepping

1　The author

2a   Leopard

2b   Wildebeest

3a Banagi

3b Mongoose

5 Scene in the Serengeti

6a A Grant gazelle

6b Cranes and Lemugrut mountain

7a Cheetah and zebra

7b Evening

from the Land Rover, I dispersed three cheetahs from their meal, and imagined I saw Gussie lying in the grass with her adhesive band around one horn. As I stared at her, my vision seemed to clear, and I found myself looking at a female *Thomson's* gazelle with horns bent one across the other, bearing not the faintest resemblance to Gussie.

We never discovered what became of our gentle gazelle. Ignorance about her fate left me always with the hope that she lived and had gone to join the herds on the plains. For a long time afterwards I missed Gussie's visits. In consequence I paid more attention to Jason, our old and much-loved Siamese cat. He fell ill shortly after Gussie's disappearance, and I was able to devote all my attention to him until he died.

For the first time I now had no animals to look after, apart from the children's dormice and tortoises, and the house felt strangely empty. Within a week this was filled by two wild orphans, and I was once again involved in the joys and anxieties of their upbringing.

That day we were visiting the game warden in Arusha, Eric Balson, when his rangers brought in two serval kittens. They had been found in a poachers' game pit, dug 6 feet into the ground and covered with grass to trap any animal that passed. Since there are usually three servals to a litter, it seemed likely the mother had managed to leap from the pit with one kitten in her mouth, leaving the other two to their fate. They lay together in a small cardboard box, two bleary-eyed, smudgily spotted bundles of fur. They were as yet unable to see or walk properly, and Myles estimated their age at a week or two.

"Are you going to keep them?" I asked, envying our friend's good fortune.

"Oh no," Eric replied, "not with our large dogs about the house. They'll probably go to the local game sanctuary." This was a small privately run zoo near Arusha.

Hardly daring to hope, I then asked if we might try to rear them at Seronera. The warden was delighted, for it meant they could later be returned to the wild. That evening we flew back to the Serengeti with our enchanting new pets cradled on my lap.

Although the kittens weighed little more than 1 pound each when they arrived and suffered the usual digestive difficulties, their weight increased by 50 percent within the first week. During this time we were camped on the Mara River in the north of the Park. The kittens slept in a box inside my mosquito net to protect them from the *siafu* ants that frequently invaded the camp. Unlike our fox, the servals slept reasonably quietly all night; but my first chore on awakening was to bathe them, for their upset digestions resulted in their box being in a deplorable mess by morning. Seeing this each day made me feel despondent about the kittens' chances of survival. Like domestic cats, however, they clung to life, and soon adjusted to their diet of canned milk, yeast, calcium, bone meal, baby cereal, vitamins, kaolin powder, and, later, small quantities of meat, liver, and egg. At six weeks they were eating live mice. Whenever their digestive systems gave them trouble, I reduced their diet to glucose water until they recovered. Within a month they had doubled in weight.

I named the cats Prince and Pixie, but they answered only to my imitation of their small birdlike chirrups. In appearance and temperament they differed completely. Of the two Prince was stronger and heavier, with larger, more defined spots; his eyes were green compared with Pixie's topaz. With her sad expression Pixie gave an impression of nervousness, and she spent most of each day above a wardrobe, peering anxiously down at anyone who called to her. She was less self-assured and not as affectionate as her brother, who purred constantly and would suck at anything available, intent upon getting the maximum of attention. Yet as time went on, Prince grew more independent and Pixie became friendlier.

At two months Pixie developed a partial paralysis of her limbs, dragging her back legs along the floor and lying semiconscious about the house. I suspected there had always been something wrong with her. Since our Research veterinarian was away, I left a notice on the messages board at the Lodge, asking any qualified tourist for help. I had begun to think Pixie could not survive much longer when an American veterinarian and his wife drove up at nine that night. Although he carried no specific drugs for animals and had experience only of domestic pets, he apparently diagnosed the trouble successfully and kindly gave me some of his own medicine. Every four hours during that night I administered the drug, breaking each tablet intended for a human being into eight pieces. The result was astonishing. Pixie changed into a bundle of energy, leaping about the room with dilated eyes and disturbing Prince by her behaviour. I thought she had quite taken leave of her senses. But in the end, after three days of intermittent paralytic attacks and treatment, she recovered completely and never had a recurrence of her mysterious illness.

Like all kittens the servals were delightful animals and never tired of playing. They enjoyed a game of rushing round to look for me whenever they heard my chirrups; then, on finding my hiding place, they would rub their heads against my legs and hands, purring ecstatically with tails held high and waving stiffly at the tips. They miaowed only if they wanted something, such as food when the refrigerator was opened. To show their displeasure, if for instance they were hugged too tightly, they gave a low rattling growl in their throats. But generally they purred at the least encouragement, loud rumbling vibrations of contentment.

The lavatory bowl especially fascinated Pixie. Each time it was flushed she would appear at once, stand on her back legs, and gaze down at the water swirling round inside. When it stopped, she always looked up with a quizzical expression, hoping the show would be repeated.

Boxing was another of the cats' favourite pastimes. Reaching out a paw with infinite care, they would clout the object and then withdraw the paw at lightning speed. If I knocked something to the ground for them to pounce on, they rubbed against me and purred, evidently waiting for me to have first go at it. Pixie was careful to lick me affectionately before biting me, sometimes quite fiercely, for she was rougher than Prince and used her sharp claws, especially on my toes under the bedclothes. Myles's dressing gown was another game they loved. If it was thrown to the floor, Pixie immediately rushed under it and Prince gathered himself up high to leap down on her from above. A furious tussle would then ensue, with Prince biting through the cloth and Pixie growling angrily underneath.

It was fascinating to see the cats pounce. I enjoyed running my hand under the bedcovers, watching the kittens rear as high as they could on their back legs. With claws outstretched and immense ears straining forwards, they would crash down suddenly upon their hurriedly withdrawn prey. If I was not quick enough, their sharp teeth and claws sometimes pierced the cloth and my skin; for however tame they seemed, the servals always retained their fierce characteristics and remained wild.

When adult, servals are exotic-looking animals, standing nearly 2 feet high and 4 feet long, with enormous pointed ears, tawny spotted coats, and long legs. Their ringed tails are shorter than those of other cats and they are slenderly built. Of our two, Prince was the more handsome, with his large green eyes and magnificent coat of spotted amber. I delighted in seeing him on the alert, with tail fluffed out and back hair raised, while Pixie lay in wait to pounce out at him in passing. He moved with a distinctive high walk, and darted like quicksilver, chasing the paper balls I pulled along by string.

We went for walks every day, the kittens rushing to retrieve the sticks I threw for them. One day I heard a disturbance outside as a flock of helmeted guinea fowl advanced towards the house, protesting loudly. Ahead of them ran our baby servals with the vociferous mob on their tails. After that sobering lesson they showed less enthusiasm for stalking the larger birds that lived around our kopjes.

The kittens were about six weeks old when I offered them their first live mouse. They fell on it, growling fiercely, and quickly ate it; but they soon became lazy about killing their prey. After waiting a few minutes for them to finish off a frightened mouse, I always ended the creature's misery, hoping the cats would eat it. Sometimes they did, although they disliked being offered dead creatures. We baited the mice in live traps and kept them in a wooden box outside the back door. Apart from the possibility of attracting snakes by their squeaks, Myles disapproved of the whole system and predicted retribution. I, too, felt unhappy about giving the cats a balanced diet like this, but was unable to think of an alternative.

As usual Myles's forebodings proved correct. The kittens were six months old when I noticed that Pixie was unusually nervous one evening, staring tensely at the refrigerator. Each time I picked her up to soothe her she struggled to be released, ran down the passageway, and immediately returned, as if drawn irresistibly to the refrigerator. I was puzzled by the alert, frightened look on her face, though she sometimes behaved in this manner if there was anything unusual in the house, such as our safari paraphernalia. This time I could see no reason for her anxiety, and I inspected the refrigerator several times in the dim light, returning to reassure Pixie, who would not be comforted. With her eyes glued to something I could not see, I was wondering if perhaps she was having one of her strange bouts of nerves, when Prince sauntered along to join us. Immediately he too froze in his tracks, his eyes riveted on the refrigerator. This time I looked more carefully and saw, to my dismay, the thick black coils of a cobra writhing in the darkness behind it. The snake had been trapped in the house after the servants had closed the back door, attracted in the first place by the squeaking of the imprisoned mice outside.

While Myles drove to the Park's armoury for a shotgun, I spent the time shutting off the rest of the house from the cobra. The kittens needed to be hidden away, too, for they were growing more venturesome by the minute, drawing nearer and nearer to the alarmed snake and provoking it into moving openly about the floor in an attempt to find an escape. Seven doors along a passageway led to the back verandah that held the refrigerator, all of which I closed before the cobra finally took refuge in the passageway. I then sealed this off by placing an upturned table against the entrance, to avoid having a bullet in our refrigerator should the cobra return there. Each time it tried to scale the table, I gently shooed it back from the other side, whereupon it reared up with spread hood and then retreated. It did not attempt to spit at me.

Myles seemed to be taking an age. Meanwhile the cobra found its way into the lavatory, passing under the door which stood 2 inches above the floor. Only a single light shone into the passageway through a glass pane in this door. The other doors were all wooden, and the passage light had long ceased to function, due to a faulty connection. As soon as the snake left the passageway, I climbed onto a stool under the electric light and struggled to put a new bulb into the broken socket. While I was thus occupied the cobra would occasionally reappear and glide past me as I froze to the stool. It scaled up the walls and doors to a height of 3 feet or more in its efforts to find a way out. In the lavatory strange noises could be heard, as something crashed to the floor, followed by soft mewing sounds of distress. I had never before heard a snake producing vocal sounds other than hissing, but this was not a product of my imagination. We discovered later that the cobra had knocked a plastic container of lavatory cleanser from the windowshelf, which lost its top and filled the room with fumes. The frightened snake had struck again and again at the container and spattered the window panes with its venom.

At last Myles returned. Telling me to shoot the cobra if it emerged, which I fervently hoped would not happen, he too tried to fit a bulb to the passage light, but without success. Finally he decided to fire at the reptile from under the lavatory door, since opening it on a disturbed cobra in a confined space might easily have been disastrous. Pointing the gun through the gap, Myles rested his cheek along the ground and saw the reflection of the cobra's body in the polished floor. He fired, and the snake immediately shot out from under the door, at the same time as I pulled Myles back into our bedroom. We then went round to the back verandah and shone a flashlight into the passageway, where the snake lay mortally wounded. Myles fired again, the shot reverberating through the house.

After this incident the kittens treated the house with suspicion, nervously investigating its interior and jumping at every movement. But their troubles were not at an end, for only three days later an even more traumatic experience resulted in tragedy.

We invited Bernd, our veterinarian friend, to dinner on his return from several weeks' holiday in Germany. The cats at six months looked almost full-grown and, having known them when they were very young, Bernd was impressed by their progress. It was already dusk. While we talked for a few moments, watching the cats playing together in the bedroom, I noticed that Fundi had forgotten to draw the curtains across the windows. This provided a clear view into the lighted room from outside. At the time I felt vaguely uneasy about it, but I paid little heed to my inner warning in the more pressing matter of greeting unexpected visitors; besides, the windows were screened by mosquito wire, and in any case Fundi would be sure to remember soon. I did not return to the room that evening, and the curtains remained undrawn.

At about ten o'clock that night Fundi opened the bedroom door to allow the cats to join us, and then went home, shutting all the outside doors to the house. The servals raced along the passageway and in and out of the rooms, playing for an hour before they tired and jumped back to rest on our beds, which lay directly under the window.

Suddenly there was a loud crash and Pixie hurtled into the sitting room and flung herself against the gauzed window by Myles's chair. Thinking the cats had knocked something over, I ran to the bedroom. Everything looked normal, but I could see no sign of Prince. Puzzled, I called his name and searched for him. It was then that I noticed a torn and gaping hole in the mosquito wire of the window above our beds. For a moment I looked at it in amazement, thinking Prince had leaped out. I called to Myles to come quickly. After taking one glance at the window, he said: "Prince couldn't have done that! Most likely a leopard has grabbed him."

Aghast at this statement I raced outside to check whether Myles could be right. There, to my horror, I saw the pug marks of a leopard in the sand directly beneath the window; a scrape of mud lay under the ledge where it had jumped. On the ledge itself was a puddle of urine, pathetically left by our frightened cat. Running out to the kopjes, I called Prince's name again and again, hoping the leopard would drop him. The thought that he might still be alive encouraged me to go on looking for him, despite Myles's warnings about buffaloes frequenting our kopjes at night. In the end I gave up hope and returned sick at heart to our remaining kitten.

The next day we were told there was a dead serval in a tree by the river, 2 miles away; but I could not bring myself to discover whether it might be Prince.

Although at the time I did not feel fortunate, Myles reiterated that I had been lucky not to come face to face with a leopard in our bedroom; evidently Prince had been on our pillows directly beneath the window, and the leopard had needed only to force his head and shoulders through the wire gauze to reach him. By leaving the curtains undrawn I felt to blame, but Myles also assured me that sooner or later the leopard would have succeeded in killing one or both cats; servals are a favourite prey of these animals. Myles felt the leopard had been waiting its chance for some time, and that it had finally leaped through the apparently open window without realizing it was screened. He reminded me, too, of his earlier forebodings, when the baby servals had sat with us in the open living room, tied by their leads to the sofa. Frequently sensing a leopard's presence outside, Myles had warned me then that one might come into the room after the cats; but I had disregarded his fears on the grounds that Jason, our Siamese cat, had survived nearly fifteen years without even wire screens on the windows during our early years in the Park.

Prince's death was a grievous shock to both Pixie and me, and she now refused to sleep any longer alone in her room. For the first time she took to jumping on my lap, purring loudly as Prince had done as a small kitten, and following me wherever I went. Once when I returned from being away ten days, she greeted me with delirious joy, miaowing sharply whenever I tried putting her in her room for the evening. During the next few days she would not let me out of her sight. I felt desperately sorry for her and gave her all the love and attention I could.

As the weeks passed, we watched our serval developing a growing antipathy towards Africans, until only Fundi could approach her without being warned to keep his distance. Pixie still roamed freely during the day; but in order to make Fundi's job easier when we were on safari, we constructed a large enclosure in which he could capture Pixie for shutting into the house at night. The enclosure was rarely used otherwise.

One day Fundi met us with a worried look and confessed he had been unable to approach Pixie. She had been "kali sana" (very fierce), resisting all his attempts to touch her. Consequently he had been obliged to leave her shut inside the house for the three days we were away. I opened the door to her room and found Pixie sitting on top of the wardrobe, surrounded by a scene of chaotic disorder. The room was a shambles. Pixie was overjoyed at our return and she greeted us with frenzied purrs and rubbings. Looking round, I realized the time had come to release her and to let her take her chance at night. Although she was only eight months old, there was now really no alternative, and I began planning for her first night in the wild with misgivings, worried that a leopard might kill her too. First we built a small door on a hinged flap into the mesh of the back verandah, and I spent hours showing Pixie how to use it. This was designed to keep other creatures from coming in after her. But she never learned how to push against the door, and we finally removed it. Pixie was free.

For a few nights all went well. Our serval would wander in and out of the house, leaping onto my bed and biting my feet through the covers. Her loud purrs and demonstrations soon drove Myles from the room; but her visits reassured me of her safety and I looked forward eagerly to them. After the fifth night she disappeared.

There was, of course, always the possibility that Pixie had found a companion and that she had gone with him to start a new life in another area; I hoped so. Only once did I see an unusually tame serval along the river, 4 miles away, but when I left the car to approach it on foot, the animal fled. It was evidently not our serval.

Chapter 9

Lions

He was a beautiful beast; very dark tawny, with a
mane that was almost black in places and gray in
others. His face was old and wise and kind—or as
kind as a lion's face can be. For no matter how be-
nevolent a lion may seem, there is always a slight
tinge of cruelty in his deep-set eyes.

—Martin Johnson, *Lion**

Of all the African game sanctuaries the Serengeti is the most
famous for its lions. At Seronera, where lions have grown indifferent to vehicles flocking round them, visitors were almost certain to see them during even the shortest stay. Stretched in the
grass, the lions slumbered for hours on end, generally ignoring
the cameras of tourists anxious for more interesting pictures. Occasionally one would roll over, huge paws dangling in the air, or
another gave a cavernous yawn, exposing formidable canine
teeth, while rays of sunlight filtered through the trees to dapple
their sleek amber forms, comatose in the shade.

Looking at them, it was difficult to regard these relaxed creatures as savagely dangerous beasts. Indeed, tourists sometimes
expressed a desire to leave their cars and stroke them. Years
ago, it was said, an American asked his wife to film him approaching one such somnolent pride. He was promptly killed,

* New York: G. P. Putnam's Sons, 1929.

while his wife continued to press the button of the movie camera, recording the entire scene.

We came on lions frequently during our years in the Serengeti. They had become accustomed to our settlement at Seronera, and sometimes stalked past the house in broad daylight to join other members of their pride. One afternoon while our serval kittens were playing outside, a lioness unexpectedly appeared around the corner of the house, followed by two half-grown cubs. The kittens froze, fur on end, then streaked past me into the bedroom. Ignoring us completely, the lioness drank thirstily from the birdbath, while the children and I stood 10 yards away and watched her. Although the cubs glanced at us uneasily from time to time, their mother moved off without once having looked in our direction.

On another occasion I awoke to an unusually quiet house. It was almost seven o'clock and Fundi had not brought our tea. There was no sign of the cook, nor of the children's ayah, all of whom normally began work at six-thirty each morning. I had started towards their quarters at the back of the house when I suddenly became aware of two magnificent lions lying 20 yards from the house beneath the clothesline. Their tawny manes rippled in the breeze as they watched me with languid interest. I hurriedly retreated to the house. Later I decided the staff could not be excused duty because two lions happened to have taken up residence with us for the day. Skirting round the lions behind the kitchen, I found the servants sheltering inside locked rooms. They followed me back to the house in single file, with little gasps of alarm. All that day while they nervously hurried about their work between the kitchen and the house, the servants were conscious of the impassive gaze of the lions. No clothes were washed, and the children played indoors. After spending the day with us, our visitors eventually wandered towards the plains in the late afternoon.

Numerous as they were, the lions of the Serengeti were not hostile towards people. Game was abundant and they did not look upon man as a source of food, though they could be dangerous if they felt threatened or were defending their cubs. I remembered an occasion on safari when we had stopped to look at a pride that contained several cubs. A lioness immediately charged the Land Rover, spitting furiously as she leaped towards us, claws outstretched. We were carrying a heavy load of equipment that day, and Myles had fortunately felt it wise not to switch off the engine; he only just managed to keep ahead of her, while the rangers on the exposed open back beseeched him to go faster. On another occasion we were pursued for some distance by a lion wounded in a fight. In pain, hungry, and hot on the treeless plains, he was not in any mood to tolerate intruders.

Generally, however, lions avoided trouble if they could, even during periods when the wildebeest and other migratory animals had moved on and game was scarce around Seronera. At such times the resident prides went through a difficult spell; their cubs sometimes starved to death, and man would have made an easy prey. Yet still they avoided him, the instinctive fear of man being strong in all animals. In other areas of Africa where game had become scarce and lions turned to people as a source of food, they became extremely dangerous, perhaps having discovered how simple it was to kill man. But to my knowledge, no instance of a man-killer ever occurred in the Serengeti until one night in July 1961.

On that evening Myles returned to Seronera after two long and tiring days in Arusha attending Parks meetings. Mr. Tig, our two-week-old hyrax, was in good health when I left for Nairobi that morning, but he died suddenly and quite unexpectedly on the journey home. The loss of our small friend saddened Myles, and he arrived at the house after dark, exhausted by the tedious drive. Joy Adamson was awaiting him on our verandah; she wanted news of the Parks' decision on the nearly full-grown cubs of Elsa, her famous lioness. Joy and George, her husband, had brought the cubs from Kenya two months previously. It had been agreed between the Parks authorities and the Adamsons that, after a period of rehabilitation, the lions were to live wild and natural lives in the Serengeti, without human interference. But one of the lions had arrived with an unpoisoned arrowhead lodged beneath the skin of its rump, fired several weeks before by an African child in Kenya; this had not been removed when the cubs were captured and caged for translocation. Joy now sought permission to capture the injured animal and have the arrowhead removed. The lions were free and had not been seen by the Adamsons for some time. Acting on the advice of experts, the Parks authorities decided the proposal was unfeasible. To locate and trap this particular animal in a heavily lion-infested valley such as the Mbalageti, and then to operate on it with the inadequate experience as yet gained of drug dosages for immobilization, could lead to the death of the lion or a mauling of the vet—quite apart from the disturbance caused to all the other animals that might be caught in the trap before the Adamsons' lion was successfully captured.

Joy, on hearing this decision, was very upset. After she had eventually left the house, Myles collapsed into bed, depressed and worn out. He slept fitfully, dreaming he was on safari and that a man was being mauled by a lion. At the same time, he could hear a voice calling urgently: "Myles! Myles! Get up, man! A visitor has been mauled by a lion!"

Suddenly he realized he was no longer dreaming, and that Gordon Poolman stood outside banging at his door. It was one o'clock in the morning. Myles leaped to his feet, threw on a coat, and rushed out.

The victim of the lion's attack was lying at the Lodge, where he had been carried from a camping site by his two companions. He was a young English farmer who, some years previously, had visited Kenya to attend a wedding and stayed on to work there. Before the country became an independent state, he decided to start a new career in England; this was to be his final safari in the wilds. He and his friends came lightly equipped with an open tent and no mosquito nets. On their first evening at Seronera they saw two lions close by, but they had camped before in wildlife areas and were not alarmed. Finishing their meal, they went to bed, paying no further attention to the lions, who were now rummaging amongst their kitchen utensils. The three visitors' heads lay in the open doorway of the tent and they slept soundly. Four hours later two of the party were awakened by the sound of a muffled scream. To their horror they saw a lion standing over their friend with his head in its jaws. At their yells, the lion dropped him and moved away. Later one of the party (in an adjacent tent) said the lion had to be kicked in the face before releasing its victim.

The young man's wounds were terrible. One arm and shoulder had been badly mauled, an eye was bitten through, and there were teeth marks across his cheeks and mouth. His scalp had been lacerated and he shivered uncontrollably, mumbling and calling out repeatedly for a doctor. While our African medical worker tried to stem the flow of blood and dress the appalling wounds, Connie sat beside him, covering him with blankets and hot water bottles. In the meantime Myles and Gordon drove off in separate Land Rovers to alert other campers in the area and obtain some morphine, which in those days was not kept in our small dispensary. They also hoped to find a doctor, but in this they were not successful. Within half an hour of the accident, the patient was injected with morphine from the Adamsons' supply, and he felt no more pain.

At that time we had no airplane, but two Rhodesian tourists had luckily flown in that day and Myles sought their help. Without hesitation they set to work removing the back seats from their aircraft and preparing a stretcher. At first light they took off for Nairobi with their unconscious passenger, and Myles watched them go with a heavy heart. Within half an hour of reaching hospital the unfortunate man died. It was a terrible day in Serengeti's history.

Early that morning the wardens tracked the lions by following their spoor and found them a mile from the victim's camp. They were both full-grown males, and one of them had a suppurating shoulder. As it was not possible to tell which lion was responsible for the attack, it was necessary to destroy them both; Myles and Gordon fired simultaneously, killing the lions instantly.

It is an accepted precaution on safari to sleep under a mosquito net when camping in an open tent. This the ill-fated visitors had not done, and they had made some fundamental errors of judgment. With their canvas beds in the open doorway of the tent, they lay with their exposed heads outwards, turned off the light, and allowed their small campfire to burn itself out. They were then in total darkness, unconscious, unprotected, and unscreened, within a few feet of two wild lions they had seen earlier that evening. Even so, and with the men sleeping peacefully, the lions had waited four hours to attack; there were no drag marks from the bed, the spoor indicating that the victim had been carried 12 feet through the air in a single bound. From then onwards the rules for camping in the Park were tightened and certain precautions enforced, such as a lamp burning all night outside each tent.

During the years we lived in the Serengeti there were no further attacks by lions, although from time to time we had reports of them playfully terrorizing tourists in their camps. One of these incidents was recorded by Myles, who wrote:

On campsite 3, a Seronera lion tore the mosquito net off a cook, who was sleeping outside the main tents of a tourist party. The cook recovered from this shock, but was again awakened by a lion pulling the groundsheet from *underneath* him! Sounds of rending groundsheet could be heard disappearing into the night. The cook, badly shaken, retired to a lorry.

On another occasion a party of Lodge visitors, sitting by the campfire one evening, were confronted by a pride of twenty-one lions gazing at them from across the flames a few yards away. Their reaction was instantaneous; they all rushed indoors, "one old lady, who was crippled by rheumatism, clearing the four-foot bar counter like a two-year-old."

The lions sometimes disturbed labour gangs; and once an entire workforce, building a dam on the Seronera River, was treed by a pride that wandered down to drink. The workers were still in the trees when the truck arrived to collect them for their lunch break.

A few weeks later the water-boring machine was hammering away at 7:00 A.M. when three lions appeared on site. The operator, in one movement, cut the motor and went straight up the sheer legs of the machinery, while the rest of the crew scattered into trees and onto the truck.

Looking back, it seemed there were more lions in our early days than when we left the Serengeti in 1972, for we sometimes saw as many as fifty in a day on safari. A single pride could number thirty, and some of the lions' manes extended halfway along their backs and down their forelegs, with great tufts of fur at the elbows. Once our Land Rover broke down alongside one of these huge prides and Myles scrambled out to see to the trouble, while I kept an uneasy watch on the lions from the car. They lay 20 yards away, but after a few moments they made off to a thick patch of bush nearby and observed us from there.

In the past lion hunting in the Serengeti had been extremely popular, and after the area was closed it continued unabated around its boundaries. This was especially so in the Ikoma district, where there was no limit on the number of lions that could be shot on licence. Other areas around the Park were divided into controlled shooting blocks, where only a specified number of lions were allowed to be killed on licence each year. We had not been three years in the Serengeti when Myles began to grow anxious about the dwindling number of lions we were seeing on our safaris. He felt sure the Serengeti's lion population was decreasing, and for weeks he would lie awake at nights, wondering how best to deal with the problem. Letters to the various Game Department offices, requesting statistics of lions shot in the hunting areas around the Park, produced no effective reply. Finally he visited each of the customs officials in surrounding townships, inspected their trophy export books, and discovered that a total of eighty-eight male lions had been shot on the periphery of the Park during the previous six months. This number was even greater than Myles had feared, and in February 1960 he issued a first warning on the situation to the Parks and Game authorities. He then took the matter further by writing monthly reports on the worsening position, which were sometimes publicized in the local press. Eventually, after months of harassment, the Ikoma area was belatedly closed to lion hunting. Although this had the effect of increasing the lion population within the Park, they never really recovered to their former levels, particularly in the narrow western Corridor.

Prior to the Serengeti achieving National Park status, lions were baited by photographers from cars, and would appear as soon as they heard a vehicle, following it in the hope of being fed. A hunter friend once took us to the northern extension before it was added to the Park, and we were given a demonstration of how this was done. The vehicle had no doors. After shooting a gazelle, the hunter tied it to his truck on a long rope and dragged the carcass through the bush. Amongst the lions that converged on us from all directions were two splendid males. They stalked within touching distance of the truck and were fully aware of us sitting inside. Not being used to the wilds in those days, I felt a little uneasy looking into the intent eyes of two hungry lions at such close range! The practice of feeding lions was eventually stopped, though in certain areas the lions still ran up hopefully for some time afterwards, and around Seronera we never knew them to show any fear of vehicles.

The only time to my knowledge that I tried the patience of our lions to the limit was one night when the children were at school and Myles had gone to Arusha. Returning alone from dinner with Ros and Hugh Lamprey, I parked the Land Rover in the garage 20 yards from the house, and realized I had forgotten my flashlight. It was a very dark and moonless night, the generator had been shut down as usual at 10:00 P.M., and no light shone from the house. But it was not the first time I had had to walk in the dark, and I stepped briskly towards the house, hoping there were no buffaloes or lions in my path. After a few paces I felt the hair begin to rise on the back of my neck and quickened my pace, reaching the back door with relief. As I pulled it open, I heard the unmistakable deep-throated growl of a lion behind me. Rushing inside, I slammed the door and hurried to the bedroom for a flashlight. To my consternation there were eighteen lions between the garage and the house; I had walked through the middle of them. Their eyes glowed back at me in the beam from my flashlight and they were so disturbed that one of them sprang towards the light, grunting angrily. Only their surprise must have prevented them from reacting to my sudden appearance in their midst. The lions had not been visible when I had swung the Land Rover into the garage from behind the kitchen; but blundering through them on the direct walk to the house, in all probability I had caused some of them to move out of my way. No sound warned me, which was fortunate, for had I hesitated or shown any fear, it is unlikely they would have behaved with such docility.

This may explain why mad people, who sometimes walked without fear in the Park, apparently came to no harm. People often walked in the Serengeti, some of them of unsound mind and no longer in control of their actions. The Africans firmly believed that wild animals would not attack a mad person, and this, from our experience, seemed to be true.

One night, while Myles and I read to an accompaniment of reverberating roars from a pride of lions close by, we were surprised to hear a sepulchral voice intoning "Hodi!" at the door. This Swahili word is used instead of a doorbell or knock, and we looked at each other in astonishment. Expecting to find a terrified passer-by seeking refuge from the lions, Myles hurried to the door; a woman stood there stark naked, smiling happily, while the lions grunted the final notes of their chorus. After wrapping her in a *kikoi* (sarong), we bundled her into the Land Rover and put her for the night into a room used for locking up prisoners. The next day Myles sent her by Land Rover to the nearest settlement, where she would be cared for by her kinsfolk. Since she had already been seen several times wandering naked in the bush, we felt sure she would soon discard the *kikoi* I had given her. We were astounded by her survival, but the Africans took a more philosophical view. "God will protect her," they said, "for He knows that she is like a small child." And certainly on that night the lions had let her walk amongst them without protest.

During all our years in the Serengeti I confronted a lion only once at close quarters. This was early one morning when I decided to take a walk before breakfast. The sun had just risen over the horizon and I was enjoying the beauty of a new day when suddenly I saw a Thomson's gazelle streaking at full speed in my direction. It stopped abruptly a few feet from me and turned to look back, all the while feverishly wagging its short black tail. To my dismay a lioness was racing towards us in pursuit of the Tommy. She pulled up just 10 yards away, with ears pressed flat against her head, her long tail lashing. In her state of concentrated fury it seemed inevitable that she would spring on me, and I was immediately paralyzed with shock. After a while the lioness appeared to relax very slightly; her gaze wandered from me and her ears pricked up. But her tail continued to lash from side to side, and when I took a tentative step backwards, she at once switched her intent eyes back onto me and I was riveted to the spot. Meanwhile the Tommy grazed quite unconcernedly a few yards away, conscious that it was no longer the object of the lioness's attention. I took another step backward, then slowly increased the distance between us step by step until I felt the lioness had lost interest. Finally I turned and walked quickly away. Looking back I saw the Tommy grazing some distance from the lioness, who was now walking in the direction she had come. There seemed little doubt that the Tommy had deliberately run towards me in the hope that the lioness would not pursue it to within such close range of a human being.

There were numerous occasions when we heard of people walking into lions in the Serengeti. One of these encounters took place at the site of a modern hotel that was to be built at Seronera, in an extensive kopje with splendid views of the surrounding countryside. A large pride of sixteen lions and newly born cubs had made this kopje their home; but none of us had thought to mention the fact to John Owen, the Parks director, or to Robert Marshall, the architect of the proposed building. Visiting the site together one morning, they left their Land Rover to walk over the kopje, and were immediately confronted by four snarling lionesses leaping towards them from the rocks. Both men took to their heels with Robert, the younger and lighter of the two, leading in the race to their vehicle. Realizing that one of the lionesses was gaining on him, John suddenly spun round and roared "*STOP!*" in a commanding tone. At the same time he flung both arms above his head, which had the effect of making his massive frame look even more formidable. The lioness pulled up a few feet away, snarling and lashing her tail while she glared angrily at John. He stared back. In the end the lioness turned and bounded towards her cubs.

Later the two men walked into the office and related their hair-raising tale to Myles. Far from showing any sympathy, Myles lightly brushed the affair aside with the words: "We all knew those lions were there."

"Well," replied our director in mild tones of reproof, "you might at least have told us."

"In Seronera, John," Myles retorted briskly, "you walk around at your own risk."

After dinner with the Chief Park Warden one evening, our director was walking to the guesthouse nearby when he stumbled upon a lioness by Sandy's verandah and beat a precipitate retreat. Sandy, on hearing the angry grunts of the lioness, rushed to a window and flung the curtains apart; whereupon the wooden pelmet immediately fell on him and added to the turmoil.

The more I learned about lions, the more I admired them. It was impossible not to feel touched by their essentially amiable nature, and I could understand why those people who had reared lions always loved them with such enthusiasm. Lions have a great capacity for affection; they are also very lazy. For me they symbolized the Serengeti, with their benign amber eyes and their bodies sprawled in abandon about the grass. The lionesses allowed any of the cubs in their pride to suckle, rolling obligingly onto their sides for the young animals to knead their fur like outsize kittens. When they came to life in the cool of the evenings, they would yawn and stretch and caress one another languorously, while their young played together and tussled with the faces and tails of their elders.

I should have welcomed the chance of rearing a cub. But the opportunity never arose; and while our children were small, this was perhaps as well. Lions could be dangerous with the very young, if only by accident when they played. Moreover, much as one liked them, they usually presented problems as they grew older and larger. Just such a case occurred when a cub raised at Seronera reached the age of six months. The animal had originally been brought to Myles as a very young cub of not more than two weeks. Its mother had an injured paw and was unable to look after her three cubs easily; eventually she abandoned one. The warden who discovered them kept watch over the tiny animal for twenty-four hours, and when the lioness did not return, he asked if he could rear the cub himself. In view of the circumstances, Myles agreed.

For the first few months the cub was an endearing pet, and our children (aged four and five at the time) frequently visited it. The little animal was allowed the run of the house; but as it grew larger and more boisterous, this raised difficulties, for the cub was not yet able to moderate its activities in keeping with its increasing size and weight. There were times when the young lion would launch itself at a visitor's back as he walked to his car, almost knocking him over and sometimes ripping his clothes with the powerful claws it had not yet learned to sheathe; or it might land suddenly in our laps, sending things flying in all directions as it played affectionately. Particularly rough at mealtimes, the cub often leaped at the owner's wife in its demands to be fed, and in struggling to keep a grip, it would tear her clothes and sometimes her skin. Finally the warden began making enquiries for a suitable home; he intended going on holiday and did not feel he could cope with the cub when travelling. After all efforts at finding a home had failed, he asked Myles to release his pet in the Park.

A lion is generally not capable of supporting itself until it is at least eighteen months old. By this time the cub was only six months, and unable to fend for itself; it also reacted nervously whenever it heard wild lions, cowering under the bed and refusing to be reassured. Myles felt doubtful about its chances of being accepted by a wild pride; but there was now no alternative to releasing it and he decided to go ahead with the experiment. Searching until he had found a large pride of lions with cubs the same age, he shot a zebra and gave it to them. Whilst they fed, he pushed the frightened cub out of the Land Rover and hoped it would be able to join the pride. None of the lions paid any attention to the newcomer, which crept into a patch of bush nearby and remained there till nightfall, alongside the surfeited lions. Early next morning Myles returned; but the lions had moved away and neither they nor the cub were seen again.

During his years as a professional hunter Myles had had many experiences with lions. There was a saying that all the cruelty of Africa could be seen in the pitiless yellow stare of a lion's eyes, and many hunters considered lions to be the most dangerous animals on earth. But in areas where they were not hunted, it was hard to imagine them as being the ruthless beasts depicted by legend. Contrary to the cold beauty of the solitary leopard, the Serengeti lions gave an impression of warmth and companionship; and if, in their struggle to survive, they were merciless and selfish, they also showed many instances of gentler emotions, nuzzling one another and enduring with patience the playful attentions of their young. There were even times when they showed tolerance towards other animals.

We were shown an instance of this one evening while we listened to the animals on our verandah and enjoyed the cool air. Although mosquitoes buzzed round us in swarms, it was worth suffering their attentions for a while to savour the magic of an African night. A pair of dikdiks stepping daintily beneath the trees suddenly gave birdlike whistles and darted towards the kopjes. Pale light filtered through the branches of the acacias to dapple shadows on the lawn, while stars crowded the dark velvet curve above us. I was musing on the infinitude of space and the meaning of eternity when Myles suddenly got to his feet and strolled across the grass. To my dismay the patches I had thought to be shadows rose up and turned into lions. There were eight of them. After standing for a moment watching Myles's motionless figure, they faded into the darkness without a sound.

"Well, that was close!" said Myles, turning towards the house.

The following morning we discovered the lions had returned during the night and utterly destroyed our badminton net, chewing not only the net itself but also the aluminum poles!

Over the years I spent many nights alone while Myles was away. Although as a rule solitude never worried me, there were the odd moments when I felt uneasy. On one of these occasions the house was being redecorated, and furniture was piled into the center of the living room. I found it depressing to work inside and took my writing materials to the verandah. It was a blustery night; wind moaned around the house and thorny acacia branches scratched the roof. The electric lamp, painted orange to deter insects, threw shadows across my table and glowed eerily, making the darkness outside seem deeper than usual. Ghostly clouds skidded across the moon. Except for the wind and the scratching on the roof, the night was unusually quiet and no animals called. I tried to ignore the strange atmosphere and to concentrate on writing, looking out every now and then for inspiration.

It was during one of these pauses that I found myself gazing at a waterbuck which stood motionless in a pool of light by the verandah steps. I watched her for a while and wondered if the light or my presence had frightened her. Suddenly there was a stampede and several other waterbuck rushed past in the darkness. With a bound the waterbuck I had been watching leaped out of sight, followed closely by a lioness who skimmed the bottom step of the verandah. More lions materialized from the shadows and disappeared silently around the house in the direction the waterbuck had taken. I could hear the drumming of hooves and a rush of running bodies, but no other sound. The heavy silence that followed seemed to indicate the lions had failed in their hunt. Once again, I thought, an animal had apparently sought refuge from a lion by standing close to a human being. This had almost been the waterbuck's undoing, since she had waited until the lioness was almost upon her before leaping away.

Deciding I had had enough, I went to bed. In the weird atmosphere of that night it seemed less sinister there than on the verandah listening to the noises of the wind and trees. Even the animals were strangely silent and no lions roared.

Chapter 10

Making Friends

During our early days at Seronera I needed to choose between making friends with our animal neighbours or growing a garden, which meant continually chasing off the birds and hyraxes that lived around us. The hyraxes showed themselves to be adept at getting over, under, or through any kind of fence. Since I preferred seeing animals undisturbed to waging a constant war against them, I soon abandoned the garden.

Hyraxes are small furry creatures that look like a cross between a large guinea pig and a rabbit. Two species belonging to the genera lived in our kopjes: *Procavia johnstoni* (rock hyrax) and *Dendrohyrax brucei* (tree hyrax). Despite their rodent-like appearance, hyraxes are actually small pachyderms whose feet and bone formation are similar to the elephant, their nearest living relative. The *Pharmaceutical Journal* of September 1850 described them as being, with the exception of the horn, "little else than rhinoceroses in miniature"!

At first we saw only a few hyraxes in our kopjes, but as time went by their numbers increased tenfold. This may have been attributable to reduced predation after we came to live in the area, and to our regular feeding of them. At the sound of my voice calling "*Chuka, chuka*" (*chakula* means food in Swahili), and of their metal feeding tray being banged, small heads would pop up over the tops of the rocks, followed by the rock hyraxes leaping and scampering across the boulders to the glade where I fed them. From the edge of the sansevieria they would eye me seriously for a moment whilst busily scratching themselves in a nervous behavioural trait known as displacement; then they would cautiously waddle out with bellies close to the ground, sometimes dragging their rear quarters in the dust. In the beginning brief fights and arguments frequently broke out, but as their confidence increased they grew more relaxed.

I fed them mainly on vegetable peelings from the kitchen, mixed with lucerne pellets, apple skins, and bananas, which seemed to be their favourite food. For these the braver animals took almost unlimited risks, suppressing their customary caution and alertness to danger.

During the severe drought of 1961 conditions were so bad that the hyraxes fed mainly on the bitter milky leaves of the aloes that grew around our house. I began feeding them at this time, and the hyraxes lost no time in accepting help. For several weeks I sat each day totally immobile for long periods of time. The hyraxes watched me from the bush, until eventually they started to venture out. However, the slightest sign of life would send them scurrying for cover, and it took a long time to entice them back again. For this reason the children and I suffered innumerable tsetse and mosquito bites, fly tickles, and nose itches without moving a hair. In the end the hyraxes came to know us, and I began keeping notes on their behaviour.

Adult rock hyraxes are about 18 inches long and weigh approximately the same as a mature domestic cat. They have small round ears, short legs, no tail, and a few long bristles spaced along their bodies. Their small rodent faces are alert and infinitely endearing, and when frightened their round bright eyes seem to roll over, leaving just the whites visible. They have four toes on each forefoot and three on each hind foot, which is armed with a curved nail "terminated by a kind of very small, thin and rounded hoof" (*Pharmaceutical Journal*, September 1850); their rubbery soles are designed for scampering up sheer rock faces and small trees.

Compared with the rock hyraxes, the tree hyraxes in our kopjes were shy and timid creatures, although from time to time one would creep cautiously out to join the rock hyraxes feeding round us. Grey in colour, with white chests and bellies, they were smaller, with narrower faces, and they fed mainly on acacia leaves.

Hyraxes are intelligent animals. They soon learned to jump onto our laps for food, sometimes even with strangers sitting alongside, and most would tolerate being stroked or scratched behind the ears. Occasionally they bit from nervousness or sudden anger, and sometimes by accident while we hand-fed them; but we soon became skilled at avoiding their strong sharp teeth. Warning rattles indicated annoyance in a dispute among themselves for a place on our laps, and it was prudent at such times to keep hands and arms well away from the battle zone. During feeding the rock hyraxes displayed very short tempers and they quarrelled constantly, frequently springing round to attack neighbours. Combatants chattered and snapped viciously, until the argument was ended usually by one hyrax briefly mounting the other to assert its dominance. Some were bolder than others and their personalities varied tremendously. I named my favourites Teddy and Poppet, the former being the dominant male of the colony, and the latter a female who later showed a trust in me that was remarkable in an adult wild animal.

Prominent also in the colony were Foxy and Percival, and of them all I liked Foxy the least, for he had an unusually long, pointed face, and tended to bully the others. He would leap onto my lap, exchange unpleasant words with his companions, and bound off again, forcing the others to jump down without having the courage to take their place. When I offered him food, he always reared onto his hind legs and snapped greedily at my hand, sometimes biting my fingers before I could snatch them away. The other hyraxes were gentler.

As the oldest member of the group that eventually numbered twenty in our early days of feeding them, Percival commanded a certain respect. He had been one of the original six when we moved to the kopjes and was among the first to become tame. Percival disliked being touched more than the others, hunching his back and rippling his skin with distaste whenever he was stroked. But he had an endearing habit of pleading up into my face for some juicy titbit, and of touching noses with me when I had nothing in my hands to offer him.

I had seldom seen hyraxes demonstrate their affection for one another and was interested one day to observe Percival greet Poppet with obvious joy. She was now living in the opposite kopje and had dashed some 40 yards across open ground to the glade where I always fed the hyraxes. This caused the feeding animals to screech their alarm signal, and Percival froze whilst scrabbling up my legs. When he saw it was only Poppet bounding towards us, he behaved in a rather unusual way, uttering soft squeaky noises in his throat and snuffling into her fur. She returned his greeting with equal enthusiasm before turning her attention to my hand and gently taking a banana. Some of the younger hyraxes also came up and sniffed under her belly, which made me think she might have young in the other kopje.

The social structure of the hyrax colony seemed to be based on a hierarchy in which each member knew its place. Generally they lived very peaceably together, with Teddy (also one of the original six) as their leader. During the drought of 1961 he was out of condition and had a large shoulder wound; but with proper feeding he grew into a fine animal and was always ready to sit on my lap, responding to being stroked without sign of displeasure. Teddy seldom showed aggression towards the others and he was the only member of the colony respected by Foxy, whose normal behaviour was to snap at every other hyrax in the vicinity.

The younger members of the community quarrelled extensively amongst themselves, using a variety of sounds which I soon learned to interpret. The mewing noises, already described, seemed to be a means of talking to one another, sometimes used with a friendly intonation, and at others in whining protest against an encroachment. The most frequently heard noise was a rattle in the throat, uttered as a warning signal which preceded a short and sharp disagreement. Often the hyrax being warned turned his back and continued to trespass without interruption. This usually provoked the aggressor into briefly mounting the offending intruder, all the while rattling with indignation.

Another hyrax sound heard at regular intervals was a short piercing shriek used as a warning of danger. At this the whole colony would race for cover, whereas similar noises such as a loud sneeze or a bird screech aroused very little interest. A young animal once raised the alarm while I fed the colony and the whole group vanished within half a second. Looking round to see what had frightened them, I saw our Siamese cat treading

cautiously across the lawn 30 yards away. This seemed to indicate the extent to which hyraxes feared cats, although in time
they lost all fear of Jason. Another expression of unease was a
dorsal spot of erectile hairs on the animal's back which, when
raised, showed up clearly against the brownish colour of their
bodies. In our early days of feeding them this patch of fur stood
permanently erect; but later they raised it only at a real or an
imagined threat.

Eagles were a source of terror to the hyraxes. We once saw a
magnificent Martial eagle swoop down upon a tree hyrax and pin
it to the ground with its huge talons. Our appearance caused the
eagle to release the terrified animal, which then raced to the
kopjes, apparently unharmed.

On another occasion the hyraxes were contentedly munching
when all at once one of them raised the alarm. Immediately the
hyraxes pointed their noses towards the sky instead of running
for cover. This was unusual. Looking up I saw a pale harrier
circling slowly in the sky 500 yards away. It was behind the
kopje and out of range of their vision, and I wondered how the
warning hyrax could possibly have known it was there. I was also
impressed by the hyraxes' communication system.

One morning when the animals failed to respond to my calls, I
heard a sudden scream and saw a caracal (African lynx) standing
amongst the sansevieria close to the feeding glade. In the beautiful cat's jaws was a hyrax that had ventured out to feed. Small
wonder my calls had not been answered! On seeing me, the
caracal dropped its prey and raced across the open glade to
another patch of bush. For a while the stricken hyrax stood
dazed, fur on end; then it scampered away to cover. All the
hyraxes were thoroughly alarmed and for a long time afterwards
they voiced their short piercing screams. A week later I heard
the same noise and crept into the bush to see again a caracal
streaking away and a petrified hyrax cringing in a crevice deep
in the rocks, just out of reach of the cat's paw.

As time went on, Poppet and Teddy grew progressively tamer
and I was soon able to call them from the house and to feed
them on the verandah, alongside any visitors who might be
present. Teddy did not really like this and would sit uneasily on
my lap, surrounded by people and voices. His nervousness
sometimes caused him to bite, but he remained reasonably con-

fident so long as I soothed him. Poppet was much braver and
would feed under any conditions, often approaching complete
strangers and sniffing at their hands or cameras in the hope they
had something to offer her. Once she allowed me to remove a
tick from the rim of her eye, which took several minutes. She
refused to keep still, and before eventually succeeding I had
made a number of attempts. By pulling the short hairs around
her eyes I must have hurt and aggravated her, but she showed
no sign of resistance or fear. She also surprised me by her
fondness for aloes, which made me doubt my belief that hyraxes
only ate them during very dry conditions; I wondered whether,
in fact, the plant had any medicinal value.

On one occasion Teddy bit me sharply on the arm, apparently
to attract my attention whilst I fed the others. I tapped him
smartly on the nose, admonishing him for his churlish behaviour, and he listened solemnly, his small round ears moving
backwards and forwards. Then, seeming to realize he had done a
foolish thing, he jumped up behind me on the wooden box I
used as a stool, and waited patiently until I put down a handful
of lucerne pellets, which he then ate unperturbedly. Hyraxes
used their long narrow tongues to collect the food and draw it
into their mouths.

There was another side to Teddy's personality, which I discovered when some pellet flour lodged in his large scarred nose. Although he was generally peaceful, all the hyraxes feared him.
Feeding supplies that day were short, and aggravated further by
the lucerne powder in his nose, Teddy suddenly vented his frus-
tration on all the hyraxes around him, his hostility finally de-
moralizing the whole group. Despite his bad mood he continued
to let me stroke him cautiously between snaps and lunges at the
other hyraxes. Foxy, the only hyrax who shared top place, was
not present that day.

Shortly afterwards when the two dominant hyraxes were mo-
nopolizing the metal tray of food on my lap and keeping all
comers at bay, it became evident that Foxy had ousted Teddy
from top place. As food supplies ran low, instead of leaving the
pickings to Teddy, Foxy rattled belligerently at him and Teddy
backed down, turning his rear end at him. Foxy never resorted
to this tactic and was openly aggressive at all times. From that
day his behaviour towards Teddy was as bossy as towards the rest

of the colony, although Foxy still permitted his former leader to share the tray. Other hyraxes who attempted to join the feeding pair pushed their way in backwards, and neither Teddy nor Foxy would react until a face came alongside. Only Percival remained a complete outsider, afraid of everyone but me; he avoided both Teddy and Foxy whenever possible, being nervous of crossing swords with either.

By this time Poppet had taken to appearing at any hour of the day in the bedroom, sitting room, or verandah. She paid not the slightest attention to our cross-eyed cat, and from the beginning she established that she would have the upper hand. The hyrax was feeding quietly on the verandah one day when I saw Jason looking intently through the glass door of the sitting room. Opening it, I watched Jason with fur bristling skirt uneasily towards the verandah gate a few feet from Poppet. The hyrax continued to feed. Only the slow rise of pale fur on her back gave any indication that she was aware of the cat. Suddenly, without any warning, she flew at him, snapping angrily, before she leaped onto the verandah parapet and raced towards the kopje. The ferocity of her attack took us both unawares, and an affronted Jason left the house, to return shortly afterwards with a large rat in his jaws. Although I tried enticing Poppet back that day, she would not be persuaded, having already eaten all she needed. But the incident did not deter her from returning to the house whenever she wanted food, and from then on Jason always gave her a wide berth.

One evening when the house was quiet, Poppet staggered out of the kopje in response to my calls. I had not seen her for three weeks. To my dismay I discovered she had a large festering wound on one side of her neck. She was very thin, with hardly enough strength to drag herself to the verandah. It appeared the wound had been caused by a bite. I rushed to find antiseptic and medicine, and Poppet seemed to realize I was trying to help, for she lay quietly while I carefully cleaned the wound, even though this must have caused her considerable pain. There was no way in which I could forcibly keep the hyrax in the house. Whenever my hand slipped beneath her belly, she resisted with a warning bite; I could not lift her by the neck because of the wound, and in any case I was afraid of alarming her. The only difference between Poppet and a domesticated animal was that she refused to be picked up. Reluctantly I let her go, and watched her move painfully back to the kopje. It was the last time I saw her.

Shortly after Poppet's disappearance I returned from holiday to find that Teddy also had vanished. I was now spending less and less time with the hyraxes, for there were many demands on my time with growing numbers of visitors and increased office work. Besides, Myles was exasperated at finding hyraxes all over the house, helping themselves to fruit or flowers and fighting with their reflections in our mirrors which they sometimes broke. Our small friends had taken over the house to such an extent that they scampered in and out at will, leaving their droppings and pungent-smelling urine everywhere.

The time had come to discourage their familiarity. Myles suggested that I stop feeding them, especially in view of their rapid increase in numbers, for we now estimated there were more than sixty rock hyraxes living in our kopjes. Three years later an infectious mite-borne disease killed most of them, and the Research vet believed this to be a direct consequence of overpopulation. Symptoms of the disease were severe itching, extreme thirst, a rapid deterioration in their general condition, and eventually the almost total loss of fur. The stricken animals looked pathetic and I found it hard to watch their suffering. When the disease finally subsided, some of our hyraxes had survived, and by 1972, when we left the Serengeti, the colony again looked healthy.

During our acquaintance with the hyraxes I made three attempts at rearing them. The first two, found during the drought of 1961, were a few days old and they were enchanting. Having been told that warmth was essential to them, I put them each night into a box in the kitchen, where the firewood stove retained its heat. Soon after their arrival Myles left the house before dawn one morning and I got up as usual to feed the little animals. To my horror I found the kitchen partially destroyed by fire and the hyraxes asphyxiated by smoke. The only house fire we ever experienced in the Serengeti had been caused by our cook leaving a roaring fire in the stove, in a misguided but kindly attempt to keep the young animals warm; a burning ember had fallen out and set light to a pile of firewood nearby, creating dense smoke in the airtight room.

Shortly afterwards we were brought another abandoned

hyrax. After feeding it successfully for nine days, its intestines ceased to function. I tried everything to cure the trouble, but sadly the tiny creature died inside my shirt where I carried it for warmth.

Our third attempt at raising a hyrax ended with its unhappy demise at Ngorongoro; this again was the result of a stomach disorder. In both cases I believe my mistake had been in feeding the tiny animals milk instead of glucose water for twenty-four hours, whilst their mothers' milk was still in their systems. But perhaps they were just too young to survive, or too weak in our harsh conditions at that time.

As well as hyraxes, a variety of birds lived in our kopjes and we fed them at a stone table on the lawn. Ruppells long-tailed starlings, speckle-fronted weavers, dusky flycatchers, and slate-coloured boubou shrikes, in particular, became very tame and would hop about our breakfast table. African pied wagtails walked within inches of Jason's crossed eyes, which on one occasion proved too great a temptation for our old cat. In the end, to protect the birds, we moved their table and bath further away from the verandah and discouraged them from coming into the house.

Each morning the cook replenished the birds' supply of water, millet, and fruit, and we enjoyed watching them drop like leaves from the trees to feed. With a whirr of wings they would all rise together when disturbed. Once I counted twenty-six different species within a few feet of the house. Their glossy plumage gleamed like jewels in the sun, and we were often dazzled by the richness of a violet-backed starling or the brilliance of a superb starling. Occasionally brightly coloured sunbirds hung from the aloes, probing their crimson flowers with long curved beaks; or hundreds of Fisher's lovebirds flew into the commiphora trees nearby, transforming the dull grey foliage into vivid green. A pair of d'Arnaud's barbets on a branch overhanging the verandah would regularly sing a duet that sounded like a child's clockwork toy, prompting one astonished visitor to comment drily: "Made in Hong Kong."

The birds around our kopjes provided a constant source of pleasure and entertainment. At their food table they were usually dominated by the Ruppells long-tailed starlings, whose raucous voices tyrannized any other birds that tried to feed with them; yet at other times these starlings could be heard whistling and singing very sweetly in the trees. The only birds that stood up to the long-tailed starlings were the smaller d'Arnaud's barbets, whose powerful beaks gave them an advantage over other birds. The timid, red-eyed Hildebrandt's starlings would soon abandon the field to their more aggressive cousins, flying to the nearest tree on humming wings. Speckle-fronted weavers and sparrows would cling to the edges of the bird table for a quick peck at any food within reach. Occasionally a purple grenadier or cordon bleu appeared on the scene, and a common sight on our lawn were the African hoopoes and lilac-breasted rollers. Without moving from the verandah, we could identify a great variety of starlings, weavers, sparrows, doves, finches, shrikes, sunbirds, hornbills, kingfishers, woodpeckers, and many other species, such as the drongo, the grey heron, and sometimes one of the birds of prey. The pale chanting goshawk and bare-faced go-away-birds were frequent visitors, and often a tawny eagle or bateleur could be seen circling above.

Once we saw an unusually fearless brown parrot perched on a branch of the wild plum tree that grew in our kopjes. We climbed up the tree and touched it, and the bird remained in a torpor, gazing at us through half-closed eyes; we decided it was intoxicated from eating the fermented fruit lying on the ground. The fruit of this splendid tree made an excellent jelly that we enjoyed eating with game meat.

A pair of spotted thicknees also lived in our kopjes, using the bare earth for a nest. Although their eggs merged well with the background, they were continually eaten by a mongoose. In the end the birds' repeated failure to rear their young distressed Myles, and he detailed a ranger to guard the nest. To our delight the thicknees finally succeeded in hatching two chicks.

At Seronera our house was surrounded by large acacias, and the singing of birds was a constant feature of life. Ruppells long-tailed starlings generally made the most noise, chattering, whistling, and singing all day long, to a background of cooing from a ring-necked dove, or the clear voice of an eastern bearded scrub robin. In the mornings we usually woke to the flutelike notes of a tropical boubou, repeated over and over again, or to the song of a chin-spot puffback flycatcher, whose nest I passed on my visits to the wild plum tree. The pure voice of a white-browed

1 Wildebeest concentrations on the plains

3a   Flood

3b   Crossing a river in the early days

4a　Snares captured on one safari

4b　A buffalo after surviving for weeks with a steel noose around his neck

5a Three old buffalo bulls at Seronera

5b A poachers' camp with dried meat, lion skins, and a poacher in the foreground

7a   Lynda travelled everywhere with us on safari

7b   Our house at Seronera

8a   Lynda feeding the hyraxes

8b   Gussie makes friends with Amos

9a Chutu, our fox, on the first day

9b Feeding Chutu at ten days

9c A very relaxed fox

10a Bernhard Grzimek with Pixie, the serval

10b Our servals

11　Mother and son

13a   Lions killed a zebra and ate it under the Grzimeks' plane

13b   A rhino about to charge

14a   **Flying over the zebras to make game census**

14b   **Drowned wildebeest after a stampede across the river**

15　Elephants drinking in the Mara

robin-chat provided another familiar sound around our kopjes, while golden-breasted buntings produced their sweet trilling songs, repeated again and again, and the Fisher's whydah called its three notes unceasingly. The repetitious calls of many of these birds, heard elsewhere, would evoke a strong sense of nostalgia.

Sometimes we saw vitelline masked weavers carry straws in their beaks to trees in the kopjes, where their nests dangled from the branches like golden decorations in the sunlight. If a female rejected a proposed home from her mate, he would immediately abandon it and begin constructing another, so that the tree soon became festooned with nests. In an acacia close to the verandah variable sunbirds popped in and out of their pendulous lichen-covered nests, which looked too delicate to survive the strong winds that sometimes rocked them; while nubian woodpeckers tapped the bark of the acacias with their beaks, searching untiringly for insects.

Some of our birds, such as swallows and sand martins, lived in the house, and I once studied the development of a family of wire-tailed swallows nesting above the doorway to our sitting room. They completed building their cup-shaped nest within four days, carrying the wet mud in their beaks and vibrating it into position for several seconds before they flew off for the next load. Within three days three eggs were laid. I attached a small mirror with adhesive tape to the ceiling and observed the activities below. At first the parent birds disliked seeing their reflections in the mirror and would cling to the outside of the nest, fluttering their wings, prepared for instant flight. Sometimes, in their nervousness, the swallows squawked and pecked at one another as they sat together on an open window frame alongside. After a few hours the mother bird settled on her eggs, but she looked up whenever she entered the nest to see if the "other" bird was still there. On one occasion I saw her peck at the mirror, giving herself such a fright that she squawked in alarm and flew away.

While keeping watch over the little family of swallows, other birds frequently distracted my attention. One day I stood at arm's length from about thirty sparrows and grey-headed social weavers which were feeding on the bird table, and a pair of laughing doves allowed me to walk within 3 feet of them before they took flight. Sparrows often crashed against the window panes of our house, and I would hold the little stunned creatures until they revived and flew away. Once we found a tropical boubou sitting on my bed, apparently wondering how best to find its way out of the room. Two golden-breasted buntings were frequently to be seen hopping about the verandah floor, paying no attention to the swallows repeatedly diving at them. When I re-secured the swallows' mirror to the ceiling with more adhesive tape, they would swoop and squawk at me too, before settling again on the eggs.

Within two weeks the eggs hatched and the baby swallows grew rapidly. Three days after hatching their little necks were straining upwards, beaks wide open for the food their parents brought every two or three minutes. Each bird was fed in turn. Every so often there would be a scuffle as one of the chicks turned itself round, baby wings flapping, and raised its tail into the air for a parent to extract the excreta which it then deposited outside. This helped to keep the nest clean, but in case a chick should accidentally fall, Myles erected a shelf underneath. By the end of a week the young birds were very large, resting their heads on the rim of the nest and depositing their droppings over the edge by themselves; a large pile started to accumulate on the shelf beneath, which I swept clean from time to time. Soon the chicks grew so big there was no space for their mother to perch on top of them, and she abandoned her young to sleep elsewhere.

Three weeks after hatching, the young swallows flew for the first time. Finding one of them in our room that evening, I tried to return it to its nest, but the frightened chick immediately flew out into the darkness, and I worried needlessly all night about its safety. The next morning I found it reunited with its family. Later that day I looked in and saw just one young swallow left in the nest. While I watched, the mother flew up and enticed it out. The chicks were now three-quarters grown and had grey heads instead of the chestnut crowns of adult birds. A week later the young swallows stopped using their nest, for they were now as large as their parents and flew with confidence. It was almost a month since they were hatched and seven weeks since the eggs had been laid.

After another ten days the parents began repairing their nest, and within a week the first new egg was laid, followed by two more. The whole cycle repeated itself in an almost identical pattern. By this time the swallows had accepted me as a friendly spectator and would calmly continue their activities despite disturbances in the house. They even remained unperturbed when the verandah light suddenly beamed on beside their nest.

Other wildlife that came to accept us were the genet cats that sometimes came into the house in search of food; the colourful agama lizards that took insects from our hands; and the timid slender mongooses that frequently explored the verandah. It was touching how quickly animals lost their fear of man when they learned there was no danger.

Chapter 11

Bush Flying

The language is short of words for the experiences
of flying, and will have to invent new words with
time.

—Karen Blixen, *Out of Africa* *

Apart from visitors flying to the Park, airplanes were not used in
the Serengeti until the arrival of Bernhard Grzimek and his son
Michael in January 1958, while we still lived at Banagi. They
were invited by the Board of Trustees, at their own expense, to
carry out an aerial count of the plains animals in the Serengeti;
to plot their main migration routes; and to advise on the proposed new boundaries of the Park. Both were dedicated conservationists, anxious to put some of the money made by their
award-winning film *No Room for Wild Animals* into protecting
African wildlife.

At first the Grzimeks had contemplated buying, as a game
sanctuary, part of Momella in Tanzania—a beautiful farm,
owned by a German named Trappe. The farm was set amongst
forests and lakes at the foot of Mount Meru and overlooked
Mount Kilimanjaro to the east. It was a paradise for game, and is
now a National Park, 42 square miles in extent.

Professor Grzimek sought the advice of Colonel Peter Molloy,
then director of Parks, who suggested that the money be used

* London: G. P. Putnam, 1937.

instead for a research project in the Serengeti. This idea appealed to Michael, who resolved that both he and his father should at once learn to fly. At that time light aircraft were not used in National Parks in East Africa. Convinced of their importance for effective game management, Myles had been pressing for an airplane since his arrival and was delighted when the Grzimeks eventually bought a six-seater Dornier DO-27. After only sixty hours flying experience apiece, the Grzimeks flew it from Germany to the Serengeti. It was a remarkable feat of courage and determination, typifying the indomitable spirit of these two outstanding men.

At Banagi we had been told they were coming, and Myles set to work to prepare an airstrip and to erect for the Grzimeks a prefabricated metal building below our house. The field was only partly completed when we heard the drone of an aircraft. Looking up, we saw a zebra-striped plane descending, and Myles hurried to meet the powerful machine as it pulled up at the end of the short runway, with only a few feet to spare. Two tall, good-looking Germans stepped out. After introducing themselves, they asked if this was Seronera Airfield, 11 miles away, and Myles assured them it was not. For a moment Bernhard and Michael just stood there in the sun, smiling in delight at being in the Serengeti on their first day of a study that interested them intensely. Myles brought them to our house for lunch, and we were all soon deep in discussion over their plans.

Dr. Grzimek's quiet distinction was a perfect foil for his son's youthful exuberance and high spirits, and their love for wild animals was very obvious. As director of the Frankfurt Zoo, Bernhard already had a deep understanding of animals and he spoke convincingly of the urgent need to take action to protect what remained of the earth's diminishing wildlife. Our task was as important, he said, as preserving the world's ancient monuments and art. I had never thought of it in that way before, but of course he was right. Impressed by our guests' impassioned beliefs, I felt the beginnings of an awareness that was to grow into a deep concern for the plight of all wild animals, be they whales, elephants, green turtles, or wolves. Bernhard made me realize for the first time the crisis that faced our wildlife, as man's demands increased. It was unthinkable to imagine life without birds and animals; yet such a prospect was not impossible. With every year that passed the rights of animals to co-exist with man grew more fragile, and everything within our power should be done to safeguard the earth's heritage before it was too late. Once exterminated, the animals could never be re-stored.

On their first day in the Serengeti the Grzimeks flew Myles to the Ngorongoro Crater, a journey which then took eight hours by Land Rover and only one by air. Myles's views on the value of aircraft in the Serengeti were soon confirmed. After flying every day with Michael, he had covered most of the Park within a week and commented jubilantly: "For the first time since coming to Western Serengeti, I know the exact location of the game."

From an airplane it was possible to establish the position and distribution of the migratory animals, and even to estimate their numbers. Until then we had kept records each month of animals seen from the Land Rover that were close enough to identify, but the value of these counts during the migrations was minimal. Myles now made meticulous notes of all animals seen from the air, and at the same time he kept a sharp lookout for poachers. Once, when two poachers were spotted, a Very light was fired to frighten them; unfortunately, it went off inside the plane and blew a hole through the windscreen.

As our knowledge increased, we grew excited by this first step towards establishing a well-run Park, a step that would enable Myles to comprehend the pattern of life in the Serengeti. Before this he had felt frustrated while driving round by Land Rover in a wilderness of 5,600 square miles, able only to collect scraps of information and to hit out almost blindly against the poachers. Although he possessed an intuition about bush life that seldom failed him, there were, for instance, occasions when he was unable to locate the wildebeest. The apparent disappearance of thousands of these animals overnight also bewildered many experienced hunters. Once a friend told us how he had driven his party amongst the migratory animals, day after day, never tiring of seeing such incredible numbers, until one morning he aroused everyone at dawn as usual and travelled across a vast stretch of country without seeing a solitary wildebeest.

With the plane the Grzimeks were able to locate the wildebeest herds at any time of the year and to follow their movements, which often took them well outside the Park boundaries. This knowledge about their migration routes was of the greatest importance to the discussions determining the demarcation of the new Serengeti boundaries. When the Serengeti was enlarged in 1957, it included a large section of country to the north bordering upon the Mara River. This linked the Park with the Kenya Mara Game Reserve and provided an additional 2,000 square miles essential to the migratory animals. They were now relatively safe in the north, though they still spilled out of the Park on its western borders; but it was too late to do anything about their routes through this country, which was already heavily settled. Another 1,000 square miles, added to the Park along its southwestern boundary, further safeguarded the migratory animals on their journey through the Duma region, which bordered upon the settlements of the Wasukuma poachers. We were distressed at this time by the exclusion of the highlands from the Park, and it was one of the Grzimeks' tasks to count the animals living in the Ngorongoro Crater.

Ten days after his arrival Michael flew back to Germany for the beginning of his university term. He returned in March for two months, and his father rejoined him in May. By then various experiments had been carried out in the use of different methods of capturing and marking animals to study their movements. Sometimes Connie and I would sit up late at night, gossiping and waiting for the men to come home, after they had spent hours marking Thomson's gazelles with broad yellow collars. They used a system of dazzling the animal at night and catching hold of it whilst it stood bewildered in the harsh glare of a powerful light.

Another method used for marking zebras was to chase the animal in a Land Rover and seize its tail. Gordon Poolman, who was an expert at game catching, would then leap from the vehicle, grip the animal's lower jaw with one hand, and with the other grasp its offside ear while someone fastened a collar about its neck. Once, when trying to do the same thing, Michael had his thumb severely bitten. His next accident was more serious.

In seeking to find a simpler method of catching zebras, the Grzimeks decided to lasso them with a rope noose attached to a long bamboo pole. After two animals had been successfully caught in this manner, Myles was winded by one end of the bamboo pole violently hitting him in the chest; the other end had dug into the ground while the Land Rover was travelling fast along the bumpy ground. Michael then took over the pole. Suddenly there was a jerk, and he fell unconscious into the car, with a hole in his neck. Again the long pole had run into the ground at high speed. Michael was flown to Musoma at once and returned the following day with the wound stitched but feeling sore. He was fortunate to have survived.

One afternoon Bernhard and Michael decided to fly down the Corridor to where they had built a blind on the Grumeti for photographing the animals that came to drink at the river. Before they left, we gave them tea and they told us of their plan. Otherwise we would not have known where to begin looking for them, should they fail to return by nightfall. This was a problem that had always worried Myles, and one that he tried to solve by persuading Michael to leave some indication of his planned flights each day. Myles's proposed system seldom worked, and we were often left ignorant of the Grzimeks' whereabouts. That evening when it grew dark and there was no sign of the plane, we packed the Land Rover with blankets, medical kit, brandy, food, and hot coffee, and set off in the direction of Musabi, with Lynda sleeping soundly in the jolting vehicle. We arrived to find Bernhard and Michael at the guardpost, smiling broadly, with two shaken rangers whom they had taken with them in the plane. Michael had run into a pig hole on landing, and broken the undercarriage and propeller. Fortunately no one was hurt. It took three weeks for mechanics from Nairobi to repair the damage on the spot with the help of a large tripod and tackle.

Shortly after this mishap there was another accident. Myles left the house early to fly with Michael, having warned me not to expect him back till dusk, as they would be counting animals all day in the Ngorongoro Crater. As the afternoon wore on, I began to worry, although I tried to persuade myself there would be good reason for their delay. It was not the first time the men had returned late. At last I heard the drone of an approaching aircraft and rushed out with relief. It was not the Dornier. Watching the strange plane disappear behind the trees on its descent to Banagi airstrip, I waited miserably for news of what had happened. Finally a Land Rover drove up to the house in the darkness, and several cheerful people jumped out: Myles, Michael, Gordon Harvey, and a Nairobi pilot. We all needed a drink. Later, while the rain pelted down, I listened to their story.

After leaving Banagi, Michael had flown to the crater, where he picked up Gordon and dropped his father. Hermann, their German photographer, was also with them. They had just taken off, when there was a loud bang and the plane went into a steep climb. They had hit something. Michael had little time to think for the plane was threatening to stall, with the rudder and elevators momentarily not working. He managed to regain some control by using his flaps and trimmer. After circling round to test the plane's performance, he decided not to land in the crater, and dropped a message down to Bernhard, who was lying half-asleep in the grass and did not see it. The plane then headed for Nairobi, about 160 miles away. None of them knew the extent of the damage, nor whether the tailplane was still in one piece. Some heavy camera batteries and other equipment were jettisoned to lighten the load, and for the best part of an hour they limped towards the airport. Finally they circled the runway at Nairobi for thirty more minutes to use up the remaining fuel on board. During this period, Myles told me, he had time to reflect on four newly dug graves in a cemetery below them, and on the array of ambulances and fire engines which were lined up to meet the damaged plane. Eventually the engine started to splutter and Michael prepared to land. He had been in constant radio contact and now knew from ground observers that one wheel was broken. The plane descended smoothly and Michael landed it perfectly on its one good wheel. After rolling normally for a while, the plane slowly keeled over and slewed round. No one was hurt, and little additional damage had been done.

By now we had known Michael for ten months. He was our friend and we felt anxious for him. Shortly after his second plane accident he left for Germany and returned to the Serengeti just before Christmas to join in our celebrations. Foolishly superstitious, I told him of my fears: that having had two narrow escapes he must at all costs avoid a third accident. He laughed at the seriousness of my expression.

A few days later Michael walked into the Poolmans' house and asked if I would like to fly with him. During my first pregnancy I had pleaded to be taken on one of his flights after the baby's birth in June. It was now December, but I no longer wanted to go; having the baby had somehow changed my attitude towards undue risk or danger. Too cowardly to admit my fears, I accepted Michael's invitation and asked Myles to drive Lynda to Banagi and to meet us there. He first accompanied us to the airfield and watched as Michael revved the engine and stood hard on his brakes. Suddenly we were off, and immediately Michael pulled back the stick. The plane lifted off almost vertically, leaving my stomach in my shoes. Having once heard me boast that I was never airsick, Michael tried everything in the book to prove me wrong. We hurtled low over Myles's Land Rover while he rolled towards Banagi and waved at him through the windows before climbing steeply away. At a safe altitude Michael throttled right back. An awful silence hung on the air as the nose gradually descended and we plunged earthwards. Michael laughed when he saw me involuntarily screw my eyes shut against the gravitational pull. As the ground rushed to meet us, he pushed in the throttle and the engine roared to life. Approaching Banagi Hill, when it seemed we were bound to collide halfway up its slopes, Michael hauled the stick back and the powerful plane rose up and over the top. Finally he swept over the Grzimeks' camp, to alert Bernhard he was home, and we landed normally at the strip. There was no car to meet us and we walked to his camp as darkness fell.

Shortly afterwards Myles and Bernhard burst in. They were glad to see us, for Bernhard had heard the plane and watched it descend for landing. Later he thought he heard it gather speed and drone away into the distance. Alarmed by the lateness of the hour and the possibility of trouble, he waited at our house and greeted Myles with the news that Michael had not landed. They drove first to the airstrip to make sure, and were relieved to find the Dornier safely tied down in its enclosure of thorn bush. We all then spent the evening together, discussing the work achieved and the Grzimeks' future plans.

I was to remember that evening. A few days later an ashen-faced Myles walked into the house and said: "I have bad news for you."

My heart lurched sickeningly, for I knew by looking at Myles that this was not just bad news but something disastrous. I was entertaining a District Officer to breakfast at the time, a cheerful young man who had arrived the evening before, his luggage consisting only of a toothbrush and one blanket. Breaking off our laughter, we both stared in silence at Myles's grim expression.

"Michael is dead."

It was some time before I discovered the details of Michael's accident. Leaving the table, I went to the nursery and stood by Lynda's cot, gazing down at her innocent face as she slept. It was impossible to believe what Myles had said. My confused mind could not grasp the fact that we would never see our friend again. I expected him at any moment to come bursting into the house. As I stood there, Myles slipped into the room and silently put his arms around me. Only then did the tears come as I realized the significance of what had happened.

Later Myles told me what he had understood from the radio. The message from Ngorongoro was that Michael had crashed the previous day, a few miles northeast of the crater on his way to Seronera. We were told that he had been seen flying low over some water wells in the Malambo area on the Salei Plains when the plane suddenly plunged vertically towards the ground and disappeared behind a small hill. The Maasai who witnessed this strange occurrence watched for a while to see if the plane would reappear, and when it did not he alerted the European in charge of the wells' construction. They drove in the direction the plane was last seen and found the shattered remains of the Dornier. Michael had been killed instantaneously.

Investigations showed that he had collided with a vulture, which resulted in a jamming of the rudder and elevator controls. At his low altitude he could barely have had time to cope with the danger of the situation. In a matter of seconds the third accident to his plane had proved fatal. Michael was buried the following day on the crater rim. A simple memorial stone bears the words:

> He gave all he possessed for the wild animals
> of Africa, including his life.

Michael's death in January 1959 brought to an end the Grzimeks' work in the Serengeti. By this time they had virtually completed their research survey. Their film won an award for the best documentary of the year, and their book *Serengeti Shall*

Not Die became a best seller. This helped more than any other factor to arouse interest in our Park; within a few years the Serengeti became famous, and people from all over the world travelled to visit it. A research laboratory was built in the Serengeti in memory of Michael's work.

When John Owen was appointed Director of Tanzania National Parks in 1960, he—like Myles—considered it essential that the Parks be equipped with airplanes. Within a year both he and Myles had learned to fly. For three years the "Serengeti Air Wing" consisted of just one aircraft, *Bravo Zulu*, a small two-seater Cessna 150 made of aluminum, with transparent doors and an engine that sounded like a sewing machine. Myles suffered from vertigo every time he looked through the doors and saw the plane's tiny wheel hanging between him and vast nothingness below. Our conversation became dominated by "hangar flying," which was largely unintelligible to me, who thought of flying as being little more than driving an automobile through the air.

Until I took out my licence, nine years later, I could not share with Myles the thrill and wonder of flying in Africa. Sitting beside him, and sometimes being permitted to take control of the plane, I enjoyed the magnificent scenery as we skimmed through the air. But the real joy did not come until I had learned to fly alone.

In time Myles found the Cessna 150 underpowered for his needs. There were now thirty bush airstrips scattered throughout the Park, and he wanted a plane that could land and take off in the shortest possible space. His needs were filled by the arrival of a Piper Super Cub, donated by the New York Zoological Society in 1964. An unpretentious two-seater aircraft, with a fabric skin and a tail wheel, the Super Cub had exceptional performance capabilities and required greater flying skill than the Cessna 150. Myles loved it. After three years he sadly handed it over in 1967 to the Serengeti Research Institute when he took on a four-seater Cessna 180. Again, this aircraft was a "tail-dragger," even harder to control than its predecessor, and it too was a superb bush plane. Myles flew the Cessna 180 until he finally left the Parks' service in 1974.

During these years John's aircraft was a four-seater Cessna

182 called *Romeo Mike*. He used it mainly for ferrying himself and others to the Parks, which saved him many hours of valuable time. Both Myles's and John's planes, so carefully tended through the years, were later destroyed. One mysteriously crash-landed in Ruaha National Park, but the occupants escaped unharmed. The other tore itself to pieces by careering through the bush after the pilot had swung the propeller by hand, leaving the magnetos switched on. History does not relate the emotions of the three rangers who were trapped inside the machine, but in the words of Sandy Field: "They could not have been bored." No one was hurt.

Myles's aviation experiences were varied. In his early flying days he once found himself over a blanket of cloud that showed no sign of breaking as he neared Arusha. Judging his position to be over Lake Manyara, he thought it would be safe to let down. A few moments later he emerged from the clouds to find he was within 50 feet of Mount Isimongor, 15 miles to the north. From such adventures he built up a store of knowledge that carried him without mishap through 3,000 hours of bush flying. Occasionally there were difficulties, such as a tire bursting on landing, or collision with a vulture in flight, but the aircraft remained in one piece and Myles took pride in looking after it. The plane was used for many purposes: anti-poaching, regular flights to the patrol posts, distant administrative meetings with officials, game counts and surveys. As the Serengeti grew more popular, Myles was also called upon to show VIPs and conservationists the migration from the air. The sight of so many animals on the plains seldom failed to impress them.

Inevitably there were times when Myles did not return by nightfall from a local flight. One morning he flew to the small township of Shinyanga to collect a Parks' trustee for a meeting at Seronera. After waiting in vain for the official to arrive, Myles eventually turned for home. It was late and he pushed the Super Cub as fast as it would go; but he had a strong head wind and luck was against him. As darkness overtook him, he landed at the Duma Guardpost on the western borders of the Park. With typical African hospitality the rangers treated him as an honoured guest, providing him from their own limited resources with clean white sheets, his own bed, a radio, and food. While Myles enjoyed a pleasant evening chatting with his men around a campfire, I tried without success to contact Shinyanga police by radio and then spent a sleepless night wondering what had happened to him. There were many possible reasons for his nonappearance, but my imagination in the long dark hours dwelt only on the worst. Finally, as the sun came up, I heard the familiar growl of the Super Cub approaching Seronera, and then a roar as Myles skimmed the roof of the house.

Once when flying from Nairobi with our schoolgirl daughter, we were confronted with heavy storms over the Loita Hills, 8,000 feet high. Turning the plane into the Great Rift Valley, Myles tried to find an alternative northward route around the storm. As we crept lower and lower under the menacing clouds, rain drove against the windscreen until our visibility had shortened to only a few yards. I felt strangely alone in a dark and ominous world and watched silently, hoping Myles would abandon his attempt to reach Keekorok before it was too late to turn back. Eventually, within 10 miles of Keekorok, he put the plane into a slow turn and headed for Narok, our nearest airfield, 60 miles away. It was raining and almost dark when we landed, and we were soon surrounded by curious Maasai chattering excitedly as they leaned on their long spears and stared at us.

We spent that night at the house of the Maasai game warden, who was making preparations to leave for Keekorok when we arrived.

"You are welcome to stay in my guestroom," he said graciously. "Just make yourselves at home." With a wave he started the Land Rover and drove away.

The guestroom had a concrete floor and a window, nothing else; with the exception of one electric bulb powered by a battery, the house was in darkness and we had no flashlight. Striking matches, I found my way to the kitchen and searched about for pans to prepare a meal. Fortunately I had brought a few provisions from Nairobi and was able to produce a glutinous mess of sausages and rice, followed by chocolate biscuits and washed down by vodka. We slept in the sitting room where there were kapok cushions and a plastic-covered sofa. It was a cold, wet, hilarious night, and we got little sleep.

The next morning the sun appeared to be suffering a hangover as it climbed over the horizon and shone weakly on a world washed clean by the deluge. Our flight to Seronera was like sailing over a swamp, with water glinting up at us all the way.

One of the hazards of flying was bad weather, as there were no radio beacons in the bush to guide pilots to an airstrip. Generally it was wiser to avoid storms altogether than attempt to plough through them. To the northeast the Loita Hills between Seronera and Nairobi sometimes formed a cloud barrier at hilltop level, which could mean detouring round a lower section of the escarpment, or climbing several thousand feet to fly above the clouds. To the southeast, between Seronera and Arusha, lay the Crater Highlands, rising to 11,000 feet; this was also an area that needed careful consideration when clouds restricted visibility. Should one turn back? Fly along under the cloud at treetop level, trusting there would be reasonable clearance? Or climb above the clouds and hope they would not exceed the altitude limitations of the plane? A mistake could be disastrous. Flying for hours over unbroken cloud and searching for a hole through which to descend, or looking for a strip on which to land after a long deviation, could result in fuel exhaustion and a forced landing in inhospitable country.

Fortunately most passengers are ignorant of the problems of flying in a light aircraft. Until I learned to fly, I had implicit faith in the skill and invincibility of all pilots. There they sat, calm and sure, making decisions without a flicker of concern on their faces, confidently flying under a blanket of cloud and sometimes saying in a matter-of-fact way when clouds and trees met: "We'll have to go back, I'm afraid." In fact they might be wondering whether the escape route was already cut off by the deteriorating weather. If I felt any nervousness at all, it was for the reliability of the aircraft itself, when we suffered a violent bump in turbulent weather or the engine spluttered with carburetor icing. Might the wings fall off? Were we about to make a forced landing because of engine failure? I learned later that the aircraft and its engine were the least of one's worries; it was rarely the machine that was at fault when things went wrong. External factors, especially pilot's error, nearly always caused the trouble.

Flying in cloud without an instrument rating was to be avoided at all costs; the pilot would almost certainly lose control when he could no longer see the horizon. On the other hand a pilot with an instrument rating could be tempted to fly through cloud which might conceal an obstruction, such as a hill, or, in unusual circumstances, lead to the break-up of the plane in a violent storm.

Although flying accidents were rare in the Serengeti, we had them from time to time. Once a warden lost control of the Parks' Cessna 180 while landing at a bush strip in a strong crosswind. The plane hurtled through the trees, tearing off a wing and shedding bits of metal before coming to rest. The African passengers were badly shaken and one of them refused ever to set foot in an airplane again.

Other accidents involved a scientist stalling his Super Cub on landing, which entailed walking 20 miles back to Seronera. His passenger had never flown in a light aircraft before, and had thought the landing normal! Another plane failed to become airborne on a short strip and wound up in the trees at the far end. Collisions with birds were fairly common. But there were amusing moments too.

Once when Myles was flying our research vet to Tororo in Uganda with a cargo of white mice, he was sorely tempted in his message to East Air Centre to report: "One thousand and two passengers on board." During that flight some of the mice escaped from their crate and scuttled to and fro in the plane.

I had flown for hundreds of hours in the right-hand seat of light planes when my opportunity to learn came in 1969, during Myles's absence at a conference in America. Far from simply driving an automobile through the air, learning to fly gave me six weeks of fright and excitement, but it was more fun than anything I had ever done before. After training on a Cherokee 140 in Myles's childhood town of Nanyuki, I completed the written work and flying instruction in Nairobi. The subjects for examination included meteorology, air law, navigation, radiotelephony, airframes and engines, and word-perfect knowledge of all air signs and signals.

Navigation meant knowing about such subjects as calibrated air speed, density altitude, drift angles, wind velocity, vector triangles, reciprocal tracks, variation, and deviation. While I have always enjoyed mathematics, I found the study of airframes and engines to be most difficult. Machinery has always been totally incomprehensible to me, and no glimmer of understanding would cross my face when the mechanics of an airplane were explained. By dint of hard work, however, I succeeded in completing the course, and returned home jubilantly with my new licence.

To my disappointment the terms of the Parks' insurance policy stipulated a minimum of 500 hours flying experience for the Cessna 180. With only fifty my hopes of helping the wardens faded; they would have welcomed an unpaid pilot to fly some of the tiresome taxi missions to and from the Serengeti. The only plane available to me was *Romeo Juliette*, the cherished Cessna 150 privately owned by Sandy Field, our Chief Park Warden. Sandy kindly allowed me to ferry people to and from Nairobi, including scientists who were training for their pilot's licences, or guests who needed a lift. Occasionally I would be asked to fly a distinguished visitor to a destination I had not visited before; on seeing me consulting my map and learning I had only recently qualified, my passenger usually lost interest in his camera and concentrated on map reading!

In those early days of flying, when I was sometimes nervous and unsure, there were times when I wondered how I could have involved myself in such a hazardous pastime; but the joys of flying far outweighed its anxieties, and with practice I gained confidence.

The longest bush flight I ever made was from Ruaha National Park, 500 miles south of the Serengeti. John Owen was planning to visit Ruaha and he offered to take me there, so that I could fly Sandy's plane back to Seronera. At certain times of the year much of the dry bush burns and the atmosphere that day was hazy. In flight John turned off course from time to time to familiarize me with the landmarks I would see on the return journey; but my thoughts were apprehensive as we drifted over that huge expanse of uninhabited country, grey and forbidding under a pall of smoke. I need not have worried.

The next day dawned bright and clear, and the plane I flew soared through the air like a bird. It was one of those occasions when it was wonderful to be alive: the sky seemed bluer, the air clearer, the colours more vivid. All that day I flew with the window open, the air streaming through my hair, and I felt a sense of freedom and exhilaration that compared with nothing else in life. I was remote from the earth below, yet in touch with it; delighted when I glimpsed a wild animal in the bush or passed over a small cluster of huts where the goats ran for cover and the villagers waved. I was keenly aware of every bird, of the clouds drifting by, the play of colour and light on the country below, of the distance and space, and of being alone.

Yet flying was not always fun. The dangers of cloud were brought home to me once when I crossed the Loita Hills with Lynda at the end of a school holiday. She had fallen asleep, and we were almost into the Rift Valley when a veil of cloud at the edge of the escarpment barred me from continuing on my course. It seemed to extend for miles, north and south, but in the direction we were travelling it looked vapoury and light. Rather than search for a long way round, I kept on, thinking I would be able to see the ground through the mist.

The cloud was deceptive, for no sooner were we committed than all visibility was lost. The plane was only 300 feet above the trees, and I had to concentrate all my attention on the artificial horizon and altimeter to check whether we were flying straight and level, climbing or descending. Airspeed also had to be watched carefully, so as not to stall. I had been told it took approximately 180 seconds for an untrained pilot to lose control in cloud. We were in cloud for only thirty seconds, but when we emerged into the sunshine, the port wing was down. During that half-minute Lynda had opened her eyes and looked into the opaque whiteness around her. Sensing my concern, she had murmured: "I don't think I like this very much," shut her eyes, and did not look again until we were flying through clear air.

Once when we were entertaining official guests in the Park, Sandy flew his plane to Kirawira "B" airstrip to join the rest of our party on the Grumeti River. When the time came to leave, after a picnic lunch, John Owen decided to drive back to Seronera, and he asked Myles to fly three of his guests in the Cessna 180 to Fort Ikoma Lodge for tea. A storm was building up as Myles took off. Sandy kindly offered me the left-hand pilot's seat of *Romeo Juliette;* but just as we were about to leave he missed his camera, which had been forgotten by the river, a mile from the airstrip. The Land Rover had already gone, and two of the rangers from a nearby post offered to retrieve the camera. By the time they had returned, the storm covered half the sky. I hurriedly took off and attempted to navigate north of the angry weather, but the turbulence was appalling and we were being driven far off course. Sandy advised me to return and to wait out the storm at Kirawira.

There were two airstrips: one at a research camp on the north bank of the river and one at a ranger post on the south. By the time we reached the first, from where we had started, it was invisible under a purple curtain of rain and we could not land. A mile or two separated the runways; should we be unsuccessful in landing at the second, our only alternative was Musoma township, 60 miles to the north. All the remaining country was enveloped in the deluge.

Sandy immediately took command. Wasting no time, he pushed the dual-controlled plane as fast as it would go towards Kirawira "A" ranger post. Without waiting to check the windsock, he swung onto short finals and landed just as the driving rain hit the end of the field. Hastily taxiing towards the post, Sandy had only enough time to clamber out and hang onto the plane before the storm broke in earnest. The rangers had raced out to help us, and I felt sorry for them grimly holding onto the plane, drenched to the skin, while I sat snugly inside. The torrential rain and wind beat about us, leaving the country under several inches of water. Within fifteen minutes the storm had passed. Shortly afterwards we heard the roar of Myles's airplane overhead, and Sandy switched on his radio. It was past six o'clock.

"What are you doing down there?" asked Myles, surprised at seeing our plane on the ranger post airstrip, only 2 miles from where he had left us.

"We got caught in the storm," Sandy answered mildly.

"Well, try to take off, and I'll watch from here," said Myles.

We started moving. Water sprayed upwards from under the wheels as we bumped along the waterlogged runway. Our speed indicator never moved from zero. As we churned past the windsock, with half the strip behind us, I yelled: "Abort!" and Sandy promptly slowed to a halt. The sound of my voice had been almost drowned in the noise of the engine and the tearing water.

"You look like a drowning duck," came Myles's dry voice over the loudspeaker. "Get the rangers to run you over to the other strip, and I'll pick you up there." He droned away into the distance.

Later we heard that Myles had returned from Ikoma to be met by John, who had expected us back much earlier. In view of the weather Myles felt he should take off at once, before nightfall at seven o'clock, and look for us along the route we should have followed. His dismay when he found no sign of the little plane at Kirawira "B" research strip turned to amusement when he flew on and saw us stranded in a sea of water at the rangers' post.

With Sandy's transfer in 1972 to Mikumi National Park in the south of Tanzania, bush flying for me virtually came to an end, although I continued to fly Sandy's plane whenever he visited us. Within a year we were transferred from the Serengeti to the Arusha National Park at Momella, where Myles continued to fly his beloved 180 until it was handed over to a newly qualified African pilot.

Chapter 12

Safaris

Shortly before my twenty-first birthday a fortune teller had told me that my life would be filled with travel, and in this she was right. The Swahili word for journey is *safari*. As soon as Myles and I were married, we spent most of our time, particularly in the early years, "on safari." We journeyed all over the Park, to the coast on our annual holidays, to places abroad on our overseas vacations, and later across long distances to visit our children at school.

The children were still very young when we returned from a holiday by the sea during the floods of early 1962. At Arusha Myles contacted Seronera by radio to enquire about the road and was encouraged to hear that they thought we could get through despite the torrential rain. In convoy with another Parks' Land Rover we started our 220-mile journey before dawn, churning up to the Crater Highlands and down to the Serengeti using four-wheel drive for most of the way. No other vehicle passed us after we left the crater, and it rained incessantly. I fed the children as we travelled, until at last we reached Naabi Hill, halfway across the Serengeti Plains. We then stopped and looked in amazement towards Seronera. The country lay completely under water and there seemed small chance of getting home along the foaming river that was once our road. Striking out across the plains, Myles decided to keep to the higher ground until we met the track from Loliondo in Kenya.

By this time the sun had dipped below the horizon and the

sky grew dark in the teeming rain. With no moon to light our way across the endless plains and no compass to guide us, I wondered how Myles could possibly navigate. Every now and then one of the Land Rovers bogged down in the sodden ground and was pulled out by the other. During such stops mosquitoes and midges swarmed round us and I covered the children with blankets from head to foot. I had frequently given them canned baby food, milk, and biscuits along the way, and they never complained, sleeping as best they could in the cramped space.

We struggled on and on, until I thought we would never reach Seronera, only 35 miles from Naabi. All at once Myles swung the Land Rover around and onto the Loliondo road, which ran in two thin streams of water across the saturated plains. We were both exhausted, and I was surprised he had noticed it. Following this track to the Maasai kopjes at the headwaters of the Seronera River, we reached the main road crossing, normally a few feet wide. The river now covered much of the country and swirled around our legs as we waded into it to gauge its depth. Suddenly two headlights flashed on and we were delighted to see Gordon Harvey standing on the opposite bank with a team of men to help us through. After considerable effort the Land Rovers surged across, their fan belts removed and several willing hands pushing from behind. Gordon's wife, Edith, had a hot meal ready and in the early hours of morning we fell thankfully into bed.

During the cataclysmal rain of 1962 I used to lie in bed and listen to the roar of the Seronera River, 2 miles away, which had burst its banks and was flooding the surrounding country. In normal times this river was a gently flowing stream leading to a series of murky pools. I wondered how the animals could be faring in such weather, but we came on only a few drowned bodies. In drier years it was not uncommon to find dozens of wildebeest floating in the river after they had stampeded across, climbing over and drowning one another in their headlong compulsion to keep moving.

There were times when the weather reached the other extreme and the country became parched after months of drought. Then fires would start, raging unchecked across miles of bush and plains. The animals preferred short grass areas, and fires were usually started by poachers to stimulate fresh growth and attract the game into their localities; burning the long grass also made it easier for the poachers to traverse the country. Sometimes honey hunters would start a fire by smoking out the bees from their hives; or a careless farmer seeking to clear his land might allow a fire to spread. But even a lighted cigarette thoughtlessly flicked through a car window could ignite the tinder-dry vegetation. Once the rangers found two poachers burned to death under a tree, which they had apparently climbed in an effort to escape a conflagration.

Bush fires were generally short-lived, however; when they passed, they left a trail of burned ostrich eggs, tortoise shells, lizards, and other slow-moving creatures. It was pathetic to see tortoises hurrying from a fire towards the nearest waterhole through the long dry grass; we always rescued them if we could. Even without seeing a distant fire, the wildlife could smell it and would start at once for safer ground. During this time Abdim's and white storks usually appeared in hundreds to feed off the grasshoppers and other insects that struggled to keep ahead of the flames.

Sometimes we had to beat a path for our Land Rover to drive safely through the blazing grass; and on one occasion we found ourselves encircled by fire in a kopje, with boulders of rock preventing our retreat. Working quickly, we made a firebreak around the Land Rover by burning back towards the fire and beating out the flames that advanced too close.

After a fire little spirals of smoke rose from smouldering undergrowth and from the ashy skeletons of trees that had fallen and burned away. With the sun seeming to beat down on the desolation more fiercely than before, a haze of heat quivered over the blackened land. Sometimes a wind whipped the ash into whirling dust devils, driving them into our tents and faces. A film of flaky black dust collected on everything, including any clothes that happened to be drying on our washing line.

From the beginning Myles introduced a system of early fire-control burning to prevent the unchecked spread of these fires during exceptionally dry seasons. As soon as it was possible after the rains had ended, he would set alight small patches of vegetation, which later acted as firebreaks when the country burned.

On safari there were some areas in the Park that gave me greater pleasure than others. One of these lay to the north, on the Kenya border. Our camp there overlooked the swirling brown waters of the Mara River, in a grove of shady trees a mile from Kogatende Guardpost. Heaving and splashing whenever they surfaced, the hippos honked and roared below us, slapping the water with their tails to scatter their dung. On some nights the moon rose with almost hallowed beauty above the trees on the opposite bank, spilling its luminous reflection across the river and bathing the scene in ghostly light. Seated at the edge of the high riverbank, we would watch the silvery clouds sail by, and the palm trees sway gently in dark silhouette against a sky made brilliant by a million stars. Once we saw an elephant gliding down to drink in the moonlight, making no sound as he stretched his trunk across the water, then raised it to his mouth. His movements were almost dreamlike as he drank, the soft light glinting along his tusks, until at last his thirst was sated and he melted again into the shadows as silently as he had come. A tiny Scops owl chirped constantly from a branch above us, while occasionally a lion grunted or a hyena moaned mournfully in the distance.

With forests, hills, rivers, and open glades, the Mara was idyllic and harboured a great variety of animals, especially buffaloes in large herds. Most of the dwindling number of rhinos in the Park were to be found there, and it was a favourite haunt for the migratory animals, too, during the long dry months when they withdrew from the plains. Once we even saw a giant forest hog near the river, unheard of before in the Serengeti, and believed to be only the second such animal recorded in Tanzania.

Although there was an atmosphere of harmony about this area, the Mara elephants seemed unusually aggressive and would charge at us with greater determination than in any other section of the Park. Bushes and small trees failed to slow one lone bull, who crashed through them with such vengeance in his heart, we only barely managed to keep ahead of him along the bumpy ground. Each time I looked round, there he was behind us, his ears flared out and trunk curled under, until at last we outdistanced him. I was unaccustomed to elephants at Seronera, and always urged Myles to go faster whenever one threatened us, while the rangers on the open back would shout: "*Kwenda! Kwenda!*" (Go on! Go on!) if the Land Rover slowed down.

Myles and I were enjoying an evening walk one day when we

saw a scrape of fresh rhino dung along the path and thought it prudent to turn back. After taking a few paces I heard the sharp crack of a breaking branch. Expecting to see a rhino, I stopped in mid-sentence and turned. To my dismay a cow elephant was bearing down upon us, with a very small calf standing beyond her. She made no sound, and charged in so determined a manner my only thought was "Run!" It never occurred to me that Myles had not heard the branch snap. He was slightly deaf from many years of shooting, and watched his fleeing wife in astonishment before becoming aware of the huge beast. Without a rifle and at such close range, Myles thought for the first time in his long experience of elephants, "This is it!" He took to his heels, and as he did so the elephant stopped and trumpeted furiously, her scream of rage lending added wings to my feet. Glancing over his shoulder as he ran, Myles saw that the elephant was more concerned for her calf, now some distance behind, than she was in continuing her pursuit. He slowed to a walk; but it was some time before he caught up with me.

Apart from Kogatende, other favourite places in the north that we used for camping included Larelemangi salt lick, where Lynda surprised her cobra. Another was the Bologonja headwaters, a most beautiful site until it became the reservoir for Seronera's water supply, 50 miles away. Stewart Edward White, when he saw the Bologonja in 1910, described it as a "paradise," "a clear stream running over pebbles and little rocks, shadowed by a lofty, vine-hung jungle of darkness, coolness, little gray monkeys, and brilliant birds," adding that "no hint of the fierceness of the equatorial sun reached us." *

Massive trees shaded the spring and crystal clear water that flowed between banks covered in wildflowers, shrubs, and ferns. With its smooth flat stones, its tadpoles, and its velvety moss, the shallow sparkling waters of the Bologonja were a child's delight. We pitched our tent beside the stream to the sound of the white-browed coucal's bubbling call, and occasionally we glimpsed a magnificent red and green Narina's trogon flitting amongst the dark shadows cast by the giant fig trees. After the heat of the sun, the peaceful seclusion of this cool forest always gave me a sense of deep contentment.

* *The Rediscovered Country.*

Once when we camped on the Bologonja with our Director, I was invited to climb the Kuka range, some 2,000 feet high, with a party that included a Kenya game warden. During the ascent the others stopped to study their maps and I hurried ahead to photograph the Serengeti scenery with the camera Myles had recently given me. It did not cross my mind there might be animals at the top of such a steep climb. The views from the crest were splendid, and as I wandered heedlessly about taking pictures, I approached a tree with low-hanging branches that reached to the ground. Suddenly two buffaloes exploded from its shadows and confronted me. They were so close I could see the flies on the ends of their shiny noses, while they snorted and swung their heads uncertainly from side to side. After what seemed a lifetime but could only have been a few seconds, they turned and lumbered away a few paces, before swinging round to face me again. The vapour of their breath steamed through their nostrils. Having swung round to face me three times during their retreat, they eventually disappeared over the crest of the hill grunting indignantly. I was rooted to the ground. It was the only time I had ever encountered buffaloes at such close range, and the experience left me limp with shock.

Another of our camps in the Mara country was at a guardpost called Wogakuria, built at the foot of an extensive rocky outcrop. This kopje stood out as a landmark in the north, and offered superb views of the surrounding country from its summit. Below the camp flowed a freshwater spring, a favourite place for old buffalo bulls, who sometimes used the camp for shelter. They became very tolerant of the rangers and twice came to the door to die, lying within 6 feet of the post. On one occasion the rangers tried to get an old bull to its feet, pushing and heaving at the enormous body until they were exhausted. The buffalo did nothing to deter them and suffered their efforts with resignation. That night it died where it lay.

We often climbed the kopje at Wogakuria to scan the country through our field glasses. This was how Africa must have looked for millennia, with animals peacefully grazing over acres of un-spoiled land while vultures cruised lazily above them, quick to spot any dead or suffering creature from thousands of feet away. Gazing at this splendid scene, and at many others on safari, I realized how privileged we were to experience the reality of living in the wild. At the same time, however, I felt an almost overwhelming despondency about all these animals who might enjoy only a limited span of time before vanishing from the earth. Each year the boundaries of their natural world grew smaller, and I found it difficult to be optimistic.

Life on safari, especially in the 1950s, was fairly spartan. We could take only a limited amount of equipment in our Land Rover, which had to carry the rangers as well. At first our camps consisted of a small tent, light canvas beds, sleeping bags, mosquito nets, hurricane lamps, a folding table, buckets, a canvas bath that doubled as a basin, two mortar ammunition boxes for carrying food (they served also as stools), a kitbag of clothes, and a small kitchen box. Later a larger Land Rover enabled us to carry more luxuries, including a bigger zip-fastened tent and camp chairs. We baked our own bread and lived mostly on canned food supplemented by the fresh meat we captured from poachers. As a paraffin tin oven took up too much space in the Land Rover, we devised a means of baking by digging a hole in the ground, with a base of burning coals. Sticks dug into the sides of the hole held the loaf tin, and over the top of the hole we placed a metal sheet covered with live coals that the cook constantly replenished.

If we camped near a river, we fished and fried the delicious tilapia, or smoked the more common catfish over an open fire. I normally took ready-baked oatmeal biscuits, pastry shells, and a fruit cake with us, and our cook made delicious pancakes and steamed puddings in camp. Garlic and paprika were safari standbys, and I never travelled without Myles's *pili-pili ho-ho* for soup—a potent brew of miniature chillies marinated for several months in gin and sherry. Lunch was generally a picnic snack; supper, the big meal of the day, included soup, meat, and pudding, which we ate beside our campfire just after the sun went down.

The cook was an essential member of our team. As well as coping with smoking fires, hauling water from the nearest stream, and producing tea at dawn, he guarded the camp against bush fires or sabotage by poachers when we were out. Our bathwater was heated in galvanized iron buckets over an open fire. The wind sometimes blew the smoke into the cook's face, or it rained, or the damp firewood refused to burn, but somehow he managed to produce an appetizing meal; food always tasted better when cooked out of doors.

For twelve years our cook in the Serengeti was a man named Paulo, who accompanied us on all our safaris into the bush. Barely able to read or write, he had a natural flair for cooking and made the lightest cakes and pastries, never forgetting any of the recipes I had taught him. Paulo had been with us for five years when he suddenly contracted sleeping sickness. Returning late from a visit to his home on the northwestern borders of the Park, his excuse was a high fever he had suffered for several days. He seemed to improve at first, but his illness was of the type that takes several months to kill, if left untreated. Paulo's symptoms were not diagnosed until he had reached the last stages of the disease preceding a coma that results in death. Although he insisted he felt well, we noticed his failing faculties and were alarmed by his deteriorating sight and hearing. Finally during one of our safaris he dropped plates to the ground instead of putting them on the table, and was oblivious to a severe gash on his leg. Myles sent him at once to Arusha Hospital. The doctors diagnosed sleeping sickness and Paulo spent two months recuperating. He would never admit to his illness, and was soon bossily supervising the rangers loading our Land Rover for safari. For mile after mile he sat precariously on top of our bedding valise in the vehicle, generally half-asleep in the sun, until one day he was brought to life when we disturbed a lone buffalo bull resting under a tree beside the track. Without a moment's hesitation the buffalo jumped up and pursued the Land Rover, hooking furiously at trees and grass while our cook rained a hail of curses on its head.

One of my favourite camps in the Serengeti was at Moru on the western edge of the central plains. This area, covering the most extensive kopjes in the Park, was believed to have been formed millions of years ago, preceding a long period of erosion that resulted in the formation of vast plains, jutting rocks, and isolated ranges. Driving from Seronera along the foot of one of these ranges, we looked across miles of open plain before coming to a lake called Magadi, meaning salt or soda. During the wet season the lake's surface was sometimes a carpet of pink flamingoes that rose and wheeled in huge flocks like thousands of petals tossed into the air. When dry, Magadi gleamed white with crusted soda which, in the early days, the rangers collected for use as salt. The lake bed itself had an overpowering smell and we were careful not to break through the brittle crust into the black mess beneath as we gathered the whitest slabs of soda, or tried to reach a fledgling flamingo trapped in the dried lake.

At Moru we often visited a pair of rare Verreaux's eagles whose nest was built on a shallow ledge at the top of a high and inaccessible boulder. By climbing an adjacent rock we could just see into this precariously balanced ramshackle structure. The nest usually held a lone chick which its parents fed with meat, mainly from the hyraxes they had killed in the kopjes.

Maasai tribesmen had adorned some of the caves in the rocks with crude paintings that were probably done within this century, for they depicted figures with hands on hips in a typically European stance, as well as sketches in red ocher of lions, elephants, and Maasai shields. Before entering the caves I always made sure no bees inhabited them, for the African stinging bee is fiercer than its European counterpart, and having in my teens suffered some fifty bee stings on the coast of Tanzania, I was anxious not to repeat the experience.

The kopjes extended for miles, dotted with candelabra Euphorbia trees that stood above the surrounding vegetation. Shrubs and trees grew profusely amidst gigantic granite boulders, golden grasslands rippled in the wind like the waves of the sea, and the sky always seemed grander there than anywhere else. Of all the scenic wonders of the Serengeti, I thought Moru the most beautiful.

Safaris included taking our children to and from their school in Kenya and visiting them at half-terms, a round trip of more than 1,000 miles. On one of these journeys we were told that the road had been closed to tourists because of heavy rain, and the children and I left before dawn so as to arrive in Nairobi for a dental appointment the following morning. Accompanying us was an old African driver, who had been with Parks for many years, driving the truck each week to Arusha for supplies. His name was Omari and he was a great and popular character, with a face like a boxer.

As the hours passed, Omari grew despondent, motoring stolidly along the deeply rutted road even when he would have done better to drive parallel to it. We ploughed on without

seeing another vehicle until at midday we reached Keekorok
Lodge on the Kenya border. Fearing we would bog down in the
mud if Omari continued to drive in this fashion, I suggested
tactfully that he had earned a rest and it was my turn to drive.
Omari shrugged and made no reply. He grew more morose the
further we journeyed from home, and from time to time suggested we turn back. Eventually he lapsed into silence.

The Land Rover crawled along the empty waterlogged road,
skidding and sliding sideways on the slippery surface. Occasionally we stopped within inches of the mud-filled depres-
sions bordering the road, and there were times when I had to
drive off it altogether, maneuvering our way through the bush
around sections that were impassable. Perhaps Omari was right:
I should have turned back, especially since Myles did not expect
me to return from Kenya for nearly a week. With the weather
deteriorating, we might be stuck for days and there would be no
traffic on the road to assist us; I had packed only a picnic lunch
and there was not enough food for the children. But we were already halfway and I struggled on, my mind filled with doubt.
Later I learned that the approaches to the causeway over the
Sand River were washed away soon after we crossed, and we
would not have been able to return to Seronera had we turned
back.

At last we reached the Uaso Nyiro River near the game post
at Narok. Normally gently flowing, the river was now a raging
torrent of brown swirling water, stretching out of sight around a
bend in the road. A few Maasai—tall lean warriors with aristo-
cratic faces—were wading into the river to gauge its depth and
the strength of the current. They were the first people we had
seen since leaving Keekorok. As I watched the water reach their
waists, I realized we had small hope of getting through. Calling
to the Maasai, I asked how long the river had been like this, and
they loped towards us with broad grins, their toga-like garments
still hitched high around their naked torsos. The river had risen
only that day, they said, but it was also likely to go down just as
rapidly; if we waited we might be able to cross. At this news
Omari's chin sank deeper into his chest, while I brought out the
lunch basket and settled down to a long wait.

After two hours the river had receded a foot. Throwing caution to the winds, Omari suggested we attempt a crossing. I agreed, and at once he became efficient and brisk, making all the necessary preparations before silently taking his place behind the wheel. He looked more like a fighter than ever, with his jaw set aggressively in his weathered old face. His whole demeanour registered disapproval of my stubborn persistence as we chugged slowly through the river like a motorboat, with water swirling over the hood and across the floor of the Land Rover as it deepened. Eventually we rose again onto higher ground, and I congratulated Omari, who managed a wan smile.

It was almost dusk when we reached the local store at Narok. The Asian there filled our Land Rover with petrol and told us no vehicles had come through that day from Nairobi. A bridge had been washed away some miles from the township, but there was a track through the bush which led to a possible fording of the river further down. It would be hardly discernible at night.

Fortunately I had brought sleeping bags for the children, and they were tucked into them before we resumed our journey. On reaching the broken bridge, I reversed slowly up the road until we found a faint track leading off into the bush. It was quite dark and rain fell incessantly as we followed this indistinct track for miles, crossed the river, and eventually regained the main road. A dense mist now covered the ground, so that I could see the road only by driving with dipped headlights. This made it impossible to avoid hitting the huge potholes that characterized the Narok road, and however slowly we moved the Land Rover crashed into them, deluging the windscreen with muddy water. It was like being at sea, with the rain lashing the windowpanes in a steady downpour and the car plunging and leaping through the storm. My eyes felt pulled from their sockets with the concentration of keeping on the mist-shrouded track, while beside me Omari slumped even further into his seat and stared glumly ahead.

Eventually we reached the main tarred road and climbed the Rift Valley escarpment to Nairobi. Our journey of less than 300 miles had lasted eighteen hours.

As the years passed I took up painting, struggling to capture the mood and atmosphere of the Park, its sweeping panoramic views and the feeling of space and light. I was an amateur, my efforts primitive, but it gave me pleasure to express creatively my appreciation of the Serengeti's unique charm.

Once when we camped at an isolated kopje amongst the migratory animals on the vast plains, I climbed to the top of the highest rock to sketch the view. It was a perfect day, and a stiff breeze cooled the fierceness of the sun. Scrambling over the last rise of the hill, I suddenly saw three lions hidden in the tall coarse grass a few yards away. Their long manes, blowing in the wind, were the colour of the grass itself; their heads were averted, and their noses were lifted into the wind to sniff the air. I watched them uneasily for a while, wondering if they might be aware of my presence. But the wind was strong and blew into my face. They had neither seen me nor caught my scent. With the sound of the wind drowning my movements, I was able to tiptoe away until I had cleared the crest of the hill. Later Sandy Field flew in to join us and saw the lions from his plane. They roared magnificently that night, enticing a pajama-clad Sandy far from his tent to listen, and causing him to hurry for refuge to his Land Rover when they grunted a warning close by.

Sometimes the force of the wind on the plains could be trying. We once watched a flock of sandgrouse flying towards the water pool in our kopje. Reaching the gap between two rocky outcrops, they were struck by the wind with such intensity they could make no further progress. The birds flapped their wings helplessly, wheeled away in a wide circle, and tried again. Eventually, after several attempts, they gave up and flew away to find an alternative pool.

Calling this camp *"Kampi ya barafu"* (Camp of ice), we pitched our tents in the lee of the rocks. There was no way of avoiding the wind that howled all night, and during the long dark hours the canvas would bang and billow over my bed. Sometimes I heard the guy ropes flapping wildly against the sides of the tent and would stagger out into the cold wind to tie them down again. When at last the dawn appeared after such a night, we emerged from our tent looking much the worse for wear. But any discomforts of camping on the plains were far outweighed by the superb scenery and the unbelievable density of wild animals; each safari amongst them was an unforgettable experience.

Driving in any direction across the open plains, we would follow the wild dogs or the vultures circling overhead, watch lions pad disdainfully past a herd of curious wildebeest, stop at an isolated kopje to explore a nest at the top of a solitary tree, or pause to observe a crowned plover guarding her eggs on the bare ground against a herd of onrushing animals—by opening and closing her white-marked wings, she was able to induce the stampeding animals to swerve aside and we never saw a nest destroyed.

Camping on the plains was in a category of its own, for unlike the rest of the Serengeti, there were no anti-poaching patrols in this area and we were seldom there on duty. During the months that the migratory animals were concentrated on the plains, we camped amongst them only on certain weekends; sometimes we set out on a Sunday before dawn to cook our breakfast in the open and spend the day with the animals. Even the millions of flies brought by the game herds failed to dampen our enthusiasm, though they could be maddening when the wind dropped, settling in swarms on our mouths, eyes, and noses. The only refuge then was inside the zipped-up tent, where we retreated for our meals. The lions, too, found the flies annoying and swatted at them with their paws while lashing their tails irritably.

After a long day out in the sun amongst the game, we would return to camp for a shallow bath in water the cook had painstakingly collected from the rain catchments in the rocks. Then, stretching our feet towards the campfire with drinks in hand, we enjoyed seeing the sun sink slowly towards the horizon and the stars appear in thousands, until it seemed there was no space in the sky for more. The sky at night felt close on the treeless plains, and it glowed with a soft and enveloping radiance that inspired a feeling of harmony with the universe. We were alone in that immense open country, and it seemed the stars displayed their brilliance solely for us. After an early supper we would be lulled to sleep by the rhythmic sound of the wildebeest bleating, interspersed by the off-key moan of a hyena or the plaintive cry of a stone curlew.

Awaking before sunrise, Myles and I liked to drive out for an hour or two to see the early morning light on the plains. Herds of wildebeest stood in stark relief against an opalescent background, the sun streaming through their beards and turning them to silver. With the mists from the highlands lying in thin veils across the country, nothing seemed quite real, and the animals appeared to hover above the ground in a magical world of their own. There was an ethereal quality about the light, while all around us the pastel shades of distant hills faded to infinity and merged with a sky that held the last pale blush of dawn. As yet there was no heat in the sun and it shone in long shafts of gold through the dewy grass, occasionally touching a lion's mane or the burnished flank of a gazelle. The animals seemed to welcome each new day, tossing their heads and pursuing one another high-spiritedly. Sometimes they paused with startled expressions to watch us pass at such an early hour, and we would speak in whispers to try to lessen our intrusion upon them; in our noisy Land Rover we felt like interlopers into their primeval world.

Once we came on two lions in the morning twilight, stirringly noble as they stood side by side against a delicate sky. Their breath steamed in the cold air and one of them began to scuff the earth with his hind legs. Then they moved together towards a horizon that glowed with the first light of the rising sun.

As the heat intensified and the colours deepened, the magic of early morning faded, and it was time to return to our camp for breakfast.

Chapter 13

Visitors

"Do zebras eat people?" asked the wide-eyed girl as we drove through the herds on the Serengeti Plains.

We were asked all kinds of questions by visitors to the Park. Would we see tigers? Did lions mate for fun? Should we not bury that dead gazelle in case it got eaten by something? Questions like these made us realize how little the average person knew about wildlife. In a National Park such ignorance could be dangerous, if it produced bravado or a lack of caution towards seemingly tame lions and leopards. When I accompanied the tourists, my heart would sometimes miss a beat if I saw a lion's eyes suddenly change from indifference to alert concentration, for it invariably meant a visitor was leaning far out of an open truck to photograph a lion family at closer range.

Visitors to the Serengeti were few until East African Airways began their excursion flights in late 1957. During the dry seasons two Dakotas from Nairobi would fly to Seronera every Sunday with about forty people on board. They would be met and driven around for the day in the Serengeti's entire fleet of vehicles: two Land Rovers and a 5-ton truck. At first the airline pilots had great difficulty in finding Seronera and we would all turn out at dawn to await their arrival. By flashing mirrors and spreading white sheets across the grass we sought to attract their attention, but our efforts often failed, and the planes would drone past a mile or two away, turn round, and head back to Nairobi. Once the pilots became familiar with Seronera, there was no further trouble.

During the first day's excursion to the Park our visitors saw
thousands of animals. As well as zebras, wildebeest, and Thomson's gazelles, they saw lions, leopards, cheetahs, wild dogs,
buffaloes, kongonis, topis, reedbuck, Grant's gazelles, impalas,
bat-eared foxes, dikdiks, warthogs, hyenas, baboons, elands, waterbuck, jackals, ostriches, and giraffes. They also saw a variety
of birds, including exotic-looking species such as crowned
cranes, kori bustards, saddle-billed storks, and secretary birds.
The Kenya papers printed a glowing report of that first excursion
to the Park, and the tours soon became a popular means of visiting the Serengeti.

To accommodate the tourists, our truck was fitted with a double row of bench seats facing outwards along the open back. A
small roof provided shade. Elderly visitors and distinguished
guests were taken round in Land Rovers. When we were not on
safari, I was employed by Parks to act as hostess to the party. As
well as answering questions as best I could and serving refresh-
ments and lunchboxes at regular intervals, my duties were to
supervise the drivers and see that everything operated as
smoothly as possible; that the vehicles were kept together and
did not wander off on their own; that visitors were counted after
each stop; and that a tactful control was kept on the tourists'
behaviour in the Park. Before starting out, I would deliver a
short talk at the airstrip, warning our guests not to take risks
with dangerous animals, explaining a little about the animals they
were likely to see and, with the aid of a map, showing them the
route we intended to follow. The tourists on the truck, many of
them young, often looked as if they were on a beach holiday
with their gay hats, scarves, and shorts. Their laughter and noise
made me marvel at the patience of our Serengeti lions and leopards, especially when photographers became too bold in their
eagerness to get more interesting pictures. To a pride of lions
stretched out asleep in the grass, a visitor might shout: "Come
on, Buster, wake up!" or "Look this way, Bonzo, and show your
teeth!"

If one of the lions yawned, everyone scrambled to take a photograph. The lions would be only a few feet from the open truck,
and no one seemed to pay any attention when a lion crouched
into position to spring. Watching its eyes and feeling the hair

begin to rise on the back of my neck, I would call out sharply:
"Please talk quietly!"

Sometimes tourists taking pictures clambered over the sides
of their truck and leaned out towards the lions, holding onto the
vehicle with one hand; then I would warn them that unruly
behaviour and disturbance of any kind were strictly forbidden.
Although visitors generally talked quietly near the animals, on
one occasion they became boisterous with a leopard, which few
of them had ever seen before. She was shy, unlike the "tame"
Seronera leopards that paid scant attention to vehicles and remained draped along branches for visitors to photograph. This
leopard took one look at us converging on her and rippled
smoothly down the tree into the long grass of a shallow gully.
Our vehicles followed her. Unfortunately the gully was not deep
enough for the leopard to hide completely, and her excited audi-
ence swarmed over the sides of the truck and reached out with
their cameras to photograph the desperate animal. I caught a
glimpse of the leopard glaring towards the tourists, and in the
split second between her decision to attack or make a dash for
freedom across an open glade, I shouted: "Get back at once into
your vehicle!"

With one accord they all returned silently to their seats and
the leopard remained in the grass. Afterwards I explained the
reason for my outburst, wondering if in fact the visitors truly appreciated their danger. Although such incidents were rare, there
were times when tourists seemed to see no difference between
photographing animals in a zoo and in a wildlife sanctuary,
where common sense and sometimes caution were needed.

During our tours amongst the game I felt as delighted as the
visitors if we found one of the rarer animals, such as a cheetah or
a leopard, which particularly interested the average tourist. On
the few occasions when we saw nothing more exciting than a solitary lion, I would share equally in their disappointment.

Once a party of millionaires from a luxury liner berthed at
Mombasa chartered a Dakota to fly them at short notice to the
Serengeti. They were elderly people, and as there was only one
Land Rover available, I climbed into the back of the truck to
look after them as well as I could. Actually the seats of the truck
were comfortable, and their elevated position made them better

for game viewing than those of a Land Rover. But my guests looked somewhat taken aback as they climbed the ladder of the truck, and I heard one of them mutter: "After paying a hundred bucks to get here, this had better be good!"

Those words were the kiss of death on the day. It was the wrong time of year for animal viewing at Seronera; most of them had migrated to the plains, and to travel there meant a drive of some 40 miles across virtually empty country. It was already mid-morning, and the airline pilot wanted to be airborne by four that afternoon. We had barely five hours in which to find the game. Seronera was the only place where they were likely to see leopards; but if we failed, the visitors would have seen very little. In the end I decided to take them to the plains, where they would at least see the migratory animals, and perhaps lions as well.

For more than an hour we saw nothing except a pair of jackals and a hyena. Irritation seemed to mount amongst my guests as the heat intensified and the bumpy road grew increasingly irksome. Promising them a sight they would never forget, I tried to keep up their spirits; but with the dust swirling round them and the truck lumbering on endlessly towards Lake Lagaja, they soon lapsed into an ominous silence. At last the wavering mirage along the horizon took shape as a line of trees and the glassy surface of the water shone up at us, tinged with pink clusters of flamingoes. We stopped for lunch; and while the tourists relaxed, I consulted with Frank, the Land Rover driver, and my old friend Omari, who drove the truck. Although we had seen only small concentrations of game at Lagaja, we decided to remain in the area in the hope of finding lions, leopards, cheetahs, wild dogs, and giraffes.

Frank set off in the lead and we followed at a more sedate pace. After a short time I saw the Land Rover swing round, flash its headlights, and disappear over the edge of a steep bank. This was our signal that something had been spotted and I passed on the information to my weary guests. Omari hurried in the direction Frank had taken and then, to my horror, he followed the Land Rover without hesitation over the bank at an angle that seemed certain to overturn us. Thorn branches whipped past our faces as we crashed down through the bush. Hanging on for support to anything or anybody within reach, I thumped frantically on the cab roof for Omari to stop. But he evidently felt in control of the situation and grimly pressed on. Like a tank the truck carved a great swathe through the bush, until we came at last to rest in a valley. But our troubles were not yet ended.

The Land Rover stood to one side, and Frank was pointing into the bush nearby. Searching round for some sign of life, I saw a lioness suddenly explode out of the undergrowth, spitting and snarling as she charged straight at us. Omari reacted instantly by reversing the truck at full speed through bushes and small trees, and he managed to remain head on to the lioness. Pulling up a few feet from his mudguard, she kept up a continuous snarl of rage, while her tail lashed furiously. Then, with ears laid back and claws unsheathed in her enormous paws, she crouched low to spring at the truck. At that moment her tiny cub emerged from the bush and called complainingly in short sharp mews. The lioness turned and bolted back to cover, growling angrily as she went. It was the end of a harrowing day; no one had managed to take a single picture of the lioness.

By now it was nearly three o'clock and we decided to return to Seronera. Few words were spoken as my guests boarded their plane, and there was no telling whether they had enjoyed their brief visit to the Serengeti. Compared with past impressions of tourists' reactions, I thought they seemed unusually subdued.

On another occasion we were driving a Nairobi excursion group towards Naabi Hill when I saw what I thought was a cheetah some distance from the road. I asked the driver to stop, and the other vehicles, including the truck, drew up behind us. While everybody looked enquiringly at me, I scanned the empty plain with field glasses. To my embarrassment the cheetah was no longer in sight, and I wondered aloud if I had seen a leopard. Unlike cheetahs, who rely on their speed to escape from danger, leopards hide by crouching low in whatever cover they can find. Adam, the driver, teased me about my imagination, since we were still some distance from Naabi Hill, the only cover on the plains for miles around; to have seen a leopard in such open country was most unlikely. Yet I felt sure I had not been mistaken and I persuaded Adam to drive towards the spot where I had first sighted the animal.

Searching the open ground, I suddenly saw a spotted pelt pressed flat into the short grass. It *was* a leopard. We stopped, and as each driver came up alongside I warned him not to go too close nor to make any noise, since the leopard had no cover of any kind and was bound to feel vulnerable. I was to regret ever finding that animal. The vehicles spread out at a distance and the visitors silently prepared to take their photographs; a German tourist in our Land Rover stood up quietly through the open hatch to focus his camera. At that moment there was a flash of movement and to my dismay I saw the leopard streaking towards our vehicle. It made no sound. There was little time for me to do anything except yell: *"Get down!"*

The German could not understand my words and calmly continued to photograph the ferocious beast as it hurtled towards us. I knew that in its frantic need to reach cover, a leopard usually strikes with lightning speed at whatever is lying in its path; and with such an obvious target, I felt sure it would spring onto the roof of our Land Rover in a single bound. During the space of that second or two, when it seemed certain the German would be hurt, I thought of our first-aid box and realized it held little that could help a man even briefly raked by a leopard's claws and teeth.

Suddenly I heard a loud thump and from the offside seat I saw the leopard streak past the front of our Land Rover and race towards Naabi Hill. The drivers immediately started to follow, and I shouted to them to leave the alarmed creature in peace. I suspected the leopard had been blinded by fear; my views were later confirmed by Adam, who told me the animal had not paused in its headlong rush and had struck its head a severe blow against the wheel. I asked him again to give me an accurate account of the incident. Had the leopard clouted the Land Rover with its paw? No, Adam insisted, it had run into the wheel with its head and had not stopped. Disturbed at this information, I hoped the driver was wrong.

Shortly afterwards one of the Park guides reported that there was an ailing leopard at Naabi. Fearing this might be the same animal we had encountered two weeks earlier, I asked Myles if I could accompany him. We drove to Naabi and found the leopard lying by the roadside. When Myles bent down from the Land Rover and threw a small pebble at it, the weak and emaciated animal tottered to its feet with a snarl, then fell over. It was beyond help and Myles shot it.

Tears stung my eyes. There could be no proof that this was the same leopard, but we knew that only a pair lived at Naabi and this was the male. The leopard I had seen with the tourists was also a male and a violent blow to the head could easily have caused its death.

One day when visiting the Lodge with friends, I heard a safari courier boasting to his clients that he had once aggravated a Seronera leopard until it sprang at his vehicle with outstretched claws. "Had my window not been wound up, I would not be here today," he said, smiling round at the group from under his hat, adorned with leopard skin.

Turning to the speaker, I told him coldly that my husband as warden in the Serengeti could have him banned from the Park for such behaviour. He looked astonished, then annoyed, and I knew with despair that my meaning was lost on him. There would always be people who exploited the game for their own reasons: prestige, sensational photographs, or a personal feeling of power.

In 1965 I was shown an instance of this when I visited my parents who had retired to Australia five years previously. Missing the Park, I took Lynda and Michael to the zoo. It was the last time I ever visited one. As we came to the lions' cage—a large concrete enclosure around a solitary tree—I noticed an attendant spraying the interior with a hose. Each time the lions leaped away from the hose, the attendant directed it onto them, until they cowered miserably beneath the full force of the water. I could hardly restrain myself from saying more than: "What are you doing?"

As if his words explained everything, the attendant said firmly: "Teaching them a good lesson. They're vicious beasts, and I don't like them."

He continued to drench the lions, while I told him about the Serengeti and about our life there. "We *like* lions," Lynda added, staring at the unhappy caged creatures with troubled eyes. With a shrug the attendant moved the hose away. His actions were probably motivated by fear and ignorance, but I wondered for how long the lions under his charge had endured such torment.

Fortunately most people love animals. Many visitors to the Serengeti spent a lifetime's savings to see animals living free, and I was frequently impressed by their inborne empathy with wild creatures. Once, during a visit by Jonathan Kenworthy, a brilliant sculptor of African wildlife, we followed a female leopard hunting through the grass at the headwaters of the Seronera River. Each time tourists moved in close to photograph the leopard, their vehicles disturbed the reedbuck she was stalking, and Jonathan would groan despairingly. Again and again the leopard crept close to her quarry, only to be foiled in her attempts by vehicles rushing from all sides. We were growing exasperated by the tourists' interference, and anxious for the leopard; but at last only four vehicles remained, the other tourists having returned to the Lodge for lunch. Now perhaps the leopard would make her kill, for surely those tourists prepared to forgo their meal were eager to see the hungry animal succeed, and would not interfere while she hunted.

After we had watched the leopard for nearly three hours, she disappeared into a clump of tall reed grass. Thirty minutes later we heard a bleat; the leopard's head shot above the grass with a baby reedbuck in her jaws. Instantly the young animal's mother leaped into view across the gully and bounded to within 2 feet of the predator. Standing there holding the fawn, with head thrown back and neck arched, the leopard stared at the fawn's mother, who was gazing in consternation at her baby; for a moment it looked as if the leopard might drop the fawn and attack the adult reedbuck. We held our breath. But in that fraction of time a Land Rover sped in front of us to photograph the scene and the animals fled in opposite directions. Later, when Jonathan had recovered from his outrage, he sketched from memory the two animals facing one another for use in a future sculpture.

Visitors to the Park sometimes experienced difficulties that could have led to disaster. One of these instances occurred in the 1950s, when Myles rescued a group of Congo refugees who had been stranded for six days in the Corridor during the rains. They had entered the Park from Lake Victoria and were lost and out of food. The roads were impassable. That morning, by a stroke of good fortune, Myles decided he would attempt taking a patrol down the Corridor for the first time in several weeks. The refugees were found writing their letters of farewell and were brought safely to Banagi.

A few years later two British nursing sisters hired a Land Rover to drive them to Seronera at the start of the late 1961 floods. During their journey from Arusha it rained ceaselessly, and their African chauffeur finally stalled the vehicle in a lake that had formed near Naabi Hill. The visitors were reduced to sitting on the tops of their seats as the waters continued to rise. For two days it rained, but their cheerful driver consoled them with assurances that they would soon be rescued. They were fed on canned foods fished from sodden boxes in the waterlogged Land Rover. Eventually, on the third day, when no vehicles had passed the driver told his passengers they would have to "hoof it" to Seronera. He carried their suitcases on his head, and they walked 25 miles across country in the rain, passing a pride of lions on the way.

In a lighter vein, a party of Asian tourists once felt they had to spend the night up a tree at Seronera, after their open truck broke down near the river crossing. The next morning they complained bitterly that they had spent a terrifying night surrounded by "thousands of buffaloes (wildebeest?) and roaring lions."

On another occasion Lodge guests were astonished to see a hyena lolloping round Seronera with a rusty metal lid from one of the Lodge dustbins jammed around its neck; history does not relate how it managed to acquire or rid itself of this adornment.

When visitors stayed with us at Banagi, I often wondered how they felt about walking out at night to the long-drop lavatory; or what they thought as they filled their baths with the muddy waters of the Mgungu River. Occasionally our ancient pipes burst and water gushed all over the bathroom floor. Small snakes and other creepy-crawlies frequently appeared in the house, and tsetse flies stung us all with unrestrained zeal. During hot and dry spells it was often difficult to sleep, and the dust could be tiresome when whining east winds blew whirlwinds into the house. At night the light of the hissing pressure lamps attracted all kinds of insects, including beetles that zoomed round like miniature jets.

"You must love it here," our guests would say. "It's so peaceful and quiet." And I would wonder how they truly felt about Banagi and about the loneliness, as the night closed in around our tiny pinpoint of light amid acres of darkness.

Sitting on the verandah, with the little swifts diving past our heads at lightning speed, we were often asked why we encouraged them to nest in the house, and Myles would answer solemnly: "When the swifts leave Banagi, the Serengeti will die."

As time passed, more and more visitors came to the Serengeti, and we met people from all walks of life: writers, actors, artists, heads of state, royalty, scientists, peers, politicians, celebrities, tycoons, and many others. During our peak visitor years from 1966 to 1970 "the Taj" guesthouse was seldom empty and life moved along at a breathless pace. Apart from running two households, entertaining official guests, and accompanying them on game tours, I was also working in the Research Institute's accounts office and as part-time secretary to the wardens.

One of the wardens' duties was to look after distinguished visitors, and our first official guests were members of the Committee of Enquiry who arrived for three days in 1957 to discuss the future boundaries of the Serengeti. The party included Sir Barclay Nihill, late President of the Court of Appeal for Eastern Africa, and Sir Landsborough Thomson, President of the Zoological Society of London. So that we could look after them, Myles and I moved from Banagi to a tent at Seronera, and each morning at dawn I would walk to the Lodge to organize meals for the day. One morning I awoke to discover that my leather handbag was missing; it contained lists of menus and notes for our guests' visit, and I searched frantically, eventually finding it in the bush where it had been chewed to pieces by a hyena. The handbag had been beside my pillow.

Other early visitors to the Park included the future President of Tanzania, the Hon. Julius Nyerere, then a Member of Legislative Council, who returned many times thereafter; and the territory's last Governor, Sir Richard Turnbull.

In 1959 an impressionist artist from South West Africa, Fritz Krampe, arrived at our house with a letter of introduction. Myles later met him at the Lodge and watched fascinated as the artist swept vigorously at a brilliant sketch of two buffaloes before throwing down the brush to greet him. A powerfully built, short man, he had immense drive and a bold creative energy. His sketchbooks were filled with wonderful drawings of animals that captured their moods and movements in a few deft lines of the pen. For many years Fritz kept in touch with us from around the world. Then one day whilst he was sketching an elephant in India, he was charged and tusked as he ran. A rescue party sent out early the following morning found the elephant still standing over Fritz's lifeless body.

After the granting of independence to Tanzania in 1961, H.R.H. Prince Philip, Duke of Edinburgh, visited the Serengeti, accompanied by Rear-Admiral Bonham-Carter and Major Aubrey Buxton. He arrived in the red Heron of the Queen's Flight at the start of the floods in late 1961 and stayed for three days at the Chief Park Warden's house. Although it poured with rain, the sun shone brilliantly between downpours, and the Prince identified nearly one hundred birds. Myles's main concern when driving was that he might hit a pothole or rock in the long grass and hurl the royal visitor from his precarious position on the roof of the Land Rover.

Other royal guests who seemed to visit the Park at the wettest times of year were the King and Queen of Denmark; the Africans called him "The Rain King." On their second safari in March 1970, which coincided with the heaviest rains we had had since the early 1962 floods, they were accompanied by their daughters, Princess Margarete (now Queen of Denmark), Princess Benedict, and Queen Anne-Marie of Greece.

At the time I was returning from Nairobi with Alan Root in his Piper Colt airplane. Alan, who was a frequent visitor to the Park with his wife Joan, had been one of the Grzimeks' team in 1957, and was among the world's finest wildlife photographers. The weather was appalling that day. Our plane crept along the Rift Valley floor as we deviated further and further south in our efforts to find a way through the clouds that covered the escarpment wall. At last we saw a gap near the Gol Mountains and sped through it, flying over miles and miles of scrubland bush in a grey fog of rain and mist. There was no sign of the open plains. I had begun to think we were too far north when I suddenly recognized the Maasai kopjes southeast of Seronera. Alan swung the plane onto our new course and then dived over his tent to let Joan know he was safely back, nearly decapitating an acacia as he pulled steeply away.

We landed, and were told that Myles was escorting the Danish royal party on a tour of the migratory animals across the saturated plains.

"All we're likely to see is a fish," murmured John Owen. A short time later they crossed the Seronera River, and saw a catfish struggling to swim upstream across the concrete causeway! The Land Rovers dug deep furrows into the ground, which remained for months; but the royal party also saw several lions, bedraggled and hunched in the pouring rain.

In 1969 the Crown Prince Carl Gustav, now King of Sweden, spent one night at the official guesthouse with his entourage.

Another royal visitor to the Park was Prince Bernhard of The Netherlands in 1972, who came on a safari conducted by Eric Balson, game warden in Arusha. Myles joined them for two weeks, enjoying the company of one of the world's leading wildlife enthusiasts in a camp on the outskirts of the Serengeti.

Among our distinguished guests were many ardent conservationists, including the late Charles Lindbergh. During one of his safaris he spent several days living with the Maasai in a *manyatta* outside the Serengeti. As their honoured guest he was accommodated in the hut of the Leguinan's (or captain's) senior wife, who would show him her beads and bangles, grinning toothlessly across the small fire that burned between their pallets. Despite the flies which abounded in the manyatta, settling in swarms over his eyes and mouth, Charles Lindbergh spent his time writing his impressions and experiences. When I talked to him of flying, he sensed my enthusiasm as a novice pilot.

"Be careful," warned the Lone Eagle. "Flying is a dangerous occupation."

Myles particularly enjoyed meeting visitors with whom he had interests in common. Among his favorite books was *Gallipoli* by Alan Moorehead, who first visited the Park in 1951 and returned many times thereafter. Another visitor was Wilfred Thesiger, whose stories of life in the desert— *Arabian Sands*—fascinated us. Robert Ardrey, author of *African Genesis*, also spoke of his books on visits to the Park.

Sir Julian Huxley visited the Serengeti in 1960, and returned on many occasions. He was interested in the scientific studies being carried out, and was always a brilliant source of information and guidance to the Serengeti Research Institute. Once

when he and Lady Huxley dined with us, it rained heavily, and
Sandy Field borrowed my umbrella to escort them to the Land
Rover. After seeing Lady Huxley safely into the middle seat, he
withdrew with the umbrella, and heard a shout. The roof hatch
was open. Hurriedly climbing to the roof, Sandy closed the
hatch in record time. To his dismay the hatch cover held gallons
of water which deluged the already drenched Lady Huxley!

Dr. Fairfield Osborne, then president of the New York Zoological Society, was another welcome visitor who greatly assisted
the Serengeti by presenting Parks with a new Piper Super Cub
aircraft on behalf of the Society.

In 1961 Herr Gerstenmeier, Speaker of the West German
Bundestag, visited the Park to open the new Michael Grzimek
Memorial Laboratory at Banagi. Sir Peter Scott and his wife
were among the guests at the opening ceremony. On his first
evening with us, before going to bed, I enquired whether Herr
Gerstenmeier would like bacon and eggs for breakfast in the
morning. With a mischievous smile he replied: "Bacon and
eggs? You British! You have won two world wars on bacon and
eggs for breakfast! I would like only rolls and coffee, thank you!"

In our early years Myles was helped considerably by the Royal
Air Force and Army Air Corps stationed in Kenya at the time.
Air Marshall Sir Charles Elworthy visited the Serengeti in 1961,
with Air Commodore Macdonald, C-in-C R.A.F. East Africa.
Once when Air Commodore Macdonald was flying a Twin Pio-
neer over the Park, a vulture came straight through the nose of
the plane and landed at his feet. With its feathers blowing in the
breeze through the hole, he thought for a moment the bird was
still alive.

In 1963 the Army Air Corps began using the Serengeti for
training purposes, assisting Myles greatly on anti-poaching
operations. After dinner with us on the first visit of General
Weston and Major Whitehead, Commanding Officer of the
Corps in Kenya, they asked if they could walk to the Lodge, a
mile away. Myles insisted on driving them, and they had not
gone halfway when they saw a pride of lions lying in the middle
of the road!

At the time that the Army Air Corps were helping Myles on
anti-poaching operations, Joy and George Adamson were in the

Serengeti, driving out each day to look for the three cubs of their famous lioness, Elsa. The nearly full-grown cubs had lived wild in Kenya for some time and were already fending for themselves; but in order to give them time to settle in their new area, the Adamsons were given permission to feed them for a few weeks. Within a short time the lions wandered away into their new environment and were not to be found. For eighteen months the Adamsons searched for them, their anxiety and deep involvement with Elsa's cubs affecting us all. Eight years later a film unit arrived to photograph sequences of *Living Free*, bringing their own lions and lion tamers, with Susan Hampshire and Nigel Davenport in the roles of Joy and George.

In 1963 the author of several popular books on Africa, Elspeth Huxley, visited the Park, and delighted Myles with stories of Kenya in her youth.

James Michener also visited the Serengeti in 1970, together with his wife. We drove about the plains in two Land Rovers on an ideal morning, but by noon it had started to rain. With eight of us crowded into one Land Rover for lunch, James Michener helped dispense drinks and plates of food to our guests.

Among those writers who frequently visited the Serengeti was Martha Gellhorn, at one time married to Ernest Hemingway. Her witty conversation enlivened many an evening at Seronera, including one spent at the campsite of Prince Sadruddin Aga Khan on a visit to the Park in 1969. The author William Styron was among the guests. Other writers who visited the Park were the late Cyril Connolly in 1968 and Peter Matthiesson in 1969 and 1970.

Many artists also came to the Serengeti, including the Australian Sidney Nolan, Ralph Thompson from England, the American wildlife artist Bob Kuhn, and David Shepherd, who gave his wholehearted and generous support to helping wild animals. Once when Myles flew David to visit his patrol posts in the north, I suggested to his wife, Avril, that we might also fly over the migratory herds on the plains. Circling above the game, we suddenly saw three dead zebras lying together by a watercourse. Later we drove to the place with Myles and David, and decided the zebras had died from a lightning strike. They were unmarked and in good condition, and there seemed no other explanation for their collapse in the same spot.

In 1970 the British actor and writer Spike Milligan visited the

Park; and in the same year, James Stewart and his wife, Gloria. They were both passionately interested in wildlife, and were frequent and delightful visitors to the parks in East Africa.

Other visitors included Marshal Tito of Yugoslavia in 1970; Olof Palme, Swedish Prime Minister, in 1969; Lee Radziwill in 1969; and the late Senator Robert Kennedy, his wife, Ethel, and some forty journalists in 1966. After her husband's tragic death Ethel Kennedy sent her son, Robert Jr., then fourteen years old, to the Serengeti in 1968. Jean Smith, sister of the late President Kennedy, also visited the Serengeti in 1970.

Many well-known Americans came to the Park, including Laurence Rockefeller, Stewart Udall, Robert McNamara, Judge Russell Train, Professor Starker Leopold, Royal Little, Charles Engelhart, McGeorge Bundy, and Robert Kleiburg. I once hitched a ride to Nairobi on Robert Kleiburg's private Grummond Gulfstream turboprop aircraft, which had brought his tape recorder to Seronera and was returning empty. As we landed at Nairobi's international airport, several people lining the waving base watched curiously to see which celebrity was arriving in the gleaming white aircraft that taxied to a halt below them. From the cockpit stepped three briskly efficient crew, and from the rear emerged one very embarrassed hitchhiker carrying an old suitcase!

On one occasion three American senators visited the privately owned camp at Lake Lagaja. Driving Senators Moss, Fong, and McGee about the plains, we answered such questions as: "What is the gestation period of a giraffe?", "How many Maasai are there in Tanzania?", "What is the name of that green shrub over there?"

In reply to the last question, although it was one of the few names I knew, it eluded me. Searching my mind for inspiration, I suddenly replied: "Yes, I remember now; it's called Hyperestes."

The American consul shot me a doubtful look. "Are you sure?" he whispered.

"Of course," I replied.

On our return to camp we were talking to John Owen when the consul suddenly turned to him and said: "By the way, what's the name of that bright green shrub that grows all over the plains?"

"You mean the one the animals don't eat?" John asked. "It's called Hyperestes."

The consul looked at me in surprise, and John was quick to sum up the situation. "Actually," he added, "its full name is Hyperestes Boloneyii Turnerii!"

In few other environments could we have had the opportunity of meeting such a diversity of personalities. Many of our visitors donated funds generously towards the Serengeti's development and to conservation in general. Without their help it would not have been possible to achieve the same degree of progress in the Parks. The atmosphere of space, sun, and animals had a way of bringing happiness to those who visited the Serengeti, and it gave us great satisfaction to see our visitors' obvious pleasure and to listen to their enthusiastic remarks. We made many friends amongst them.

Chapter 14

Last Days

Our years in the Serengeti drew to a close in 1972. Towards the end several changes were made in the Parks' administration. By 1970, when John Owen had virtually achieved all of his aims, he felt his continued presence to be no longer beneficial for Parks. In an effort to secure greater political stability for the organization he had done so much to build, he surrendered his post to a citizen of the country and remained in the background for another year to help in any way he could. John finally returned to England in 1971, leaving behind a sense of irreplaceable loss among those who valued his remarkable achievements and admired his qualities.

The Conservator of Ngorongoro, Solomon ole Saibull, took charge of the Parks in 1970 (he is now Minister of Natural Resources and Tourism); and in 1972 a former Minister of Agriculture, the Hon. Derek Bryceson, MP, was appointed Director.

Between these two events there were periods of unrest and confusion that finally strengthened Myles's resolve to relinquish his duties to a citizen of the country. As an expatriate he was fortunate in that he had worked eleven years in the Parks' service since 1961, when Tanzania became a self-governing sovereign state; the time had now come for us to leave the Serengeti, and for the administration of the Parks to be in the hands of the Tanzanian people.

In April 1972 Myles tendered his resignation to the Board of Trustees. Although it had been a hard decision to make, we

knew it to be inevitable. In their ultimate wish to replace all expatriate wardens, the trustees understood and accepted Myles's
resignation; but we were pleased when they asked him to serve
for an additional two years in another Park in Tanzania. This letter was signed by the Chairman of the Board, Chief Adam Sapi
Mkwawa (now also Minister for Capital Development in Tanzania), whom we had known for many years and greatly respected.

In agreeing to stay on, Myles asked to be transferred to the
Arusha National Park where he would be in a position to lend
advisory assistance to the wardens in the northern Parks, including the Serengeti. His colleague, John Stephenson, the only
other remaining expatriate warden (who had replaced Sandy
Field as Chief Park Warden in 1971), was transferred for his
final two years to his former post in the southern parks at Mikumi.

David Stevens Babu, the Park warden at Lake Manyara National Park, now became Chief Park Warden in the Serengeti,
and Myles's position as Deputy Chief Park Warden in charge of
all fieldwork was eventually filled by Elias Kapolondo, a young
Maasai graduate from the Wildlife Management College at
Mweka in Tanzania.

In the Research Institute, Hugh Lamprey was replaced in
1972 by Dr. Tumaina Mcharo, a Tanzanian; many of our friends
also left the Serengeti after completing their research studies,
and were replaced by other ecologists from different parts of the
world. Within a few months our whole way of life had altered
drastically. At Seronera a modern hotel that catered for 150
guests neared completion, and the conversion of the old Seronera Lodge into staff quarters had already begun.

During 1972, and until we left in December, Myles concentrated his efforts upon teaching his newly appointed successor all
that he knew about the Park, and in particular about how to organize and handle the armed ranger force. He had for some time
foreseen his replacement, so that his task of training cadet wardens had already been started; he now intensified it. In addition
to learning the practical aspects of administration and fieldwork,
four of the eight African wardens—seven of them graduates from
Mweka College—were taught to fly, and Myles gave his successor further instruction on the technique of bush flying. Allow-

ing himself no feelings of regret or grievances, Myles disregarded the past and countered his depression by a sense of fatalism and an appreciative awareness of all the years he had been privileged to live in the Serengeti. All that mattered to him now was the Serengeti's continued survival, which required an efficient management to take charge of the administration of the world's most spectacular wildlife sanctuary. To this end he devoted his remaining months of service in the Serengeti.

In the same way that Myles refused to let sadness overwhelm him, so too did I seek to avoid unhappiness by burying myself in a world of make-believe. Never having thought seriously about living anywhere else, I could not now bring myself to accept the fact we were leaving the Serengeti, and I engrossed my thoughts and energies in a feverish burst of painting. By using every available hour to recapture the familiar views we loved so well, I was too preoccupied and exhausted to think deeply about our move, or to make plans for our future; as the date for our departure drew nearer, my paintings grew larger and more ambitious.

"When will you begin to pack?" Myles sometimes asked; our possessions during sixteen years had accumulated to sizable proportions.

"Soon," I would answer vaguely. "It won't take long, once I start."

Subconsciously I rejected the idea of our leaving and continued to live as if no change were taking place, wishfully believing that some intervention would reverse the whole inexorable chain of events. With growing concern Myles watched me postpone the packing until our final two weeks at Seronera. During those last hurried days, when I was too busy to think, I lived in a dreamlike world of unreality and was not unhappy.

Only later, when we were settled at Momella, did I begin to feel our loss. This mountain park, with Mount Meru (nearly 15,000 feet high) towering behind our house, was so different from those great warm savannah plains. For the first time I felt oppressed by a sense of unfamiliarity and rootlessness. Despite the beauty of our surroundings depression hung over me like a cloud, and I would lie awake at night listening to buffaloes munching on the grass, and to Myles who tossed restlessly in his sleep. No lions roared and no hyenas called; at times I would listen for them before realizing, with a sinking sensation in my stomach, that we no longer lived at Seronera. For three months I lived within a prison of despondency that became habitual as I grew accustomed to my new way of life—until one day Myles flew me to the Serengeti.

As the aircraft crossed the plains and the familiar hills took shape, a sudden sense of lightness came over me. It was as if a weight had been physically lifted from my mind, and I felt all at once more alive and aware of happiness flooding back into my dulled heart. We were home. I realized then how heavily my life had been overshadowed by nostalgia. Even as these thoughts went through my mind, and we swept low over the plains, I heard Myles say: "My God! The *magic* of this country!"

This was our Africa, the great wide views and dry colours, the heat and clear sky with its ever-changing clouds, the clarity of air, and the exhilarating freedom. The animals below us were waiting for the long rains to begin and the plains pulsated with life and vigour.

This was our Serengeti. I had almost forgotten how emotive it could be and how radiant.

We stepped from the airplane onto Seronera's familiar ground, and I breathed deeply and turned my face to the sun, feeling its warmth and vitality fill my numbed soul. We had been away too long. All we needed now was to drive home and pick up the broken threads of our life. Instead we waited for a Land Rover to meet us, and were taken to "the Taj" guesthouse, where the driver left us and drove away. We were just another couple of guests; outsiders paying a short visit to the Park.

With chilling force I realized we no longer belonged here, and that the Serengeti, which had been my life for sixteen years, no longer belonged to us. For the first time, sitting alone on the verandah and looking towards the kopjes where the roof of our house was just visible, I felt bereft and forsaken. Those three days were dismal; but during that time, while Myles instructed his successor in flying, I came to terms with reality and let the tears wash away the last of my self-deception. There would be no more clinging to the past, nor foolish hopes. Our Serengeti years were over.

We returned many times after that, and each time I was impressed again by the Serengeti's nobility, never tiring of its immense landscapes, spectacular sunsets, light and sky; and of the animals and great wild herds that enhanced its beauty.

I loved to see Tommies standing on a plain, their short tails flicking and legs stamping while they watched us pass; or streaking alongside the Land Rover as if they enjoyed a race and the chance to jink and swerve without hitting us. I enjoyed watching cheetahs move elegantly across the plains, their slender bodies, small proud heads, and long legs designed for speed; and seeing giraffes pause to gaze serenely at us over the tops of bushes, before breaking into long cantering strides with tails gently twirling.

I felt an almost atavistic sense of belonging amongst the animals when walking alone in that vast wide country, watching elephants tread majestically across a glade, their great feet touching the earth as if afraid to crush a nest or a fawn lying hidden in the grass.

We had lived for sixteen years in the Serengeti, and there were images imprinted upon my mind: glowing yellow thorn trees, and acacias in blossom, their branches tracing delicate patterns against a cobalt sky; skulking hyenas looking furtively over their shoulders; a magnificent leopard crouched above the open hatch of our Land Rover with lips curled back in a savage snarl; Lemugrut mountain in a soft mauve light across the great distance; topi bulls standing on anthills to proclaim their kingdoms; Marabou storks pacing like old solicitors with hands clasped behind them; and a giant fig tree standing alone in a valley on the empty plains.

I remembered seeing an impala vault effortlessly from one side of the road to the other above the hood of our moving Land Rover; another impala that was pursued by a pack of wild dogs into our camp, where she stood trembling a few feet from us until the dogs left her; a bull giraffe, 18 feet tall, that stood by our bedroom window, with his great knobbly legs extending out of sight while he chewed the acacia branches above the roof and paused to listen whenever the lions roared. Once we found five cheetah cubs lying hidden beneath a bush, peering out at us with small wistful faces.

Wherever we might live I would be reminded of the Serengeti if I heard the high wild cry of a fish eagle, smelled the warm earth after a first shower of rain, or saw the silvery sheen of spiky thorns on an *Acacia drepanolobium* tree with the wind whistling through its hollow galls. There were impressions that would live forever in my mind: the matchless grace of a leopard turning to look at us with expressionless yellow eyes as it flowed soundlessly through the wheatlike grass; stately waterbuck standing beside their equally proud calves; kori bustards strutting with puffed-out white necks, and tails spread over their backs in boastful display; the dust on the plains; the sound of vultures plummeting earthwards; and a small black crake busily probing the shallows of a pool.

In the words of Anthony Smith: "The Serengeti is a legacy that must always be. Whatever the difficulties, it must survive: its destruction is unthinkable. For anyone who imagines otherwise, let him go there, and let him be enriched by it." *

We had left the Serengeti and we lived in a totally different environment. But we soon grew to love our mountain park in the two years that we lived at Momella. At night the elephants would rip the fig creeper from the house, and Myles always woke if I opened the creaky door to chase them off. Climbing through a window, I would whisper "Shoo!" to an elephant standing beside our bedroom, and watch it shuffle away hurriedly into the darkness. Then, creeping back to bed, I would hear Myles enquire wearily: *"Now* what are you doing?"

My story is not intended as a guidebook to the Serengeti; I do not know enough to write one. In writing this book, I seek to cheat time by capturing our adventures and experiences before time dims them; but also, I hope, to convey my own love and enthusiasm for the Serengeti, so that in a small way I might encourage an appreciation of our world's diminishing wildlife and thus help the cause of conservation.

The animal artist Ralph Thompson once wrote:

In a concrete-threatened world, mankind will increasingly need the refreshment that wildlife and the wilderness can offer. This goes far beyond nationality or politics. Nor is it just a few wild animals like the fabulous tigers that are at risk. The fate of all living creatures, including man, is inextricably interwoven. We must maintain a balanced system and a stable environment. I am convinced that, once this is more generally understood, there will be action.†

* *Throw Out Two Hands*, London: George Allen & Unwin, 1963.
† In an article in *The Christian Science Monitor*.

The Serengeti is a land that cannot be equalled for its natural richness. It is a sanctuary that is desperately vulnerable to the whims of man. Its future lies in the hands of Tanzania's people. Amongst other conflicting demands on her limited resources, the Government is striving to meet its pledge to support the country's wildlife and National Parks. Tanzania is not an affluent country and will have a hard struggle in the years ahead to provide for her development and for a higher standard of living for her people, as well as for her priceless wildlife heritage. Sincerity and honest endeavour are exemplified by Tanzania's President, Mwalimu Julius Nyerere, who, in his Arusha Manifesto of September 1961, declared that: "In accepting the trusteeship of our wildlife, we solemnly declare that we will do everything in our power to make sure that our children's grandchildren will be able to enjoy this rich and precious inheritance."

Those words embody our hopes that the Serengeti will continue to be cherished and protected; that it will withstand all human pressures; and that those who follow in our footsteps will always appreciate the wonder of the Serengeti and its inestimable importance to mankind.

Epilogue

It is two years since Myles and I left Momella in 1974, where we spent the last two of our eighteen years in the Tanzania National Parks. In September that year we moved to the house that had once belonged to Myles's mother in Nanyuki, Kenya. It was here that my husband had spent his childhood, and it held for him many pleasant memories of a bygone age, when wild animals were almost as abundant as they are in the Serengeti.

We had hoped to continue working for conservation in East Africa, but it was increasingly difficult for an expatriate to obtain a wildlife post in newly independent African countries. Once when Myles was asked at a conference in America which species of animal in Africa he would consider endangered, he grinned and replied: "The expatriate game warden tops the list."

In 1975, after seven months of anxiety, Myles was offered a post in Malawi as regional game warden in their Department of National Parks and Wild Life. Our children were still at school in England, and we were not in a position to delay our decision. Myles accepted the offer, and was sent to the Nyika National Park, where we now live at an altitude of 8,000 feet in northern Malawi. For much of the year the clouds swirl low over the great Nyika plateau and a cold wind blows. It is a far cry from the Serengeti.

The undulating grasslands of the Nyika are bare of trees, but valleys hold patches of relic evergreen forest. Large mammals are limited mostly to roan antelopes, eland, reedbuck, and zebras, and leopards are frequently seen. There are no elephants, buffaloes, or lions on the plateau.

At our headquarters there is a small settlement of some two hundred Africans and two Europeans who respectively supervise the Park's administration and the ecological research work of the area. Myles is in charge of the whole northern region of Malawi. At present he is enlarging the Nyika National Park from 360 to 1,215 square miles. The main object of this extension is to protect the entire plateau, which forms the water catchment area of northern Malawi, and contains the sources of four major river systems. Marking the new boundaries of the Park sometimes entails foot safaris along the base of the plateau, with porters carrying our loads on their heads.

Once again our house is built of mud, there is no electricity, and our nearest township lies more than 100 miles away. Few tourists visit the Park, which is mainly scenic, with superb views on a clear day across to Zambia in the west and Tanzania to the north. Life on the Nyika plateau is almost as remote as when we lived at Banagi twenty years ago.

We have not been back to the Serengeti since we left Tanzania in 1974; but one day we will return.

Index

Adamson, George, 130, 197-198
Adamson, Joy, 130-131, 197-198
Agama lizards, 153
Aircraft, 61, 97, 99, 154-170
Amboseli Game Reserve, 15
Anne-Marie, Queen of Greece, 195
Antelopes, roan, 35
Ants, driver, 64-65
Ardrey, Robert, 196
Arrows, poisoned, 59-60
Arusha Manifesto of September 1961, 207
Arusha National Park, Momella, 154, 170, 202, 203, 206

Babu, David Stevens, 202
Badgers, honey, 91-92
Balson, Eric, 119, 196
Banagi, 1-12, 27-40, 83, 193-194
Bat-eared fox, 102-110
Baumann, Oscar, 18
Benedict, Princess of Denmark, 195
Bernhard, Prince of The Netherlands, 196
Bilharziasis, 8, 57
Birds, 149-153
Bologonja River, 175-176
Bonham-Carter, Christopher, 195
Bryceson, Derek, 201
Bubu, 32-34
Buffaloes, 10, 13-14, 35, 89, 174, 176
Bundy, McGeorge, 199
Bush fires, 172-173
Buxton, Aubrey, 195

Carl Gustav, King of Sweden, 196
Chandlers reedbuck, 35
Climate, 22-23, 96, 142, 172-173

Committee of Enquiry (1957), 11, 12, 20, 194
Connolly, Cyril, 198
Corridor, 11, 25, 158, 192

Deinotherium, 4
Disease, 8, 57
Dogs, wild, 24, 25, 112
Dormice, 111-112
Downey, Sydney, 14, 86
Driver ants, 64-65
Drought, 96, 142, 172-173
Duma region, 46-48, 157

East African Airways, 185
Elephants, 16-17, 174-175
Elworthy, Sir Charles, 197
Engelhart, Charles, 199

Fauna Preservation Society, 11
Field, Sandy, 99, 163, 167-170, 182, 197
Fires, 172-173
Flooding, 171-172
Fong, Hiram L., 199
Forest hog, 174
Fox, bat-eared, 102-110
Frederik IX, King of Denmark, 195
Friends of the Serengeti, The (Owen), 95
Fundi, 34, 52-53, 66, 67, 71, 90, 91, 116, 124, 125, 126

Game catching and marking, 157-158
Game census, 38
Game Ordinance (1940), 20
Gazelles, 62, 114-119
Gellhorn, Martha, 198

211

Genet cats, 153
Gerstenmeier, Herr, 197
Giraffes, 35
Gol Mountains, 4
Grant's gazelle, 114-119
Great Rift Mountains, 18
Great Rift Valley, 3
Grumeti River, 44, 55-57, 158
Grzimek, Bernhard, 94, 154-160
Grzimek, Michael, 72, 83, 154-161

Harthoorn, Tony, 103
Hartley, Carr, 100
Harvey, Edith, 39, 40, 172
Harvey, Gordon, 39-40, 99, 159
Hog, forest, 174
Honey badgers, 91-92
Huxley, Elspeth, 198
Huxley, Sir Julian, 196
Huxley, Lady, 196-197
Hyraxes (rock rabbit), 83-84, 141-149

Ikoma district, 133-134
Ikoma village, 1
Impalas, 35
Ingrid, Queen of Denmark, 195

Kapolondo, Elias, 202
Kennedy, Ethel, 199
Kennedy, Robert, 199
Kennedy, Robert, Jr., 106, 199
Kenworthy, Jonathan, 192
Kenya Game Department, 13-14
Ker, Donald, 14
Ker & Downey Safaris, Ltd., 14
Kibakari area, 100
Kilimafeza (Hill of Gold), 33
Kleiburg, Robert, 199
Klein, Al, 52
Kogatende Guardpost, 174
Kopjes, 21, 22
Krampe, Fritz, 194-195
Kruuk, Hans, 96
Kruuk, Jane, 98
Kuhn, Bob, 198
Kuka range, 176

Lake Lagaja, 24, 188
Lake Magadi, 178-179
Lake Manyara, 3
Lamai Wedge Game Reserve, 60-61
Lamprey, Hugh, 97, 202
Lamprey, Ros, 98
Larelemangi salt lick, 84-85, 175
Leakey, Louis, 4
Leakey, Mary, 4
L'engai Crater, 72-73

Leopards, 20, 66, 79, 100, 125-126, 187, 189-190
Leopold, Starker, 199
Lindbergh, Charles, 196
Lions, 7, 10-11, 19-20, 21, 25, 35, 36-37, 51-52, 113, 128-140, 186, 189
Little, Royal, 199
Living Free (film), 198
Lizards, 153
Lobo Springs, 51-52
Loita Hills, 165

Maasai people, 11-12, 20, 164, 179, 180
Macdonald, Air Commodore, 197
McGee, Gale W., 199
McNamara, Robert, 199
Malambo area, 161
Malaria, 8
Malawi, 209-210
Mara Game Reserve, 157
Mara River, 26, 174
Margarete, Queen of Denmark, 195
Marshall, Robert, 137
Matthiesson, Peter, 198
Mblageti Valley, 25
Mcharo, Tumaina, 202
Medical care, 31-34, 93
Metachizotherium, 4
Mgungu River, 10, 43
Michener, James, 198
Migration of animals, 5, 12, 21, 23, 25-26, 156
Milligan, Spike, 198
Mkwawa, Adam Sapi, 202
Molloy, Peter, 94, 154
Momella, 154, 170, 202, 203, 206
Mongooses, 111, 153
Moore, Audrey, 15
Moore, "Monty," 20
Moorehead, Alan, 196
Moru, 178-179
Moss, Frank E., 199
Mount Meru, 203
Mugumu village, 52, 53
Muhenge area, 18
Musoma township, 1, 31
Mwanza township, 100
Mweka College of Wildlife Management, 97

Naabi Hill, 5, 171, 189
National Parks Ordinance (1948), 20
New York Zoological Society, 162
Ngorongoro Crater, 2, 3-4, 18, 156, 157
Ngorongoro Crater Highlands, 11, 12, 20, 165, 171
Ngorongoro Game Reserve, 20

Nihill, Sir Barclay, 194
No Room for Wild Animals (film), 154, 161
Nolan, Sidney, 198
Norton-Griffiths, Ann, 98
Norton-Griffiths, Mike, 97
Nyerere, Mwalimu Julius, 194, 207
Nyika National Park, 209-210

Olduvai Gorge, 4-5
Orangi River, 10
Order of the Golden Ark, 94
Osborne, Fairfield, 197
Overgrazing, 96
Owen, John, 61, 93-97, 99, 137, 162-163, 167, 168, 196, 200, 201
Owen, Patricia, 94

Pahlavi, Abdorreza, Prince of Iran, 1, 18
Palme, Olof, 199
Paulo, 34, 178
Pearsall, W. H., 11, 12
Pets, 63-71, 102-127, 141-153
Philip, Duke of Edinburgh, 195
Poaching, 21, 41-62, 95, 156
Poisoned arrows, 59-60
Poolman, Connie, 38, 39, 65-66, 74, 75, 80, 132
Poolman, Gordon, 37-38, 75, 80, 89, 131, 132, 157
Professional Hunters' Committee, 14

Rabbits, rock, 83-84, 141-149
Radziwill, Lee, 199
Rediscovered Country, The (White), 19
Regeneration of trees, 96
Rhinoceroses, 89, 100, 174
Roan antelopes, 35
Rockefeller, Laurence, 199
Root, Alan, 195
Root, Joan, 195
Rundgren, Eric, 15-16

Safaris, 14-17, 51-52, 55-57, 171-184
Saibull, Solomon ole, 201
Schaller, George, 96, 113
Schaller, Kay, 98
Schiemann, Bernd, 70, 71, 124
Scorpions, 74-75
Scott, Sir Peter, 197
Serengeti Closed Reserve, 20
Serengeti National Park
    aircraft, 61, 97, 99, 154-170
    Banagi, 1-12, 27-40, 83, 193-194
    boundaries of, 11-12, 20-21, 55, 156
    bush fires, 172-173
    climate, 22-23, 96, 142, 172-173
    Corridor, 11, 25, 158, 192

exploration of, 18-20
    game catching and marking, 157-158
    game census, 38
    geography, 21-22
    Maasai people and, 11-12, 20
    medical care, 31-34, 93
    migration of animals, 5, 12, 21, 23, 25-26, 156
    plains, 4, 5, 11, 21, 23-25, 182-184
    poaching, 21, 41-62, 95, 156
    Research Institute, 97-98, 162
    Seronera, 1, 12, 25, 77, 83, 88-101
    supplies, 31, 92-93
    tourism, 33, 83, 94-95, 97, 99, 128, 185-200
    vegetation, 22, 23
    water supply, 93
    woodlands, 6
    See also names of animals
Serengeti Plains, 4, 5, 11, 21, 23-25, 182-184
Serengeti Research Institute, 97-98, 162
Serengeti Shall Not Die (Grzimek and Grzimek), 161-162
Seronera, 1, 12, 25, 77, 83, 88-101
Servals, 119-127
Shaw and Hunter Trophy, 18
Shepherd, David, 198
Shifting Sands hill, 5
Simpson, Leslie, 19
Sinclair, Anne, 98
Sinclair, Tony, 96
Sivatherium, 4
Smith, Anthony, 206
Smith, Jean, 199
Snakes, 35-36, 77-79, 83-86, 90, 123-124
Sorcery, 43
Spiders, 74
Stephenson, John, 202
Stewart, Gloria, 199
Stewart, James, 199
Styron, William, 198
Sukumaland, 43
Superstition, 42-43
Supplies, 31, 92-93

Tanganyika Game Department, 18, 20, 46
Tanganyika National Parks, 18
Thesiger, Wilfred, 196
Thompson, Ralph, 198, 206
Thomson, George, 13
Thomson, Sir Landsborough, 194
Thomson's gazelle, 115-116
Tibrandi, 77
Tito, Marshal, 199
Tourism, 33, 83, 94-95, 97, 99, 128, 185-200

Train, Russell, 199
Trypanosomiasis, 8
Tsetse flies, 8
Turnbull, Sir Richard, 194
Turner, Lynda, 57, 65, 73-80, 82, 83, 85-87, 89, 98, 101, 168, 171, 172, 191
Turner, Michael, 68, 79, 80-87, 89, 98, 101, 171, 172, 191

Uaso Nyiro River, 180
Udall, Stewart, 199

Verschuren, Jacques, 96

Water supply, 93
Waterbuck, 35
Weston, General, 197
White, Stewart Edward, 18, 19, 175
White hunters, 14
Whitehead, Major, 197
Wild dogs, 24, 25, 112
Wildebeest, 23-24, 35, 62, 97, 156, 171
Wire snaring, 44, 46-50, 62
Wogakuria Guardpost, 176
World Wildlife Fund, 94

Zebras, 35, 62
Zorillas (striped polecats), 110-111